PREFACE

1. Scope

Joint Publication 5-0, *Joint Operation Planning,* reflects current guidance for planning military operations and, as a keystone publication, forms the core of joint doctrine for joint operation planning throughout the range of military operations.

2. Purpose

This publication has been prepared under the direction of the Chairman of the Joint Chiefs of Staff. It sets forth joint doctrine to govern the activities and performance of the Armed Forces of the United States in joint operations and provides the doctrinal basis for interagency coordination and for US military involvement in multinational operations. It provides military guidance for the exercise of authority by combatant commanders and other joint force commanders (JFCs) and prescribes joint doctrine for operations, education, and training. It provides military guidance for use by the Armed Forces in preparing their appropriate plans. It is not the intent of this publication to restrict the authority of the JFC from organizing the force and executing the mission in a manner the JFC deems most appropriate to ensure unity of effort in the accomplishment of the overall objective.

3. Application

a. Joint doctrine established in this publication applies to the joint staff, commanders of combatant commands, subunified commands, joint task forces, subordinate components of these commands, the Services, and combat support agencies.

b. The guidance in this publication is authoritative; as such, this doctrine will be followed except when, in the judgment of the commander, exceptional circumstances dictate otherwise. If conflicts arise between the contents of this publication and the contents of Service publications, this publication will take precedence unless the Chairman of the Joint Chiefs of Staff, normally in coordination with the other members of the Joint Chiefs of Staff, has provided more current and specific guidance. Commanders of forces operating as part of a multinational (alliance or coalition) military command should follow multinational doctrine and procedures ratified by the United States. For doctrine and procedures not ratified by the United States, commanders should evaluate and follow the multinational command's doctrine and procedures, where applicable and consistent with US law, regulations, and doctrine.

Intentionally Blank

SUMMARY OF CHANGES
REVISION OF JOINT PUBLICATION 5-0
DATED 26 DECEMBER 2006

- Reorders and reorients chapters to provide a more logical flow and better reflect planning practice today.

- Adds additional appendices to provide ready reference for best practices and process specificity.

- Includes the new planning construct introduced in the 2008 Guidance for Employment of the Force.

- Reflects the Department of Defense's evolution from Joint Operation Planning and Execution System to Adaptive Planning and Execution system.

- Reintroduces the term deliberate planning to cover all plans developed in non-crisis situations.

- Reduces redundancies and improves continuity between Joint Publication (JP) 5-0 and JP 1, *Doctrine for the Armed Forces of the United States.*

- Reduces redundancies and improves continuity between JP 5-0 and JP 3-0, *Joint Operations.*

Intentionally Blank

TABLE OF CONTENTS

EXECUTIVE SUMMARY
COMMANDER'S OVERVIEW

- **Discusses the Role of Joint Operation Planning**

- **Explains the Adaptive Planning and Execution (APEX) system**

- **Explains the Composition of Strategic Direction and Joint Operation Planning**

- **Describes Operational Art, Operational Design, the Operational Design Elements, and the Relationship to Joint Operation Planning Process**

- **Describes the Joint Operation Planning Process**

Role of Joint Operation Planning

Joint Operation Planning

Joint operation planning consists of planning activities associated with joint military operations by combatant commanders (CCDRs) and their subordinate joint force commanders (JFCs) in response to contingencies and crises. It transforms national strategic objectives into activities by development of operational products that include planning for the mobilization, deployment, employment, sustainment, redeployment, and demobilization of joint forces.

Strategic Direction

Strategic direction is the common thread that integrates and synchronizes the planning activities and operations of the Joint Staff (JS), combatant commands (CCMDs), Services, JFCs, combat support agencies (CSAs), and other Department of Defense (DOD) agencies. It provides purpose and focus to the planning for employment of military force. As an overarching term, strategic direction encompasses the processes and manner by which the President and the Secretary of Defense (SecDef) provide strategic guidance to the joint force.

Providing Common Basis for Understanding and Adaptation

Joint operation planning occurs within Adaptive Planning and Execution (APEX), which is the department-level system of joint policies, processes, procedures, and reporting structures. APEX is supported by communications and information technology that is used by the joint planning and

Clear strategic guidance and frequent interaction among senior leaders, combatant commanders (CCDRs), and subordinate joint force commanders (JFCs) promotes early understanding of, and agreement on, strategic and military end states, objectives, planning assumptions, risks, and other key factors.

execution community (JPEC) to monitor, plan, and execute mobilization, deployment, employment, sustainment, redeployment, and demobilization activities associated with joint operations. APEX formally integrates the planning activities of the JPEC and facilitates the JFC's seamless transition from planning to execution during times of crisis. APEX activities span many organizational levels, but the focus is on the interaction between SecDef and CCDRs, which ultimately helps the President and SecDef decide when, where, and how to commit US military forces.

Creating Understanding and Reducing Uncertainty

In conducting joint operation planning, commanders and staff apply operational art to operational design using the joint operation planning process (JOPP). Planners apply operational design to provide the conceptual framework that will underpin joint operation or campaign plans and their subsequent execution. The application of operational art and operational design further reduces uncertainty and adequately orders complex problems to allow for more detailed planning.

Providing Options, Aligning Resources, and Mitigating Risks

The planning staff uses JOPP to conduct detailed planning to fully develop options, identify resources, and identify and mitigate risk. Planners develop the concept of operations (CONOPS), force plans, deployment plans, and supporting plans that contain multiple options in order to provide the flexibility to adapt to changing conditions and remain consistent with the JFC's intent.

Constant Change, Learning, and Adaptation

Joint operation planning plays a fundamental role in securing the Nation's interests in a continuously changing operational environment. Through structured review, assessment, and modification, plans are constantly assessed and updated by the JFC and reviewed by the broader JPEC and senior DOD leadership. The open and collaborative planning process provides common understanding across multiple levels of organizations and the basis for adaptation and change.

Strategic Direction and Joint Operation Planning

Strategic Guidance and Planning Overview

Joint plans and orders are developed with the strategic and military end states in mind. The commander and planners derive their understanding of those end states from strategic guidance. Joint operation planning is an adaptive process. It occurs in a networked, collaborative environment, which requires dialogue among senior leaders, concurrent and parallel plan development, and collaboration across multiple planning levels. Clear strategic guidance and frequent interaction between senior leaders and planners promote an early, shared understanding of the complex operational problem presented, strategic and military end states, objectives, mission, planning assumptions, considerations, risks, and other key guidance factors.

National, Defense, and Military Guidance

The National Security Council (NSC) is the President's principal forum for considering national security and foreign policy matters with the senior national security advisors and cabinet officials. For DOD, the President's decisions drive strategic guidance promulgated by the Office of the Secretary of Defense (OSD) and refined by the Joint Strategic Planning System (JSPS). To carry out Title 10, United States Code (USC), statutory responsibilities, the Chairman of the Joint Chiefs of Staff (CJCS) utilizes the JSPS to provide a formal structure in aligning ends, ways, and means, and to identify and mitigate risk for the military in shaping the best assessments, advice, and direction of the Armed Forces for the President and SecDef.

National Security Council System

The NSC system is the principal forum for interagency deliberation of national security policy issues requiring Presidential decision. The NSC prepares national security guidance that, with Presidential approval, becomes national security policy, and when implemented, these policy decisions provide the guidance for military planning and programming.

National Security Strategy (NSS)

The **National Security Strategy (NSS)** is a comprehensive report required annually by Title 50, USC, Section 404a. It is prepared by the executive branch of the government for Congress and outlines the major national security concerns of the US and how the administration plans to address them using all instruments of national power. The document is purposely general in content, and its implementation relies on elaborating guidance provided in supporting documents (such as the National Defense Strategy [NDS], the Guidance for Employment of the Force [GEF], and the National Military Strategy [NMS]).

Department of Defense

National Defense Strategy. The NDS addresses how the Armed Forces of the United States will fight and win America's wars and describes how DOD will support the objectives outlined in the NSS. It also provides a framework for other DOD strategic guidance, specifically on deliberate planning, force development, and intelligence.

Existing legislation requires Secretary of Defense (SecDef) to conduct a Quadrennial Defense Review (QDR) and to submit a report on the QDR to Congress every four years.

Quadrennial Defense Review (QDR). The QDR articulates a national defense strategy consistent with the most recent NSS by defining force structure, modernization plans, and a budget plan allowing the military to successfully execute the full range of missions within that strategy.

The Unified Command Plan, signed by the President, sets forth basic guidance to all CCDRs.

Unified Command Plan (UCP). The UCP establishes CCMD missions and responsibilities; addresses assignment of forces; delineates geographic areas of responsibility for geographic combatant commanders (GCCs); and specifies responsibilities for functional combatant commanders.

Guidance for Employment of the Force. The GEF provides two-year direction to CCMDs for operational planning, force management, security cooperation, and posture planning. The GEF is the method through which OSD translates strategic priorities set in the NSS, NDS, and QDR into implementable direction for operational activities.

Joint Strategic Planning System (JSPS)

The JSPS is the primary system by which the CJCS, in coordination with the other members of the Joint Chiefs of Staff (JCS) and the CCDRs, conducts deliberate planning and provides military advice to the President and SecDef.

JSPS products—such as the National Military Strategy and the Joint Strategic

National Military Strategy. The NMS, derived from the NSS and NDS, prioritizes and focuses the efforts of the Armed Forces of the United States while conveying

Capabilities Plan—provide guidance and instructions on military policy, strategy, plans, forces, and resource requirements and allocations essential to successful execution of the NSS and other Presidential directives.

the CJCS's advice with regard to the security environment and the necessary military actions to protect vital US interests. The NMS defines the national military objectives (i.e., ends), how to accomplish these objectives (i.e., ways), and addresses the military capabilities required to execute the strategy (i.e., means).

Joint Strategic Capabilities Plan (JSCP). The JSCP is the primary vehicle through which the CJCS exercises responsibility for directing the preparation of joint plans. The JSCP **provides military strategic and operational guidance** to CCDRs, Service Chiefs, CSAs, and applicable DOD agencies for preparation of campaign plans and contingency plans **based on current military capabilities.** It serves as the link between strategic guidance provided in the GEF and the joint operation planning activities and products that accomplish that guidance.

Global Force Management Implementation Guidance (GFMIG). The GFMIG integrates complementary assignment, apportionment, and allocation information into a single GFM document. GFM aligns force assignment, apportionment, and allocation methodologies in support of the NDS, joint force availability requirements, and joint force assessments. It provides comprehensive insights into the global availability of US military resources and provides senior decision makers a process to quickly and accurately assess the impact and risk of proposed changes in forces assignment, apportionment, and allocation.

Geographic Combatant Commanders

Strategic Estimate. The strategic estimate is a tool available to CCMDs and subunified commands as they design and develop campaign plans and subordinate campaign plans or operation plans (OPLANs). CCDRs use strategic estimates developed in peacetime to facilitate the employment of military forces across the range of military operations.

Theater Strategy. GCCs develop a theater strategy focused on achieving specified end states for their theaters. A theater strategy is a broad statement of the commander's long-term vision for the area of responsibility. It is the bridge between national strategic guidance and the joint operation planning required to achieve national and regional objectives and end states. Specifically, it links CCMD activities, operations, and resources to United States Government (USG) policy and strategic guidance.

Interagency Considerations

Commanders and planners must identify the desired contributions of other agencies and organizations and communicate needs to Office of the Secretary of Defense.

Achieving national strategic objectives requires effective unified action resulting in unity of effort. This is accomplished by collaboration, synchronization, and coordination in the use of the diplomatic, informational, military, and economic instruments of national power. To accomplish this integration, the Services and DOD agencies interact with non-DOD agencies and organizations to ensure mutual understanding of the capabilities, limitations, and consequences of military and nonmilitary actions as well as the understanding of end state and termination requirements.

Strategic Communication(SC)

Every JFC has the responsibility to develop a coordinated and synchronized communications strategy that links to, and supports, planning and execution of coherent national and SC effort.

Strategic communication (SC) refers to focused USG efforts to understand and engage key audiences to create, strengthen, or preserve conditions favorable for the advancement of USG interests, policies, and objectives through the use of coordinated programs, plans, themes, messages, and products synchronized with and leveraging the actions of all instruments of national power. The US military plays an important supporting role in SC, primarily through information operations, public affairs, and defense support to public diplomacy. SC considerations should be included in all joint operational planning for military operations from routine, recurring military activities in peacetime through major operations.

Strategic Guidance for Multinational Operations

When directed, designated US commanders participate directly with the armed forces

Multinational operations start with the diplomatic efforts to create a coalition or spur an alliance into action. Discussion and coordination between potential participants initially address basic questions at the national strategic level. These senior-level discussions could involve intergovernmental organizations (IGOs) such as the United Nations or the North Atlantic Treaty Organization, existing multinational forces (MNFs), or individual nations. In support of each MNF, a hierarchy of bilateral or multilateral bodies is

of other nations in preparing bilateral contingency plans.

established to define strategic and military end states and objectives, to develop strategies, and to coordinate strategic guidance for planning and executing multinational operations.

Application of Guidance

The headquarters, commands, and agencies involved in joint operation planning or committed to a joint operation are collectively termed the **JPEC.** Although not a standing or regularly meeting entity, the JPEC consists of the CJCS and other members of the JCS, JS, the Services and their major commands, the CCMDs and their subordinate commands, and the CSAs.

Adaptive Planning and Execution System

Joint operation planning is accomplished through the APEX system. The JPEC uses the APEX system to monitor, plan, and execute mobilization, deployment, employment, sustainment, redeployment, and demobilization activities associated with joint operations. The APEX system operates in a networked, collaborative environment, which facilitates dialogue among senior leaders, concurrent and parallel plan development, and collaboration across multiple planning levels. Joint operation planning encompasses a number of elements, including three broad **operational activities,** four **planning functions,** and a number of related products.

Operational Activities

Situational awareness addresses procedures for describing the operational environment, including threats to national security. This occurs during continuous monitoring of the national and international political and military situations so that JFCs and their staffs can determine and analyze emerging crises, notify decision makers, and determine the specific nature of the threat.

Planning continues during execution, with an initial emphasis on refining the existing plan and producing the operations order and refining the force flow utilizing employed assigned and allocated forces.

Planning translates strategic guidance and direction into campaign plans, level 1–4 plans, and operation orders (OPORDs). Joint operation planning may be based on defined tasks identified in the GEF and the JSCP. Alternatively, joint operation planning may be based on the need for a military response to an unforeseen current event, emergency, or time-sensitive crisis.

Execution begins when the President decides to use a military option to resolve a crisis. Only the President or SecDef can authorize the CJCS to issue an execute order (EXORD). Depending upon time constraints, an EXORD may be the only order a JFC receives. The EXORD defines the time to initiate operations and conveys guidance not provided earlier. Execution continues until the operation is terminated or the mission is accomplished.

Planning Functions

Although the **four planning functions of strategic guidance, concept development, plan development, and plan assessment** are generally sequential, they often run simultaneously in the effort to accelerate the overall planning process.

SecDef or the CCDR may direct the planning staff to refine or adapt a plan by reentering the planning process at any of the earlier functions.

Strategic Guidance. This function is used to formulate politico-military assessments at the strategic level, develop and evaluate military strategy and objectives, apportion and allocate forces and other resources, formulate concepts and strategic military options, and develop planning guidance leading to the preparation of courses of action (COAs).

Concept Development. During deliberate planning, the supported commander develops several COAs, each containing an initial CONOPS that identifies, at a minimum, major capabilities required and task organization, major operational tasks to be accomplished by components, a concept of employment, and assessment of risk for each COA. Each COA should contain embedded options that describe multiple alternatives to accomplish designated end states as conditions change (e.g., operational environment, problem, strategic direction).

Plan Development. This function is used to fully develop campaign plans, contingency plans, or orders, with applicable supporting annexes, and to refine preliminary feasibility analysis. This function fully integrates mobilization, deployment, employment, sustainment, conflict termination, redeployment, and demobilization activities through the six-phase joint operation construct (Phases 0–V). The CCDR briefs the final plan to SecDef (or a designated representative) during the final plan approval in-progress review (IPR), referred to as IPR F. CCDRs may repeat the IPR F, as needed until approval is granted. The primary product is an approved plan or order.

Plan Assessment (Refine, Adapt, Terminate, Execute—RATE). The supported commander continually reviews and assesses the complete plan, resulting in four possible outcomes: revise (R), adapt (A), terminate (T), or execute (E).

Deliberate Planning and Crisis Action Planning (CAP) Products

Deliberate planning encompasses the preparation of plans that occur in non-crisis situations. It is used to develop campaign and contingency plans for a broad range of activities based on requirements identified in the GEF, JSCP, or other planning directives. **Theater and global campaign plans** are the centerpiece of DOD's planning construct. They provide the means to translate CCMD theater or functional strategies into executable plans.

CAP activities are similar to deliberate planning activities, but CAP is based on dynamic, real-world conditions.

Crisis action planning (CAP) provides the CJCS and CCDRs a process for getting vital decision-making information up the chain of command to the President and SecDef. It also outlines the mechanisms for monitoring the execution of the operation. CAP encompasses the activities associated with the time-sensitive development of OPORDs for the deployment, employment, and sustainment of assigned, attached, and allocated forces and capabilities in response to a situation that may result in actual military operations. CAP procedures provide for the rapid and effective exchange of information and analysis, the timely preparation of military COAs for consideration by the President or SecDef, and the prompt transmission of their decisions to the JPEC.

CAP activities may be performed sequentially or in parallel, with supporting and subordinate plans or operation orders (OPORDs) being developed concurrently.

Contingency Plans

Contingency plans are developed in anticipation of a potential crisis outside of crisis conditions. There are four levels of planning detail for contingency plans, with an associated planning product for each level.

A contingency is a situation that likely would involve military forces in response to natural and man-made

Level 1 Planning Detail—Commander's Estimate. This level of planning involves the least amount of detail and focuses on producing multiple COAs to address a contingency. The product for this level can

disasters, terrorists, subversives, military operations by foreign powers, or other situations as directed by the President or SecDef.

be a COA briefing, command directive, commander's estimate, or a memorandum.

Level 2 Planning Detail—Base Plan (BPLAN). A BPLAN describes the CONOPS, major forces, concepts of support, and anticipated timelines for completing the mission. It normally does not include annexes or time-phased force and deployment data (TPFDD).

Level 3 Planning Detail—Concept Plan (CONPLAN). A CONPLAN is an OPLAN in an abbreviated format that may require considerable expansion or alteration to convert it into an OPLAN or OPORD. It may also produce a TPFDD if applicable.

Level 4 Planning Detail—OPLAN. An OPLAN is a complete and detailed joint plan containing a full description of the CONOPS, all annexes applicable to the plan, and a TPFDD. It identifies the specific forces, functional support, and resources required to execute the plan and provide closure estimates for their flow into the theater.

Interorganizational Planning and Coordination

Interorganizational planning and coordination is the interaction that occurs among elements of DOD; engaged USG departments and agencies; state, territorial, local, and tribal agencies; foreign military forces and government agencies; IGOs; nongovernmental organizations (NGOs); and the private sector for the purpose of accomplishing an objective. Successful interorganizational coordination of plans facilitates unity of effort among multiple organizations by promoting common understanding of the capabilities, limitations, and consequences of military and civilian actions.

Interagency Planning and Coordination

Interagency coordination is the interaction that occurs among USG departments and agencies, including DOD, for the purpose of accomplishing an objective. Interagency coordination forges the vital link between the US military and the other instruments of national power.

Multinational Planning and Coordination

Multinational operations is a collective term to describe military actions conducted by forces of two or

Agreement on clearly identified strategic and military end states for the multinational force is essential to guide all multinational coordination, planning, and execution.

more nations. Such operations are usually undertaken within the structure of a coalition or alliance, although other possible arrangements include supervision by an IGO (such as the United Nations or Organization for Security and Cooperation in Europe). **Key to any multinational operation is the achievement of unity of effort** among political and military leaders of member nations emphasizing common objectives and shared interests as well as mutual support and respect.

Review of Multinational Plans

Multilateral contingency plans routinely require national-level US approval.

US joint strategic plans or contingency plans prepared in support of multinational plans are developed, reviewed, and approved exclusively within US operational channels. They may or may not be shared in total with multinational partners. The formal review and approval of multinational plans is accomplished in accordance with specific procedures adopted by each multinational organization and may or may not include separate US review or approval.

Operational Art and Operational Design

Commanders who are skilled in the use of operational art provide the vision that links tactical actions to strategic objectives.

The JFC and staff develop plans and orders through the application of operational art and operational design and by using JOPP. They combine art and science to develop products that describe how (ways) the joint force will employ its capabilities (means) to achieve the military end state (ends). The interaction of operational art and operational design provides a bridge between strategy and tactics, linking national strategic aims to tactical combat and noncombat operations that must be executed to accomplish these aims.

The Commander's Role

The commander is the central figure in operational art, due not only to education and experience, but also because the commander's judgment and decisions are required to guide the staff through the process. Commanders compare similarities of their current situations with their own experiences or history to distinguish the unique features that require innovative or adaptive solutions. **Operational design requires the commander to encourage discourse and leverage dialogue and collaboration to identify and solve complex, ill-defined problems.** To that end, the commander must empower organizational learning and develop methods to determine if modifying the operational approach is necessary during the course of an operation.

Developing the Operational Approach

The operational approach is a commander's description of the broad actions the force must take to achieve the desired military end state. The operational approach is based largely on an understanding of the operational environment and the problem facing the JFC. Once the JFC approves the approach, it provides the basis for beginning, continuing, or completing detailed planning.

Methodology

Three distinct aspects of a methodology collectively assist with producing an operational approach.

Understand the Strategic Direction. The President, SecDef, CJCS, and CCDRs all promulgate strategic guidance. In general, this guidance provides long-term as well as intermediate or ancillary objectives. It should define what constitutes "victory" or success **(ends)** and allocate adequate forces and resources **(means)** to achieve strategic objectives. The operational approach **(ways)** of employing military capabilities to achieve the ends is for the supported JFC to develop and propose. Connecting resources and tactical actions to strategic ends is the responsibility of the operational commander.

Understand the Operational Environment. The operational environment is the composite of the conditions, circumstances, and influences that affect the employment of capabilities and bear on the decisions of the commander. It encompasses physical areas and factors of the air, land, maritime, and space domains and the information environment (which includes cyberspace). Understanding the operational environment helps the JFC to better identify the problem; anticipate potential outcomes; and understand the results of various friendly, adversary, and neutral actions and how these actions affect achieving the military end state.

Define the Problem. Defining the problem is essential to solving the problem. It involves understanding and isolating the root causes of the issue at hand—defining the essence of a complex, ill-defined problem. Defining the problem begins with a review of the tendencies and potentials of all the concerned actors and identifying tensions among the existing conditions and the desired end state.

Elements of Operational Design

Operational design employs various **elements** to develop and refine the commander's operational approach. These conceptual tools help commanders and their staffs think through the challenges of understanding the operational environment, defining the problem, and developing this approach, which guides planning and shapes the CONOPS.

Termination. To plan effectively for termination, the supported JFC must know how the President and SecDef intend to terminate the joint operation and ensure that its outcomes endure.

Military End State. Military end state is the set of required conditions that defines achievement of all military objectives.

Objectives. An objective is a clearly defined, decisive, and attainable goal toward which every military operation should be directed.

Effects. An effect is a physical and/or behavioral state of a system that results from an action, a set of actions, or another effect. A desired effect can also be thought of as a condition that can support achieving an associated objective, while an undesired effect is a condition that can inhibit progress toward an objective.

Center of Gravity (COG). A COG is a source of power that provides moral or physical strength, freedom of action, or will to act. An objective is always linked to a COG. In identifying COGs it is important to remember that irregular warfare focuses on legitimacy and influence over a population, unlike traditional warfare, which employs direct military confrontation to defeat an adversary's armed forces, destroy an adversary's war-making capacity, or seize or retain territory to force a change in an adversary's government or policies.

Decisive Points. A *decisive point* is a geographic place, specific key event, critical factor, or function that, when acted upon, allows a commander to gain a marked advantage over an adversary or contributes materially to achieving success (e.g., creating a desired effect, achieving an objective).

Lines of Operation (LOOs) and Lines of Effort. A *LOO* defines the interior or exterior orientation of the force in relation to the enemy or that connects actions on nodes and/or decisive points related in time and space to an objective(s). A *line of effort* links multiple tasks and missions using the logic of purpose—cause and effect—to focus efforts toward establishing operational and strategic conditions.

Direct and Indirect Approach. The *approach* is the manner in which a commander contends with a COG. A **direct approach** attacks the enemy's COG or principal strength by applying combat power directly against it. An **indirect approach** attacks the enemy's COG by applying combat power against a series of decisive points that lead to the defeat of the COG while avoiding enemy strength.

Anticipation. Anticipation is key to effective planning. JFCs must consider what might happen and look for the signs that may bring the possible event to pass.

Operational Reach. Operational reach is the distance and duration across which a joint force can successfully employ military capabilities.

Culmination. *Culmination* is that point in time and/or space at which the operation can no longer maintain momentum.

Arranging Operations. Commanders must determine the best arrangement of joint force and component operations to conduct the assigned tasks and joint force mission. This arrangement often will be a combination of simultaneous and sequential operations to reach the end state conditions with the least cost in personnel and other resources.

Forces and Functions. Commanders and planners can design campaigns and operations that focus on defeating either *adversary forces, functions, or a combination of both.*

Phasing

As a general rule, the phasing of the campaign or operation should be conceived in condition-driven rather than time-driven terms.

Phases are distinct in time, space, and/or purpose from one another, but must be planned in support of each other and should represent a natural progression and subdivision of the campaign or operation. Each phase should have a set of starting conditions (that define the start of the phase) and ending conditions (that define the end of the phase). The ending conditions of one phase are the starting conditions for the next phase.

Number, Sequence, and Overlap

The JFC adjusts the phases to exploit opportunities presented by the adversary or operational situation or to react to unforeseen conditions.

Working within the phasing construct, the actual phases used will vary (compressed, expanded, or omitted entirely) with the joint campaign or operation and be determined by the JFC. During planning, the JFC establishes conditions, objectives, or events for transitioning from one phase to another and plans sequels and branches for potential contingencies. Phases are designed to be conducted sequentially, but some activities from a phase may begin in a previous phase and continue into subsequent phases.

Transitions

Transitions between phases are designed to be distinct shifts in focus by the joint force, often accompanied by changes in command or support relationships. The need to move into another phase normally is identified by assessing that a set of objectives are achieved or that the enemy has acted in a manner that requires a major change in focus for the joint force and is therefore usually event driven, not time driven.

Phasing Model

Although the commander will determine the number and actual phases used during a campaign or operation, use of the phases [shape, deter, seize the initiative, dominate, stability, and enable civil authority] provides a flexible model to arrange combat and stability operations.

The six-phase model is not intended to be a universally prescriptive template for all conceivable joint operations

Shape (Phase 0). Joint and multinational operations—inclusive of normal and routine military activities—and various interagency activities are performed to dissuade or deter potential adversaries and to assure or solidify

and may be tailored to the character and duration of the operation to which it applies.

relationships with friends and allies.

Deter (Phase I). The intent of this phase is to deter undesirable adversary action by demonstrating the capabilities and resolve of the joint force. It includes activities to prepare forces and set conditions for deployment and employment of forces in the event that deterrence is not successful.

Seize Initiative (Phase II). JFCs seek to seize the initiative through the application of appropriate joint force capabilities.

Dominate (Phase III). The *dominate* phase focuses on breaking the enemy's will for organized resistance or, in noncombat situations, control of the operational environment.

Stabilize (Phase IV). The *stabilize* phase is required when there is no fully functional, legitimate civil governing authority present. The joint force may be required to perform limited local governance, integrating the efforts of other supporting/ contributing multinational, IGO, NGO, or USG department and agency participants until legitimate local entities are functioning.

Enable Civil Authority (Phase V). This phase is predominantly characterized by joint force support to legitimate civil governance in theater. The goal is for the joint force to enable the viability of the civil authority and its provision of essential services to the largest number of people in the region.

Assessment

Assessment is the continuous monitoring and evaluation of the current situation and progress of a joint operation toward mission accomplishment. It involves deliberately comparing forecasted outcomes to actual events to determine the overall effectiveness of force employment. In general, assessments should answer two questions: Is the JFC doing things right? Is the JFC doing the right things?

Application of Assessment

Assessment and learning enable incremental improvements to the commander's operational approach and the campaign or contingency plan. Once JFCs understand the problem and what needs to be

Assessment entails two distinct tasks: continuously monitoring the situation and the progress of the operations and evaluating the operation against measures of effectiveness and measures of performance to determine progress relative to the mission, objectives, and end states.

accomplished to succeed, they identify the means to assess effectiveness and the related information requirements that support assessment. This feedback becomes the basis for learning, adaptation, and subsequent adjustment. Effective assessment requires criteria for evaluating the degree of success in accomplishing the mission. Criteria can be expressed as measures of effectiveness (MOEs) and measures of performance (MOPs). A *MOE* is a criterion used to assess changes in system behavior, capability, or operational environment that is tied to measuring the attainment of an end state, an objective, or the creation of an effect. It measures the relevance of actions being performed. A *MOP* is a criterion used to assess friendly actions that is tied to measuring task accomplishment.

Joint Operation Planning Process

Joint Operation Planning Process

JOPP is an orderly, analytical process, which consists of a set of logical steps to examine a mission; develop, analyze, and compare alternative COAs; select the best COA; and produce a plan or order. **JOPP** provides a proven process to organize the work of the commander, staff, subordinate commanders, and other partners, to develop plans that will appropriately address the problem to be solved. It focuses on defining the military mission and development and synchronization of detailed plans to accomplish that mission

Operational Art and Operational Design Interface with the Joint Operation Planning Process

Operational design and JOPP are complementary elements of the overall planning process. Operational design provides an iterative process that allows for the commander's vision and mastery of operational art to help planners answer ends–ways–means–risk questions and appropriately structure campaigns and operations. The commander, supported by the staff, gains an understanding of the operational environment, defines the problem, and develops an operational approach for the campaign or operation through the application of operational design during the initiation step of JOPP. Commanders communicate their operational approach to their staff, subordinates, supporting commands, agencies, and multinational/nongovernmental entities as required in their initial planning guidance so that their approach can be translated into executable plans.

This iterative process between the commander's maturing operational approach and the development of the mission and CONOPS through JOPP facilitates the continuing development of possible COAs and their refinement into eventual CONOPS and executable plans.

Planning Initiation

The JFC typically will provide initial planning guidance based upon current understanding of the operational environment, the problem, and the initial operational approach for the campaign or operation.

Joint operation planning begins when an appropriate authority recognizes potential for military capability to be employed in response to a potential or actual crisis. **At the strategic level, that authority—the President, SecDef, or CJCS—initiates planning by deciding to develop military options.** The GEF, JSCP, and related strategic guidance documents (when applicable) serve as the primary guidance to begin deliberate planning. Analyses of developing or immediate crises may result in the President, SecDef, or CJCS initiating military planning through a warning order or other planning directive.

Mission Analysis

The joint force's mission is the task or set of tasks, together with the purpose, that clearly indicates the action to be taken and the reason for doing so.

Mission analysis is used to study the assigned tasks and to identify all other tasks necessary to accomplish the mission. Mission analysis is critical because it provides direction to the commander and the staff, enabling them to focus effectively on the problem at hand. **The primary inputs to mission analysis** are the higher headquarters' planning directive, other strategic guidance, and the commander's initial planning guidance, which may include a description of the operational environment, a definition of the problem, the operational approach, initial intent, and the joint intelligence preparation of the operational. **The primary products of mission analysis** are staff estimates, the mission statement, a refined operational approach, the commander's intent statement, updated planning guidance, and commander's critical information requirements.

Course of Action (COA) Development

A good COA accomplishes the mission within the commander's guidance, provides flexibility to meet

A COA is a potential way (solution, method) to accomplish the assigned mission. The staff develops COAs to provide unique choices to the commander, all oriented on accomplishing the military end state. Since the *operational approach* contains the JFC's broad approach to solve the problem at hand, each COA will expand this concept with the additional details that describe **who** will take the action, **what type** of

unforeseen events during execution, and positions the joint force for future operations.

military action will occur, **when** the action will begin, **where** the action will occur, **why** the action is required (purpose), and **how** the action will occur (method of employment of forces).

COA Analysis

COA analysis is the process of closely examining potential COAs to reveal details that will allow the commander and staff to tentatively identify COAs that are valid, and then compare these COAs. COA analysis identifies advantages and disadvantages of each proposed friendly COA. The commander and staff analyze each tentative COA separately according to the commander's guidance. **Wargaming** is a primary means to conduct this analysis. Wargaming is a conscious attempt to visualize the flow of the operation, given joint force strengths and dispositions, adversary capabilities and possible COAs, the operational area, and other aspects of the operational environment.

While time-consuming, COA analysis should answer two primary questions: Is the COA feasible, and is it acceptable?

COA Comparison

COA comparison is a subjective process whereby COAs are considered independently and evaluated/compared against a set of criteria that are established by the staff and commander. The goal is to identify and recommend the COA that has the highest probability of success against the enemy COA that is of the most concern to the commander. COA comparison facilitates the commander's decision-making process by balancing the **ends, means, ways, and risk** of each COA. The end product of this task is a briefing to the commander on a COA recommendation and a decision by the commander.

Plan or Order Development

During plan or order development, the commander and staff, in collaboration with subordinate and supporting components and organizations, expand the approved COA into a detailed joint contingency plan or OPORD by first developing an executable CONOPS—the eventual centerpiece of the contingency plan or OPORD. The CONOPS clearly and concisely expresses what the JFC intends to accomplish and how it will be done using available resources. It describes how the actions of the joint force components and supporting organizations will be integrated, synchronized, and phased to accomplish the mission, including potential branches and sequels.

Deliberate planning will result in plan development, while CAP typically will lead directly to OPORD development.

For plans and orders developed per JSCP direction or as a result of a Presidential or SecDef tasking (normally transmitted through the CJCS), the CJCS, in coordination with the supported and supporting commanders and other members of the JCS, monitors planning activities, resolves shortfalls when required, and reviews the supported commander's contingency plan for adequacy, feasibility, acceptability, completeness, and compliance with joint doctrine.

CONCLUSION

This publication reflects current guidance for planning military operations and, as a keystone publication, forms the core of joint doctrine for joint operation planning throughout the range of military operations.

CHAPTER I
ROLE OF JOINT OPERATION PLANNING

> *"In preparing for battle I have always found that plans are useless, but planning is indispensable."*
>
> **General Dwight D. Eisenhower**
> *34th president of the United States, 1953–1961 (1890–1969)*

1. Overview

a. Joint operation planning consists of planning activities associated with joint military operations by combatant commanders (CCDRs) and their subordinate joint force commanders (JFCs) in response to contingencies and crises. It transforms national strategic objectives into activities by development of operational products that include planning for the mobilization, deployment, employment, sustainment, redeployment, and demobilization of joint forces. It ties the military instrument of national power to the achievement of national security goals and objectives and is essential to securing strategic end states across the range of military operations. Planning begins with the end state in mind, providing a unifying purpose around which actions and resources are focused. The primary focus of this document is planning at the operational level.

b. Joint operation planning provides a common basis for discussion, understanding, and change for the joint force, its subordinate and higher headquarters, the joint planning and execution community (JPEC), and the national leadership. The Adaptive Planning and Execution (APEX) system facilitates iterative dialogue and collaborative planning between the multiple echelons of command to ensure that the military instrument of national power is employed in accordance with national priorities, and that the plan is continuously reviewed and updated as required and adapted according to changes in strategic guidance, resources, or the operational environment. Joint operation planning also identifies capabilities outside Department of Defense (DOD) required for achieving the strategic objectives to reach the end state by providing a forum that facilitates the interorganizational coordination that enables unified action.

c. The pursuit and attainment of the US national strategic objectives in today's environment requires critical and creative thinking about the challenges facing the joint force. Joint operation planning fosters understanding, allowing commanders and their staffs to provide adequate order to ill-defined problems, reduce uncertainty, and enable further detailed planning. The planning process, both iterative and collaborative, enables understanding and facilitates the development of options to effectively meet the complex challenges facing joint forces throughout the world.

d. The body of knowledge and understanding created during planning allows JFCs and their staffs to monitor, assess, and adapt to uncertain and changing environments and to anticipate and proactively act in crisis situations. Joint operation planning produces multiple options to employ the US military and to integrate US military actions with other instruments of US national power in time, space, and purpose to achieve national strategic end states. Achieving operational military victory may be only a step toward achieving the overall national strategic goals and objectives, as demonstrated by events in Operations IRAQI FREEDOM and ENDURING FREEDOM. Additionally, planning identifies and aligns resources with military actions, providing a framework to identify and mitigate risk.

e. Assessing risk and identifying mitigation strategies are fundamental to joint operation planning. In the course of developing multiple options to meet the strategic end state, JFCs and their planning staffs, as well as the larger JPEC, identify and communicate shortfalls in DOD's ability to resource, execute, and sustain the military operations contained in the plan as well as the necessary actions to reduce, control, or accept risk with knowledge of potential consequences. JFCs communicate risk to senior leadership during in-progress reviews (IPRs) of the plan.

2. Strategic Direction

a. **Strategic direction** is the common thread that integrates and synchronizes the planning activities and operations of the Joint Staff (JS), combatant commands (CCMDs), Services, JFCs, combat support agencies (CSAs), and other DOD agencies. It provides purpose and focus to the planning for employment of military force. As an overarching term, strategic direction encompasses the processes and manner by which the President and the Secretary of Defense (SecDef) provide strategic guidance to the joint force.

b. The President provides strategic guidance through the National Security Strategy (NSS), Presidential policy directives (PPDs), executive orders, and other strategic documents in conjunction with additional guidance and refinement from the National Security Council (NSC). The President also signs the Unified Command Plan (UCP) and the contingency planning guidance in the SecDef-signed Guidance for Employment of the Force (GEF), which are both developed by DOD. The UCP establishes CCMD missions, responsibilities, and areas of responsibility (AORs), while the GEF provides the written policy guidance and priorities to the Chairman of the Joint Chiefs of Staff (CJCS) and CCDRs for reviewing and preparing campaign and contingency plans (see Chapter II, "Strategic Direction and Joint Operation Planning," paragraph 15a[2], "Contingency Plans"). At times, JFCs may not receive clear strategic guidance and will need to engage the strategic leadership in order to assist with plan development and the proposal of a feasible strategic end state.

c. SecDef provides civilian oversight and control of the joint force and establishes defense policy to guide military action in support of national strategic objectives. SecDef controls the joint force through Title 10, United States Code (USC), specified responsibilities to approve assignment of forces as specified in the Forces for Unified Commands Memorandum as incorporated in the Global Force Management Implementation Guidance (GFMIG). The GFMIG also addresses the allocation of forces. Additionally, SecDef oversees the development of broad defense policy goals and priorities for the development, employment, and sustainment of US military forces based on the NSS.

d. The CJCS provides independent assessments, serves as principal military advisor to the President and the NSC, and assists the President and SecDef with providing unified strategic direction to the Armed Forces. In this capacity, the CJCS develops the National Military Strategy (NMS) and the Joint Strategic Capabilities Plan (JSCP), which provide military implementation strategies and deliberate planning direction based on Office of the Secretary of Defense (OSD) policy guidance.

Chapter II, "Strategic Direction and Joint Operation Planning," discusses strategic guidance in more detail.

3. Providing Common Basis for Understanding and Adaptation

a. Joint operation planning occurs within APEX, which is the department-level system of joint policies, processes, procedures, and reporting structures. APEX is supported by communications and information technology that is used by the JPEC to monitor, plan, and execute mobilization, deployment, employment, sustainment, redeployment, and demobilization activities associated with joint operations. APEX formally integrates the planning activities of the JPEC and facilitates the JFC's seamless transition from planning to execution during times of crisis. The integration of joint operation planning with interagency and multinational partners begins with national strategic direction. APEX activities span many organizational levels, but **the focus is on the interaction between SecDef and CCDRs, which ultimately helps the President and SecDef decide when, where, and how to commit US military forces.** The interactive and collaborative process at the national level guides the way in which planning and execution occurs throughout the Armed Forces.

b. Clear strategic guidance and frequent interaction among senior leaders, CCDRs, and subordinate JFCs promotes early understanding of, and agreement on, strategic and military end states, objectives, planning assumptions, risks, and other key factors. Based on guidance from this iterative dialogue, planners develop multiple viable options to achieve end states while providing commanders and national leaders flexibility in how they shape the situation and respond to contingencies. Collaborative and iterative assessment and recurring dialogue between commanders and senior national leadership facilitates responsive plan development and modification, resulting in plans that are continually updated. APEX also promotes early, robust, and frequent discourse between DOD planners and their interagency and multinational counterparts throughout the planning process. Dialogue, collaboration, and integration with civilian agencies and multinational partners are essential to address the increasing complexity of national security challenges while incorporating multiple instruments of national power into planning and execution efforts.

c. Joint operation planning provides a common intellectual framework for the joint force, its subordinate and higher headquarters, the JPEC, and DOD leadership from which to adapt to the dynamic operational environment. APEX incorporates planning detail, frequent IPRs, continuous assessment, and collaborative technology, which provide increased opportunities for consultation and guidance during the planning process (see Figure I-1).

d. IPRs constitute a disciplined dialogue between commanders and their higher headquarters and are a part of the formal adaptive planning review and approval process for campaign and contingency plans. Plan development will include as many IPRs as necessary. Topics for discussion may include clarification of the problem, strategic and military end

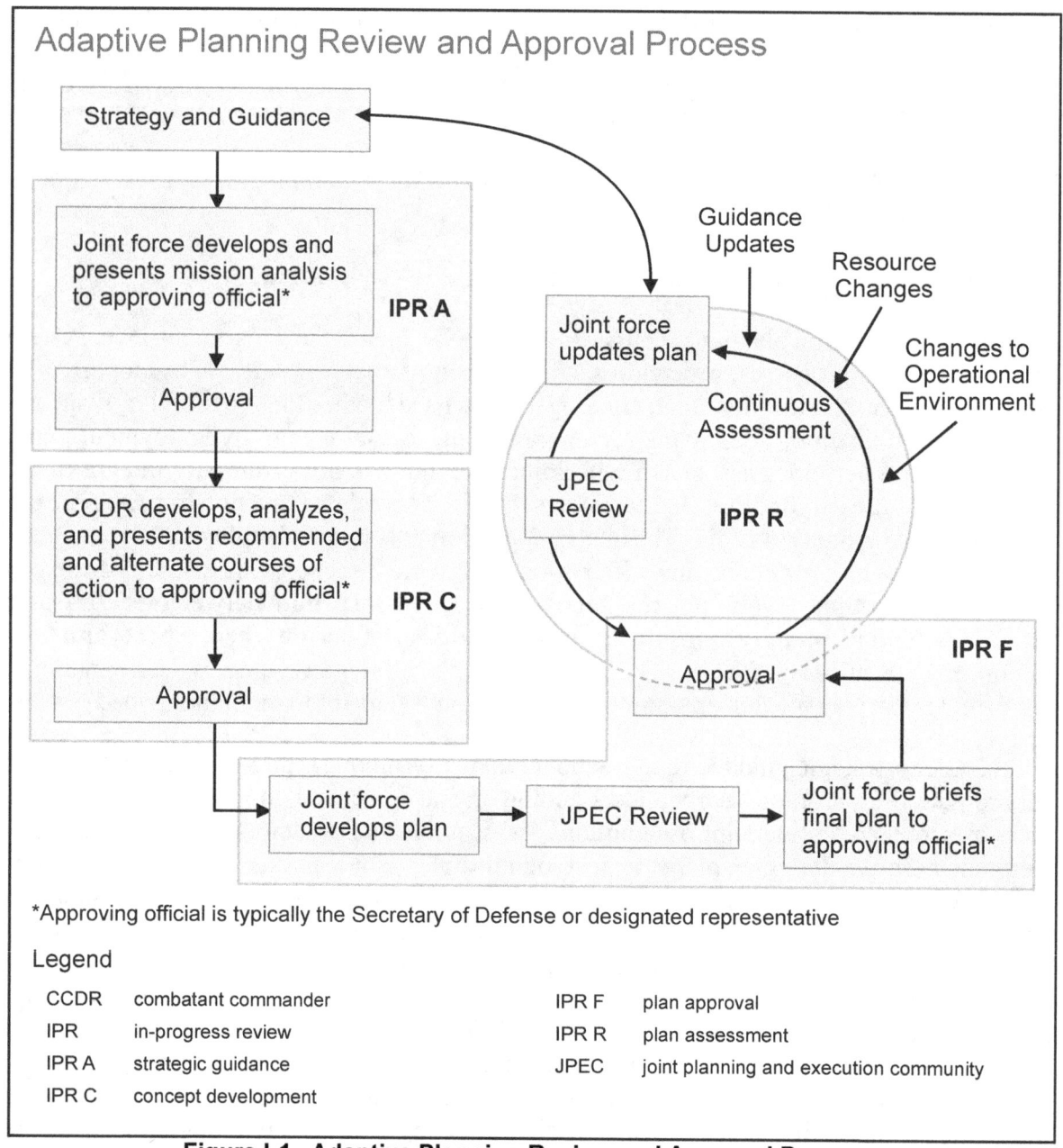

Figure I-1. Adaptive Planning Review and Approval Process

states, military objectives, confirmation of intelligence and the operational environment, mission, facts and assumptions, courses of action (COAs), capabilities and force requirements, areas of risk, identification and removal of planning obstacles, required supporting and supported activities, guidance on coordination with the interagency and multinational communities, and the resolution of planning conflicts. Further, IPRs facilitate planning by ensuring that the plan addresses the most current strategic assessments and needs. They also generate valuable feedback for planning staffs and provide a common vision between national and military leadership.

Chapter II, "Strategic Direction and Joint Operation Planning," discusses APEX in more detail.

4. Creating Understanding and Reducing Uncertainty

a. In conducting joint operation planning, commanders and staff blend operational art, operational design, and the joint operation planning process (JOPP) in complementary fashion as part of the overall process that produces the eventual plan or order that drives the joint operation. Both the conceptual thinking and detailed planning that occur during the development of joint plans and orders produce a body of information and understanding across the entire JPEC, which prepares commanders and staffs to adapt and act quickly and effectively. Operational art, **the creative thinking used to design strategies, campaigns, and major operations and to organize and employ military force,** allows commanders to better understand the challenges facing them and to conceptualize an approach for achieving their strategic objectives. The thought process helps commanders and their staffs to lessen the ambiguity and uncertainty of a complex operational environment, understand the military problem facing them, and visualize how best to effectively employ military capabilities to accomplish their mission. This is the essence of operational art.

b. Planners apply operational design to provide the conceptual framework that will underpin joint operation or campaign plans and their subsequent execution. The application of operational art and operational design further reduces uncertainty and adequately orders complex problems to allow for more detailed planning.

c. Based on understanding gained through the application of operational design, more detailed planning takes place within the steps of JOPP. JOPP is an orderly, analytical process that consists of a set of logical steps to analyze a mission; develop, analyze, and compare alternative COAs; select the best COA; and produce a plan or order. Through JOPP, planners effectively translate the commander's planning guidance into a feasible COA and concept of operations (CONOPS) by which the joint force can achieve its assigned mission and military end state. This, in turn, links tactical actions, through operational planning and execution, to the accomplishment of national strategic objectives in support of the strategic end state. Planners align actions and resources in time and space to complete the plan. In doing so, they should take into account the details of force requirements, force availability, task organization, and sustainment and deployment concepts. They should also take into account the capacity and objectives of the other instruments of national power, risk, and functional elements of the plan (i.e., personnel, intelligence, logistics).

Chapter III, "Operational Art and Operational Design," discusses operational art and design in more detail, and Chapter IV, "Joint Operation Planning Process," outlines the steps of JOPP.

5. Providing Options, Aligning Resources, and Mitigating Risks

a. The planning staff uses JOPP to conduct detailed planning to fully develop options, identify resources, and identify and mitigate risk. Planners develop the CONOPS, force plans, deployment plans, and supporting plans that contain multiple options in order to provide the flexibility to adapt to changing conditions and remain consistent with the JFC's intent.

b. The detailed planning that occurs during force planning allows CCDRs to assess risks associated with executing those plans directed to have time-phased force and deployment data (TPFDD). The supported CCDR, working with the component commanders, determines required force capabilities to accomplish an assigned mission. The Military Departments, Services, Service component commands of the CCMDs, and CSAs assist with developing forces lists, sourcing and tailoring required force capabilities with actual units, identifying and resolving shortfalls, and determining the routing and time-phasing of forces into the operational area (OA). Force planning begins early during CONOPS development and focuses on applying the right force to the mission while providing force visibility, force mobility, and adaptability throughout the duration of the operation. This detailed planning is essential to aligning resources to missions and to identifying and mitigating risks to plans.

c. Risk identification and mitigation is first conducted in the initial steps of JOPP during mission analysis and continued and updated throughout the planning process. Assumptions are made to continue planning and are continually evaluated. When sufficient information or intelligence is received to invalidate an assumption, at a minimum it becomes an additional risk to the operation, although it could result in execution of a branch or sequel or the development of a new COA or plan. Along with hazard and threat analysis, shortfall identification is performed throughout the plan development process. The supported commander continuously identifies limiting factors, capability shortfalls, and associated risks as plan development progresses. Where possible, the supported commander resolves the shortfalls through planning adjustments and coordination with supporting commanders. If the shortfalls and necessary controls and countermeasures cannot be reconciled or the resources provided are inadequate to perform the assigned task, the supported commander reports these limiting factors and assessment of the associated risk to the CJCS. The CJCS, Service Chiefs, and joint force providers (JFPs) consider shortfalls and limiting factors reported by the supported commander and coordinate resolution. However, the completion of assigned plans is not delayed pending the resolution of shortfalls, and the commander remains responsible for developing strategies for mitigating the risk.

Chapter IV, "Joint Operation Planning Process," discusses JOPP in more detail.

6. Constant Change, Learning, and Adaptation

"An important difference between a military operation and a surgical operation is that the patient is not tied down. But it is a common fault of generalship to assume that he is."

B. H. Liddell Hart, *Thoughts on War*

a. Joint operation planning plays a fundamental role in securing the Nation's interests in a continuously changing operational environment. Through structured review, assessment, and modification, plans are constantly assessed and updated by the JFC and reviewed by the broader JPEC and senior DOD leadership. The open and collaborative planning process provides common understanding across multiple levels of organizations and the basis for adaptation and change.

   b. Assessment of plans is a critical element of planning. Given the nonstatic nature of conflict and war and a dynamic operational environment, the joint force must continually assess and learn during execution in order to adapt and update plans to ensure that military actions are effectively contributing toward the achievement of the strategic end state. Furthermore, planners must constantly assess whether the military actions remain relevant to the attainment of a military end state. Plans must account for changes to the operational environment, strategic guidance, or the challenges facing the joint force, all of which drive the requirement for constant assessment. Feedback, generated from the assessment process, forms the basis for learning, adaptation, and subsequent refinements to the commander's guidance and operational concept. The commander and staff must constantly make certain that military actions are effective, correctly aligned with resources, and are contributing to the accomplishment of directed strategic and military end states.

Chapter III, "Operational Art and Operational Design," and Appendix D, "Assessment," discuss the assessment process in more detail.

Intentionally Blank

CHAPTER II
STRATEGIC DIRECTION AND JOINT OPERATION PLANNING

> *"The higher level of grand strategy [is] that of conducting war with a far-sighted regard to the state of the peace that will follow."*
>
> **B. H. Liddell Hart, *Strategy***

1. Strategic Guidance and Planning Overview

a. Joint planning is end state oriented. Joint plans and orders are developed with the strategic and military end states in mind. The commander and planners derive their understanding of those end states from strategic guidance. Strategic guidance comes in many forms and provides the purpose and focus of joint operation planning. Joint operation planners must know where to look for the guidance to ensure that plans are consistent with national priorities and are directed toward achieving national security goals and objectives.

b. Joint operation planning is an adaptive process. It occurs in a networked, collaborative environment, which requires dialogue among senior leaders, concurrent and parallel plan development, and collaboration across multiple planning levels. Clear strategic guidance and frequent interaction between senior leaders and planners promote an early, shared understanding of the complex operational problem presented, strategic and military end states, objectives, mission, planning assumptions, considerations, risks, and other key guidance factors. This facilitates responsive plan development and modification, resulting in constantly up-to-date plans. The focus is on developing plans that contain a variety of viable, flexible options for commanders, and in the case of top priority JSCP tasked plans, for SecDef to consider.

c. JFCs and staffs should consider how to involve interagency and multinational partners and relevant intergovernmental organizations (IGOs) and nongovernmental organizations (NGOs) in the planning process; how to coordinate and synchronize joint force actions with the operations of these organizations; and the military actions and resources required to fulfill their functions when they are unavailable, consistent with existing legal authorities. Regardless of the level of involvement during the planning process, commanders and staffs must consider their impact on joint operations.

d. This chapter introduces some of the major sources of planning guidance available to the commander and staff. It also provides information on how the commander and staff, using the APEX system, can apply strategic and operational guidance within the JPEC to produce joint plans and orders. Finally, it discusses how to integrate other departments, agencies, and multinational partners into overall joint planning efforts.

SECTION A. NATIONAL, DEFENSE, AND MILITARY GUIDANCE

2. Introduction

National security policy is developed at the NSC and approved by the President. The NSC is the President's principal forum for considering national security and foreign policy matters with the senior national security advisors and cabinet officials. NSC decisions may be directed to any of the member departments or agencies. The President chairs the NSC. Its regular attendees (both statutory and nonstatutory) are the Vice President, Secretary of State, Secretary of the Treasury, SecDef, Secretary of Homeland Security, and Assistant to the President for National Security Affairs. CJCS is the statutory military advisor to the NSC, and the Director of National Intelligence is the intelligence advisor. For DOD, the President's decisions drive strategic guidance promulgated by OSD and refined by the Joint Strategic Planning System (JSPS). To carry out Title 10, USC, statutory responsibilities, the CJCS utilizes the JSPS to provide a formal structure in aligning ends, ways, and means, and to identify and mitigate risk for the military in shaping the best assessments, advice, and direction of the Armed Forces for the President and SecDef. This section describes strategic guidance documents and other considerations.

3. National Security Council System

The NSC system is the principal forum for interagency deliberation of national security policy issues requiring Presidential decision. In addition to NSC meetings chaired by the President, the current NSC organization includes the Principals Committee, Deputies Committee, and Interagency Policy Committees. Specific issue interagency working groups support these higher-level committees. Although the actual structure of the NSC varies among administrations, its purpose is to develop and refine issues while attempting to gain interagency consensus prior to forwarding to the President for decision. The NSC prepares national security guidance that, with Presidential approval, becomes national security policy, and when implemented, these policy decisions provide the guidance for military planning and programming.

For additional information, see PPD-1, Organization of the National Security System, *and Chairman of the Joint Chiefs of Staff Instruction (CJCSI) 5715.01B,* Joint Staff Participation in Interagency Affairs.

4. National Security Strategy

a. The **NSS** is a comprehensive report required annually by Title 50, USC, Section 404a. It is prepared by the executive branch of the government for Congress and outlines the major national security concerns of the US and how the administration plans to address them using all instruments of national power. The document is purposely general in content, and its implementation relies on elaborating guidance provided in supporting documents (such as the National Defense Strategy [NDS], GEF, and NMS).

b. JFCs and their staffs can derive the broad overarching policy of the US from the NSS, but must check other DOD and military sources for refined guidance. Even though the

NSS is an annual requirement, it typically is not updated for several years at a time and may be superseded by other strategic documents and policy statements.

5. Department of Defense

a. **National Defense Strategy.** The NDS flows from the NSS, informs the NMS, and provides the foundation for building the legislatively mandated quadrennial defense review (QDR), which focuses the DOD's strategies, capabilities, and forces on operations of today and tomorrow. The NDS addresses how the Armed Forces of the United States will fight and win America's wars and describes how DOD will support the objectives outlined in the NSS. It also provides a framework for other DOD strategic guidance, specifically on deliberate planning, force development, and intelligence.

b. **Quadrennial Defense Review.** Existing legislation requires SecDef to conduct a QDR and to submit a report on the QDR to Congress every four years. The QDR articulates a national defense strategy consistent with the most recent NSS by defining force structure, modernization plans, and a budget plan allowing the military to successfully execute the full range of missions within that strategy. The report includes an evaluation by SecDef and CJCS of the military's ability to successfully execute its missions at a low-to-moderate level of risk within the forecasted budget plan.

c. **Unified Command Plan.** The UCP, signed by the President, sets forth basic guidance to all CCDRs. The UCP establishes CCMD missions and responsibilities; addresses assignment of forces; delineates geographic AORs for geographic combatant commanders (GCCs); and specifies responsibilities for functional combatant commanders (FCCs). The unified command structure identified in the UCP is flexible and changes as required to accommodate evolving US national security needs. Title 10, USC, Section 161, tasks CJCS to conduct a review of the UCP "not less often than every two years" and submit recommended changes to the President through SecDef. This document provides broad guidance that CCDRs and planners can use to derive tasks and missions during the development and modification of CCMD plans.

d. **Guidance for Employment of the Force.** The GEF provides two-year direction to CCMDs for operational planning, force management, security cooperation, and posture planning. The GEF is the method through which OSD translates strategic priorities set in the NSS, NDS, and QDR into implementable direction for operational activities. It consolidates and integrates DOD planning guidance related to operations and other military activities into a single, overarching guidance document. It replaces guidance DOD previously promulgated through the Contingency Planning Guidance, Security Cooperation Guidance, Policy Guidance for the Employment of Nuclear Weapons, and various policy memoranda related to Global Force Management (GFM) and Global Defense Posture. The GEF is an essential document for CCMD planners as it provides the strategic end states for the deliberate planning of campaign plans and contingency plans. It also directs the level of planning detail as well as assumptions, which must be considered during the development of plans.

(1) **Campaign Plans.** Global campaign plans and theater campaign plans (TCPs) are the centerpiece of the planning construct and "operationalize" CCMD theater or

functional strategies. Campaign plans should focus on the command's steady-state activities, which include ongoing operations, military engagement, security cooperation, deterrence, and other shaping or preventive activities. Campaign plans provide the vehicle for linking steady-state shaping activities to the attainment of strategic and military end states.

(2) **Contingency Plans.** The GEF guides the development of contingency plans, which address potential threats that put one or more end states at risk in ways that warrant military operations. Contingency plans are built to account for the possibility that steady-state activities could fail to prevent aggression, preclude large-scale instability in a key state or region, or mitigate the effects of a major disaster. Under the GEF's campaign planning concept, contingency plans are conceptually considered branches of the overarching campaign plans.

(3) **Global Posture.** Provides DOD-wide global defense posture (forces, footprint, and agreements) realignment guidance, to include DOD's broad strategic themes for posture changes and overarching posture planning guidance, which inform the JSCP theater posture planning guidance. Global posture establishes the requirement for CCDRs to submit theater posture plans annually to support TCPs and contingency plans. Posture plans align basing and forces to ensure theater and global security, respond to contingency scenarios, and provide strategic flexibility.

(4) **Global Force Management.** Guides the global sourcing processes of CCMD force requirements. It provides JS and force providers a decision framework for making assignment and allocation recommendations to SecDef and apportionment recommendations to CJCS. It also allows SecDef to make proactive, risk informed force management decisions.

6. Joint Strategic Planning System

The JSPS is the primary system by which the CJCS, in coordination with the other members of the Joint Chiefs of Staff (JCS) and the CCDRs, conducts deliberate planning and provides military advice to the President and SecDef. JSPS products—such as the NMS and the JSCP—provide guidance and instructions on military policy, strategy, plans, forces, and resource requirements and allocations essential to successful execution of the NSS and other Presidential directives. They also provide a means to evaluate extant US military capabilities, to assess the adequacy and risk associated with current programs and budgets, and to propose changes for consideration by the President, SecDef, and Congress. Other elements of JSPS, such as the CJCS Risk Assessment, the Joint Strategy Review, and the Comprehensive Joint Assessment, inform decision making and identify new contingencies that may warrant deliberate planning and the commitment of resources. Figure II-1 illustrates the relationship between national strategic guidance and joint operation plans (OPLANs) developed in the APEX system.

The JSPS is described in detail in CJCSI 3100.01B, Joint Strategic Planning System.

a. **National Military Strategy.** The NMS, derived from the NSS and NDS, prioritizes and focuses the efforts of the Armed Forces of the United States while conveying the CJCS's

Figure II-1. National Strategic Direction

advice with regard to the security environment and the necessary military actions to protect vital US interests. The NMS defines the national military objectives (i.e., ends), how to accomplish these objectives (i.e., ways), and addresses the military capabilities required to execute the strategy (i.e., means). The NMS provides focus for military activities by defining a set of interrelated military objectives and joint operating concepts from which the Service Chiefs and CCDRs identify desired capabilities and against which the CJCS assesses risk. Subordinate to the NMS are branch national military strategies. For example, the National Military Strategy to Combat Weapons of Mass Destruction (WMD) further develops the combating WMD guidance in the NMS by establishing military strategic objectives and military mission areas, and defining the guiding principles and strategic enablers for the military's role in combating WMD.

b. **Joint Strategic Capabilities Plan.** The JSCP is the primary vehicle through which the CJCS exercises responsibility for directing the preparation of joint plans. The JSCP **provides military strategic and operational guidance** to CCDRs, Service Chiefs, CSAs, and applicable DOD agencies for preparation of campaign plans and contingency plans **based on current military capabilities.** It serves **as the link between strategic guidance provided in the GEF and the joint operation planning activities and products that accomplish that guidance.** In addition to communicating to the CCMDs specific planning guidance necessary for deliberate planning, the JSCP also translates strategic policy end states from the GEF into military campaign and contingency plan guidance for CCDRs and expands guidance to include global defense posture, security cooperation, and other steady-state activities.

The JSCP is described in detail in CJCSI 3110.01G, Joint Strategic Capabilities Plan *(classified).*

c. **Global Force Management Implementation Guidance.** The GFMIG is a critical source document for force planning and execution. The GFMIG integrates complementary assignment, apportionment, and allocation information into a single GFM document. GFM aligns force assignment, apportionment, and allocation methodologies in support of the NDS, joint force availability requirements, and joint force assessments. It provides comprehensive insights into the global availability of US military resources and provides senior decision makers a process to quickly and accurately assess the impact and risk of proposed changes in forces assignment, apportionment, and allocation. JS prepares the document with the JS Director for Force Structure, Resource, and Assessment (J-8) overseeing the assignment and apportionment of forces and the JS Operations Directorate overseeing the allocation of forces. It is updated every two years and approved by SecDef. The GFMIG provides planners essential information for aligning resources to the military actions. It contains direction on assignment of forces to CCDRs, specifies the force allocation process that provides access to all available forces (including military, DOD, and other federal departments and agency resources), and includes apportionment tables used by CCDRs for sourcing plans requiring designation of forces. The GFMIG includes the Forces for Unified Commands Memorandum (referenced as the Forces For memorandum or the Forces For assignment tables). The memorandum provides SecDef's direction to the Secretaries of the Military Departments for assigning forces to CCMDs and serves as the record of force assignments.

See Appendix H, "Global Force Management," for additional information and descriptions.

7. **Geographic Combatant Commanders**

a. **Strategic Estimate**

(1) The strategic estimate is a tool available to CCMDs and subunified commands as they design and develop campaign plans and subordinate campaign or OPLANs. CCDRs use strategic estimates developed in peacetime to facilitate the employment of military forces across the range of military operations. The strategic estimate is more comprehensive in

scope than estimates of subordinate commanders, encompasses all aspects of the CCDR's operational environment, and is the basis for the development of the GCC theater strategy.

(2) The CCDR, the CCDR's staff, and supporting commands and agencies assess the broad strategic factors that influence the theater strategic environment, thus informing the theater strategy.

(3) The estimate should include an analysis of strategic direction received from the President, SecDef, or the authoritative body of a multinational force (MNF); an analysis of all states, groups, or organizations in the operational environment that may threaten or challenge the CCMD's ability to advance and defend US interests in the region; visualization of the relevant geopolitical, geoeconomic, and cultural factors in the region; an assessment of major strategic and operational challenges facing the CCMD; an analysis of known or anticipated opportunities the CCMD can leverage; and an assessment of risks inherent in the operational environment.

(4) The result of the strategic estimate is a visualization and better understanding of the operational environment to include allies, partners, neutrals, and potential adversaries. The strategic estimate process is continuous and provides input used for designing and developing strategies and implementing plans. The broad strategic estimate is also the starting point for conducting the commander's estimate of the situation for a specific operation.

(5) Supported and supporting CCDRs and subunified commanders all prepare strategic estimates based on assigned tasks. CCDRs who support multiple JFCs prepare estimates for each supporting operation.

See Appendix B, "Strategic Estimate," for a notional strategic estimate format.

b. **Theater Strategy.** GCCs develop a theater strategy focused on achieving specified end states for their theaters. A theater strategy is a broad statement of the commander's long-term vision for the AOR. It is the bridge between national strategic guidance and the joint operation planning required to achieve national and regional objectives and end states. Specifically, it links CCMD activities, operations, and resources to United States Government (USG) policy and strategic guidance. The theater strategy should describe the regional end state and the objectives, ways, and means to achieve it. The theater strategy should begin with the strategic estimate. Although there is no prescribed format for a theater strategy, it may include the commander's vision, mission, challenges, trends, assumptions, objectives, and resources. GCCs employ theater strategy to align and focus efforts and resources to mitigate and prepare for conflict and contingencies in their AOR and support and advance US interests. To support this goal, theater strategies normally emphasize security cooperation activities, building partner capacity, force posture, and preparation for contingencies. Theater strategies typically employ military and regional engagement, close cooperation with the Department of State (DOS), embassies, and other federal departments and agencies as ways to achieve theater objectives. Theater strategy should be informed by the means or resources available to support the accomplishment of designated end states and may include military resources, programs, policies, and available funding (see Figure II-2).

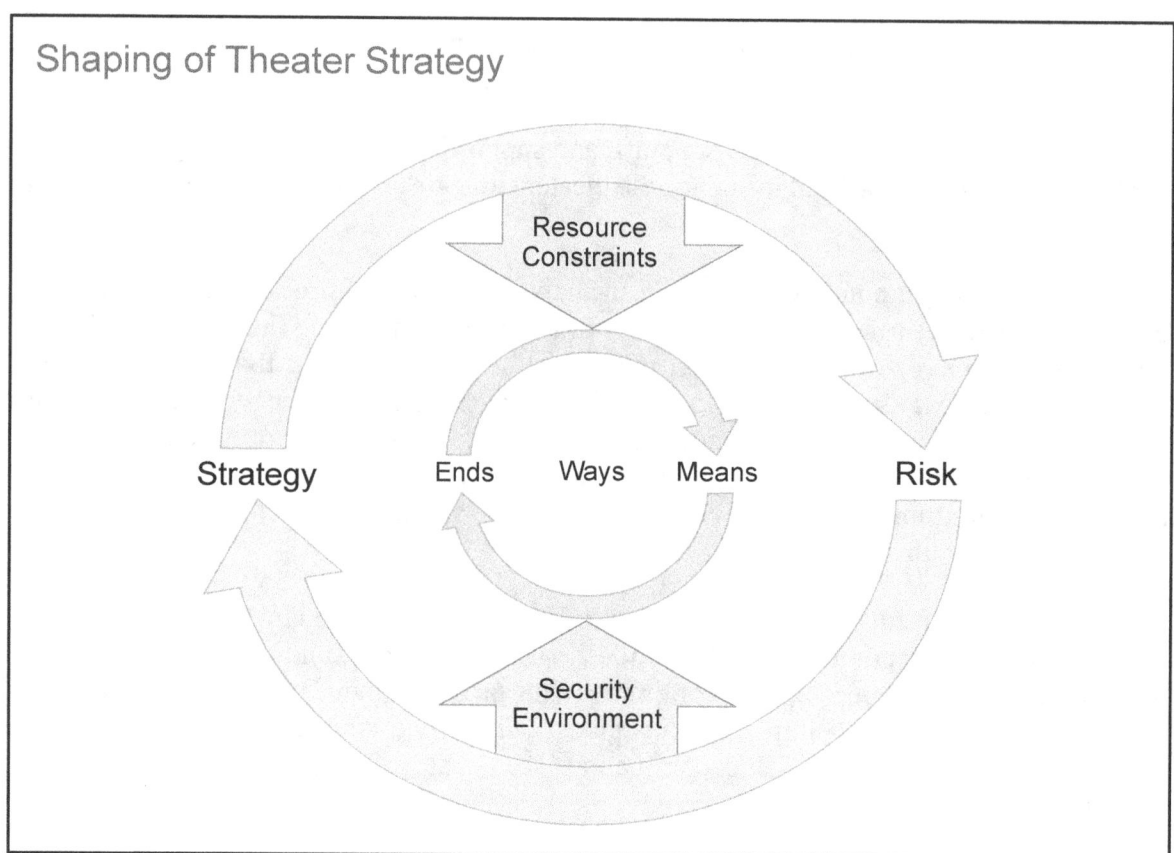

Figure II-2. Shaping of Theater Strategy

GCCs publish the theater strategy to provide guidance to subordinates and supporting commands/agencies and improve coordination with other federal departments and agencies and regional partners. The detailed execution of the theater strategy is accomplished through the TCP.

8. Interagency Considerations

a. **Achieving national strategic objectives** requires effective unified action resulting in unity of effort. This is accomplished by collaboration, synchronization, and coordination in the use of the diplomatic, informational, military, and economic instruments of national power. In such situations, military power is used in conjunction with the other instruments of national power to advance and defend US values, interests, and objectives. To accomplish this integration, the Services and DOD agencies interact with non-DOD agencies and organizations to ensure mutual understanding of the capabilities, limitations, and consequences of military and nonmilitary actions as well as the understanding of end state and termination requirements. They also identify the ways in which military and civilian capabilities best complement each other. The NSC plays a key role in the integration of all instruments of national power by facilitating mutual understanding and cooperation and is responsible for overseeing the interagency planning efforts. Further, military and civilian organizations sharing information, cooperating, and striving together to accomplish a common goal is the essence of multi-organizational coordination that makes unity of effort possible. In operations involving interagency partners and other stakeholders, where the commander may not control all elements, the commander seeks cooperation and builds consensus to achieve unity of effort. Consensus building is the key element to unity of effort.

For additional information on interagency considerations, see Joint Publication (JP) 3-08, Interorganizational Coordination During Joint Operations.

b. Commanders and planners must identify the desired contributions of other agencies and organizations and communicate needs to OSD. Further, commanders and planners should integrate limitations into their planning, such as indicating where agencies cannot act. It is critical to identify and communicate risk to mission accomplishment. Potential mitigation strategies should include COAs that do not entail the use of the military.

c. The President, assisted by the NSC, provides strategic direction to guide the efforts of USG departments and agencies and organizations that represent other instruments of national power. See Figure II-3 for other sources of strategic direction that joint planners may consider.

9. Strategic Communication

a. **Strategic communication (SC)** refers to focused USG efforts to understand and engage key audiences to create, strengthen, or preserve conditions favorable for the advancement of USG interests, policies, and objectives through the use of coordinated programs, plans, themes, messages, and products synchronized with and leveraging the actions of all instruments of national power. SC combines actions, words, and images to influence key audiences.

b. Within the USG, the DOS's Office of the Under Secretary for Public Diplomacy and Public Affairs has the lead for SC. DOS established an interagency coordination body with primary responsibility for SC oversight, called the Interagency Policy Committee on Public Diplomacy and Strategic Communication. It is led by the Under Secretary for Public Diplomacy and Public Affairs and is the overall mechanism by which the USG coordinates public diplomacy across the interagency community. A key product of this committee is the US National Strategy for Public Diplomacy and Strategic Communication. This document provides USG-level guidance, intent, strategic imperatives, and core messages under which DOD can nest its themes, messages, images, and activities.

c. The US military plays an important **supporting role** in SC, primarily through information operations (IO), public affairs, and defense support to public diplomacy. SC considerations should be included in all joint operational planning for military operations from routine, recurring military activities in peacetime through major operations.

d. Every JFC has the responsibility to develop a coordinated and synchronized **communications strategy** that links to, and supports, planning and execution of coherent national and SC effort.

e. Developing an effective communications strategy requires a comprehensive process that synchronizes all means of communication and information delivery. In addition to

---

Additional Sources of Strategic Guidance

- National Security Strategy

- National Strategy for Combating Terrorism

- National Strategy for Public Diplomacy and Strategic Communication

- National Counterintelligence Strategy

- National Intelligence Strategy

- National Strategy to Combat Weapons of Mass Destruction

- National Strategy to Combat Terrorist Travel

- National Strategy to Secure Cyberspace

- National Strategy for Homeland Security

- National Strategy for Maritime Security

- National Strategy for Information Sharing

- National Strategy for Victory in Iraq

- National Strategy for Pandemic Influenza

- National Strategy for Physical Protection of Critical Infrastructure

- National Strategy for Countering Biological Threats

List is not all inclusive.

Figure II-3. Additional Sources of Strategic Guidance

synchronizing the communications activities within the joint force, an effective communications strategy is developed in concert with other USG organizations, partner nations, and NGOs as appropriate. CCDRs should develop staff procedures for implementing SC guidance into all operational planning and targeting processes as well as collaborative processes for integrating SC activities with nonmilitary partners and subject matter experts.

See JP 1, Doctrine for the Armed Forces of the United States, *JP 3-0,* Joint Operations, *and JP 3-61,* Public Affairs, *for additional information.*

10. Strategic Guidance for Multinational Operations

a. Multinational operations start with the diplomatic efforts to create a coalition or spur an alliance into action. Discussion and coordination between potential participants initially address basic questions at the national strategic level. These senior-level discussions could

---

involve IGOs such as the United Nations or the North Atlantic Treaty Organization (NATO), existing MNFs, or individual nations. The result of these discussions should:

(1) Determine the nature and limits of the response.

(2) Determine the command structure of the response force.

(3) Determine the essential strategic guidance for the response force to include military objectives and the desired strategic and military end states.

b. In support of each MNF, a hierarchy of bilateral or multilateral bodies is established to define strategic and military end states and objectives, to develop strategies, and to coordinate strategic guidance for planning and executing multinational operations. Through dual involvement in national and multinational security processes, US national leaders integrate national and theater strategic planning with that of the MNF. Within the multinational structure, US participants work to develop objectives and strategy that complement US interests and assigned missions and tasks for participating US forces that are compatible with US capabilities. Within the US national structure, international commitments impact the development of the NMS and CCDRs should adequately address relevant concerns in strategic guidance for joint operation planning.

c. Much of the information and guidance provided for unified action and joint operations remains applicable to multinational operations. However, commanders and staffs consider differences in partners' laws, doctrine, organization, weapons, equipment, terminology, culture, politics, religion, language, and caveats on authorized military action throughout the entire operation. CCDRs and JFCs develop plans to align US forces, actions, and resources in support of the multinational plan.

d. When directed, designated US commanders participate directly with the armed forces of other nations in preparing bilateral contingency plans. Commanders assess the potential constraints, security risks, and any additional vulnerabilities resulting from bilateral planning, and how these plans impact the ability of the US to achieve its end states. Bilateral planning involves the preparation of combined, mutually developed and approved plans governing the employment of the forces of two nations for a common contingency. Bilateral planning may be accomplished within the framework of a treaty or alliance or in the absence of such arrangements. Bilateral planning is accomplished in accordance with specific guidance provided by the President, SecDef, or CJCS and captured in a bilateral strategic guidance statement (SGS) signed by the leadership of both countries.

SECTION B. APPLICATION OF GUIDANCE

11. Joint Planning and Execution Community

a. The headquarters, commands, and agencies involved in joint operation planning or committed to a joint operation are collectively termed the **JPEC.** Although not a standing or regularly meeting entity, the JPEC consists of the CJCS and other members of the JCS, JS, the Services and their major commands, the CCMDs and their subordinate commands, and the CSAs (see Figure II-4).

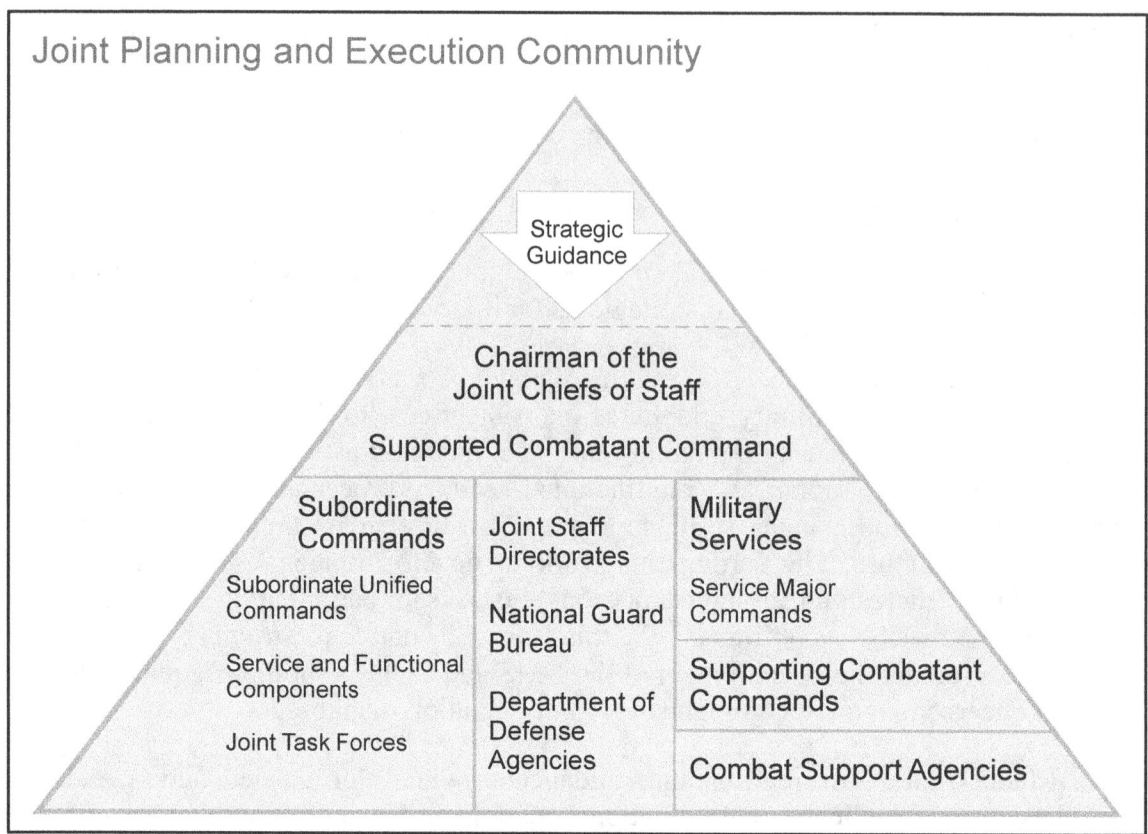

Figure II-4. Joint Planning and Execution Community

(1) The **supported CCDR** has primary responsibility for all aspects of a task assigned by the GEF, the JSCP, or other joint operation planning directives. In the context of joint operation planning, the supported commander prepares plans and orders in response to requirements generated by the President or SecDef. Once approved by SecDef or the CJCS, the designated supporting commanders provide planning assistance, forces, or other resources to a supported commander.

(2) **Supporting commanders** provide forces, assistance, or other resources to a supported commander in accordance with the principles set forth in JP 1, *Doctrine for the Armed Forces of the United States*. Supporting commanders prepare supporting plans as required. A commander may be a supporting commander for one operation while being a supported commander for another.

b. In the planning process, the President and SecDef issue policy, strategic guidance, and direction. The President, assisted by the NSC, also issues policy and strategic direction to guide the planning efforts of federal departments and agencies that represent other instruments of national power. SecDef, with the advice and assistance of the CJCS, organizes the JPEC for joint operation planning by establishing appropriate command relationships among the CCDRs. A supported commander is identified for each planning task, and supporting CCDRs, Services, and CSAs are designated as appropriate. This process provides for increased unity of command in the planning and execution of joint operations and facilitates unity of effort within the JPEC.

See CJCSI 3141.01D, Management and Review of Campaign and Contingency Plans, *for a more complete discussion of the JPEC. See JP 1,* Doctrine for the Armed Forces of the United States, *and JP 3-0,* Joint Operations, *for a more complete discussion of command relationships.*

12. Adaptive Planning and Execution System

a. Joint operation planning is accomplished through the APEX system. The JPEC uses the APEX system to monitor, plan, and execute mobilization, deployment, employment, sustainment, redeployment, and demobilization activities associated with joint operations. The APEX system operates in a networked, collaborative environment, which facilitates dialogue among senior leaders, concurrent and parallel plan development, and collaboration across multiple planning levels. Clear strategic guidance and frequent interaction between senior leaders and planners promote early understanding of, and agreement on, planning assumptions, considerations, risks, and other key factors. The focus is on developing plans that contain a variety of viable, embedded options for the President and SecDef to leverage as they seek to shape the situation and respond to contingencies. This facilitates responsive plan development and modification, resulting in continually up-to-date plans. The APEX system also promotes involvement with other USG departments and agencies and multinational partners.

b. While joint operation planning has the inherent flexibility to adjust to changing requirements, the APEX system incorporates initiatives to make the planning process even more responsive. These initiatives—such as levels of planning detail, the requirement for more frequent IPRs between CCDRs and SecDef, routine assessments, and the use of collaboration technology—provide more and better options during plan development, increase opportunities for consultation and guidance during the planning process, and promote increased agility in plan implementation.

c. Joint operation planning encompasses a number of elements, including three broad **operational activities,** four **planning functions,** and a number of related **products** (see Figure II-5). Each of these planning functions will include as many IPRs as necessary to complete the plan. IPR participants are based on the initiating authority/level. For example, formal plans directed by the JSCP require SecDef-level IPRs while plans directed by a CCDR may require only CCDR-level review.

d. IPRs constitute a disciplined dialogue among strategic leaders (most notably the CCDRs, CJCS, SecDef, and, when approved, senior DOS and other key department/agency leadership or their representatives) to shape the plan as it is developed. Topics such as guidance on coordination with the interagency and multinational communities, required supporting and supported activities, identification and removal of planning obstacles, clarification of desired objectives and strategic and military end states, key capability shortfalls, areas of risk, and resolution of planning conflicts may be discussed. Further, IPRs expedite planning by ensuring that the plan addresses the most current strategic assessments and needs. They also generate valuable feedback for planning staffs.

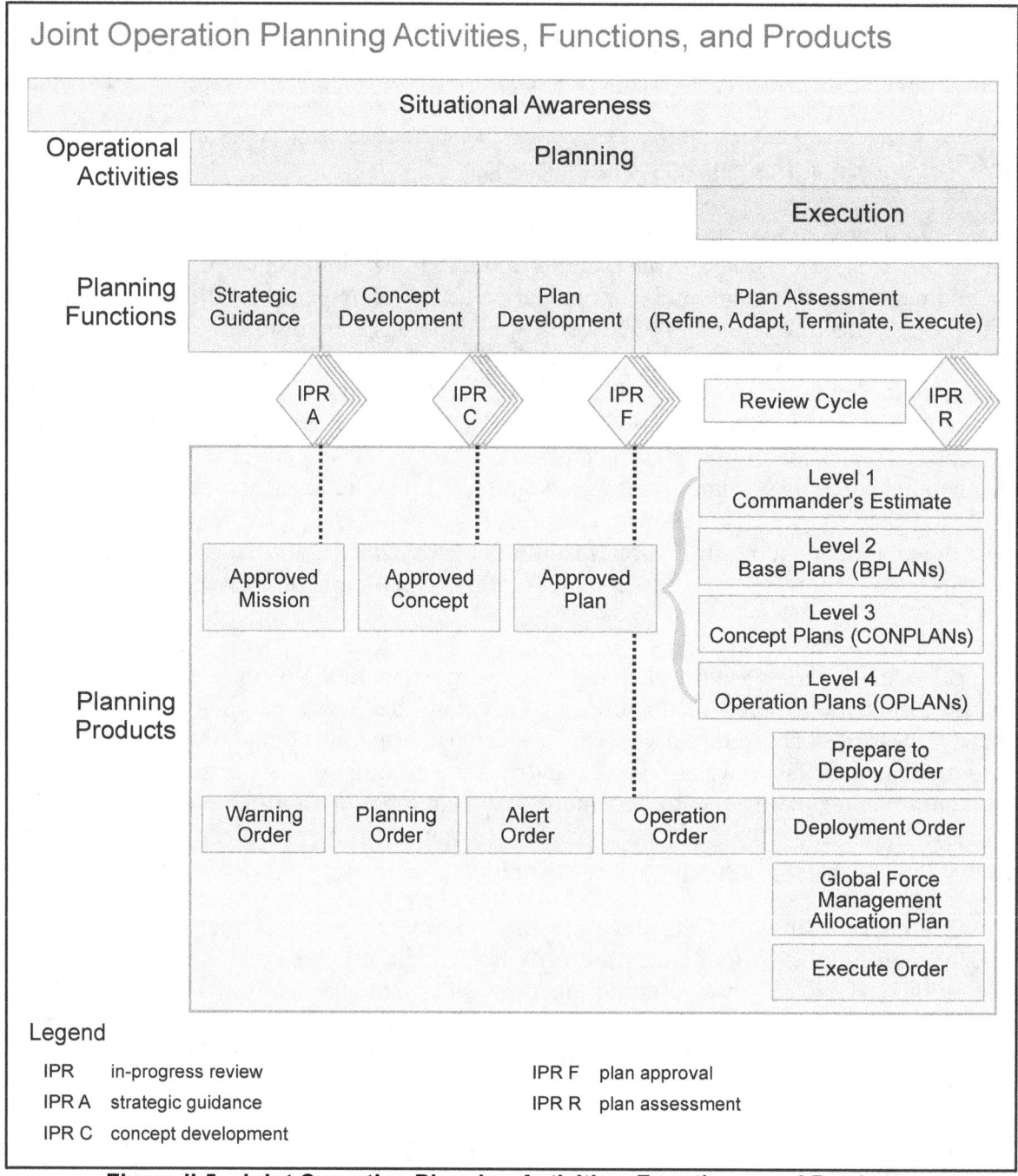

Figure II-5. Joint Operation Planning Activities, Functions, and Products

e. Generally, the IPR process will regulate the interagency dialogue and coordination, with SecDef receiving an update on the scope and scale of planning exchanges with civilian and multinational counterparts and having the opportunity to provide guidance or direction.

13. Operational Activities

a. Situational Awareness

(1) Situational awareness addresses procedures for describing the operational environment, including threats to national security. This occurs during continuous monitoring of the national and international political and military situations so that JFCs and their staffs can determine and analyze emerging crises, notify decision makers, and determine the specific nature of the threat.

(2) Situational awareness actions support both deliberate planning and crisis action planning (CAP). Situational awareness encompasses five related activities: monitoring the global situation; identifying that an event has occurred; recognizing that the event is a problem or a potential problem; reporting the event; and reviewing all-source intelligence and information to include the Defense Intelligence Agency-produced dynamic threat assessment (DTA) or the CCMD's running intelligence estimate. An event is a national or international occurrence assessed as unusual and viewed as potentially having an adverse impact on US national interests and national security. The recognition of the event as a problem or potential problem follows from the observation.

b. **Planning**

(1) Planning translates strategic guidance and direction into campaign plans, contingency plans, and operation orders (OPORDs). Joint operation planning may be based on defined tasks identified in the GEF and the JSCP. Alternatively, joint operation planning may be based on the need for a military response to an unforeseen current event, emergency, or time-sensitive crisis.

(2) Planning for contingencies is normally initiated by a GEF, JSCP, or planning directive tasking. It is based on assigned planning guidance, derived assumptions, and apportioned forces and combat support activities.

(3) Planning for crises is initiated to respond to an unforeseen current event, emergency, or time-sensitive crisis. It is based on planning guidance, actual circumstances, and usually limits force planning considerations to apportioned forces. Supported commanders evaluate the availability of their assigned and previously allocated forces to respond to the event. They also plan for potential force contributions from CSAs.

c. **Execution**

(1) **Execution begins when the President decides to use a military option to resolve a crisis.** Only the President or SecDef can authorize the CJCS to issue an execute order (EXORD). **Depending upon time constraints, an EXORD may be the only order a JFC receives. The EXORD defines the time to initiate operations and conveys guidance not provided earlier.**

(2) The CJCS monitors the deployment and employment of forces, makes recommendations to SecDef to resolve shortfalls, and tasks directed actions by SecDef and the President to support the successful execution of military operations. **Execution continues until the operation is terminated or the mission is accomplished.** In execution, the planning process is repeated continuously as circumstances and missions change.

(3) During execution, the supported CCDR assesses the deployment and employment of forces, measures progress toward mission accomplishment, and adapts and adjusts operations as required to reach the end states. This continual assessment and adjustment of operations creates an organizational environment of learning and adaptation. This adaptation can range from minor operational adjustments to a radical change of approach. **When fundamental changes have occurred that challenge existing understanding or indicate a shift in the operational environment/problem, commanders and staffs may develop a new operational approach that recognizes that the initial problem has changed, thus requiring a different approach to solving the problem. The change to the operational environment could be so significant that it may require a review of the global strategic, theater strategic, and military end states and discussions with higher authority to determine if the end states are still viable.**

(4) Early in execution, changes to the original plan may be necessary because of tactical, intelligence, and environmental considerations, force and non-unit cargo availability, availability of strategic lift assets, and port capabilities. Therefore, ongoing refinement and adjustment of deployment requirements and schedules and close coordination and monitoring of deployment activities are required.

(5) The CJCS-published EXORD defines the unnamed day on which operations commence or are scheduled to commence (D-day) and the specific time an operation begins (H-hour) and directs execution of the OPORD. While OPORD operations commence on the specified D-day and H-hour, deployments providing forces, equipment, and sustainment to support such are defined by C-day, an unnamed day on which a deployment operation begins, and a specific hour on C-day at which a deployment operation commences or is to commence (L-hour). The CJCS's EXORD is a record communication that authorizes execution of the COA approved by the President or SecDef and detailed in the supported commander's OPORD. It may include further guidance, instructions, or amplifying orders. In a fast-developing crisis, the EXORD may be the first record communication generated by the CJCS. The record communication may be preceded by a voice authorization. **The issuance of the EXORD is time-sensitive.** The format may differ depending on the amount of previous correspondence and the applicability of prior guidance. The Chairman of the Joint Chiefs of Staff Manual (CJCSM) 3122.01 series volumes contain the format for the EXORD. Information already communicated in previous orders should not be repeated unless previous orders were not made available to all concerned. The EXORD need only contain the authority to execute the operation and any additional essential guidance, such as D-day and H-hour.

(6) Throughout execution, JS, JFPs, Services, supported JFCs, and CSAs monitor movements, assess accomplishment of tasks, and resolve shortfalls as necessary. This allows the CJCS, in conjunction with the supported commander, to change guidance, modify plans, and, if necessary, recommend changes to the termination criteria.

(7) The supported commander issues an EXORD to subordinate and supporting commanders upon receipt of the CJCS's EXORD. It may give the detailed planning guidance resulting from updated or amplifying orders, instructions, or guidance that the CJCS's EXORD does not cover. The supported commander also assesses and reports

achievement of objectives and replans, redeploys, or terminates operations as necessary, in compliance with termination criteria directed by the President or SecDef. **If significant changes in the operational environment or the problem are identified, which call into question viability of the current operational approach or end states, the supported commander should consult with subordinate and supporting commanders and higher authority.**

(8) The supported commander's force requests are allocated in the CJCS Global Force Management Allocation Plan (GFMAP) annex, and the JFP publishes the GFMAP Annex Schedule to order forces to deploy. The JFP GFMAP Annex Schedule serves as the deployment order (DEPORD) for all global allocations.

(9) GCCs coordinate with United States Transportation Command (USTRANSCOM), supporting CCDRs, JS, and force providers to provide an integrated transportation system from origin to destination. Surface Deployment and Distribution Command and Military Sealift Command coordinate common user sea and land movements while Air Mobility Command coordinates common user air movements for supported GCCs. The GCCs control the flow into and out of theater using the appropriate TPFDD validation process. The geographic service components incrementally select and validate unit line numbers throughout the flow into and out of theater.

d. **Planning During Execution**

(1) Planning continues during execution, with an initial emphasis on refining the existing plan and producing the OPORD and refining the force flow utilizing employed assigned and allocated forces. As the operation progresses, planning generally occurs in three distinct but overlapping timeframes: future plans, future operations, and current operations, as Figure II-6 depicts.

(a) **The plans directorate of a joint staff (J-5) focuses on *future plans*.** The timeframe of focus for this effort varies according to the level of command, type of operation, JFC desires, and other factors. Typically, the emphasis of the future plans effort is on planning the next phase of operations or **sequels** to the current operation. In a campaign, this could be planning the next major operation or the next phase of the campaign.

(b) Planning also occurs for **branches** to current operations (*future operations planning*). The timeframe of focus for *future operations* planning varies according to the factors listed for *future plans*, but the period typically is more near-term than the *future plans* timeframe. *Future* planning normally occurs in the J-5 or joint planning group (JPG), while *future operations* planning normally occurs in the operations directorate of a joint staff (J-3).

(c) Finally, ***current operations*** planning addresses the immediate or very near-term planning issues associated with ongoing operations. This occurs in the joint operations center or J-3.

(2) During execution, progress in meeting the commander's intent and successful accomplishment of tasks will be monitored and measured, along with the input of new data

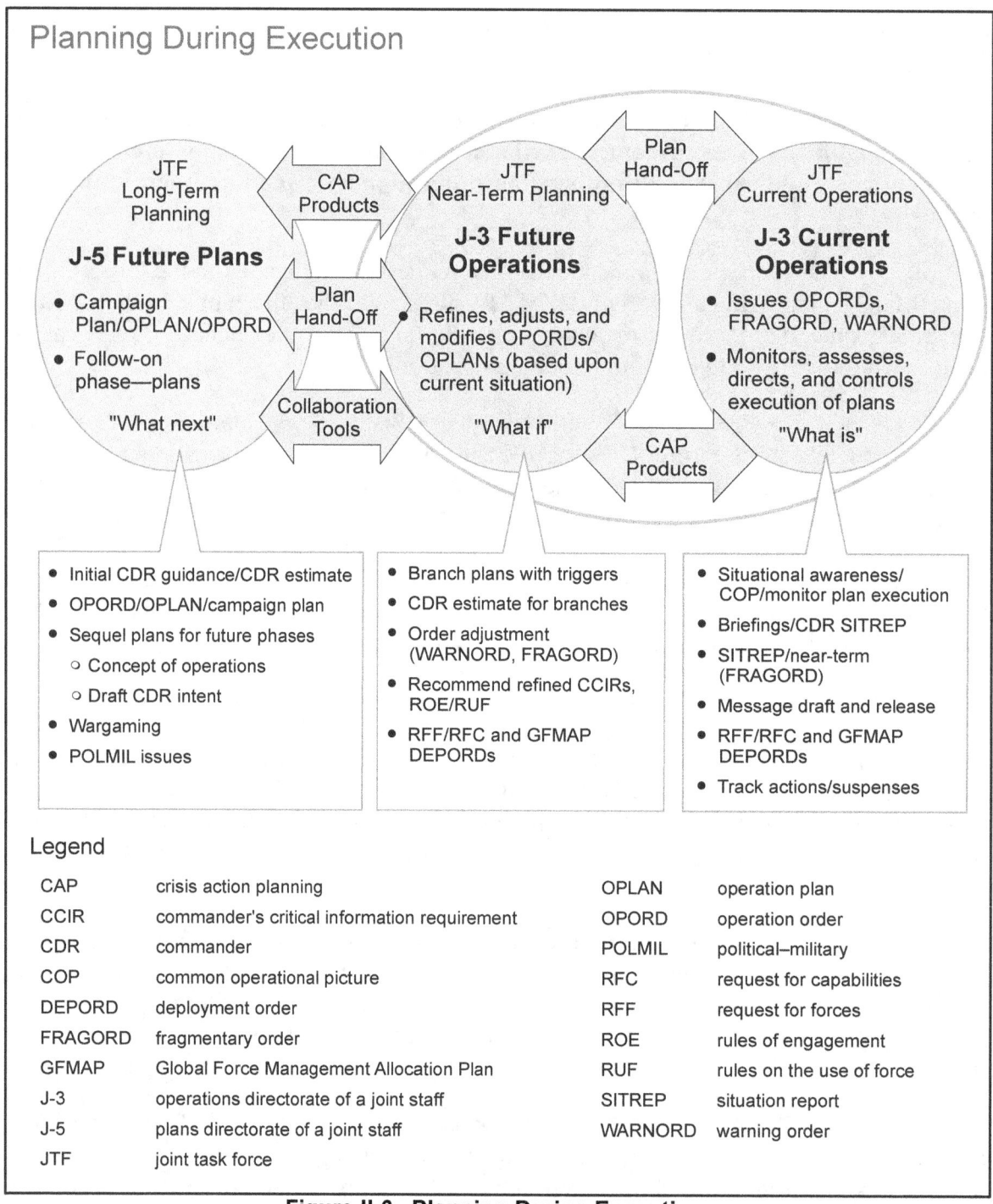

Planning During Execution

J-5 Future Plans
JTF Long-Term Planning
- Campaign Plan/OPLAN/OPORD
- Follow-on phase—plans

"What next"

CAP Products

Plan Hand-Off

Collaboration Tools

J-3 Future Operations
JTF Near-Term Planning
- Refines, adjusts, and modifies OPORDs/OPLANs (based upon current situation)

"What if"

Plan Hand-Off

CAP Products

J-3 Current Operations
JTF Current Operations
- Issues OPORDs, FRAGORD, WARNORD
- Monitors, assesses, directs, and controls execution of plans

"What is"

- Initial CDR guidance/CDR estimate
- OPORD/OPLAN/campaign plan
- Sequel plans for future phases
  - Concept of operations
  - Draft CDR intent
- Wargaming
- POLMIL issues

- Branch plans with triggers
- CDR estimate for branches
- Order adjustment (WARNORD, FRAGORD)
- Recommend refined CCIRs, ROE/RUF
- RFF/RFC and GFMAP DEPORDs

- Situational awareness/ COP/monitor plan execution
- Briefings/CDR SITREP
- SITREP/near-term (FRAGORD)
- Message draft and release
- RFF/RFC and GFMAP DEPORDs
- Track actions/suspenses

Legend

CAP	crisis action planning	OPLAN	operation plan
CCIR	commander's critical information requirement	OPORD	operation order
CDR	commander	POLMIL	political–military
COP	common operational picture	RFC	request for capabilities
DEPORD	deployment order	RFF	request for forces
FRAGORD	fragmentary order	ROE	rules of engagement
GFMAP	Global Force Management Allocation Plan	RUF	rules on the use of force
J-3	operations directorate of a joint staff	SITREP	situation report
J-5	plans directorate of a joint staff	WARNORD	warning order
JTF	joint task force		

Figure II-6. Planning During Execution

and information as it is obtained to facilitate decision making and allow for selection of branches or sequels, if applicable, or the plan to be modified as necessary.

(3) Future planners must also look for opportunities or unforeseen challenges that suggest that the current mission may require revision and that a different operational approach may be required to achieve the desired end state. They should also look for indicators that the desired end state is not achievable or no longer desirable. Subsequently,

these circumstances may result in a reframing of the problem and the development or execution of a branch plan or new COA.

(4) Execution of a plan does not end the planning process. The planning cycle may be reentered at any point to receive new guidance, provide an IPR, modify the plan, decide if and when to execute branches or sequels, or terminate the operation. Planning also continues for future operations.

14. Planning Functions

a. Although the four planning functions of strategic guidance, concept development, plan development, and plan assessment are generally sequential, they often run simultaneously in the effort to accelerate the overall planning process. SecDef or the CCDR may direct the planning staff to refine or adapt a plan by reentering the planning process at any of the earlier functions. The time spent accomplishing each activity and function depends on the nature of the crisis.

(1) In time-sensitive cases, activities and functions may be accomplished simultaneously and compressed so that all decisions are reached in open forum and orders are combined and initially may be issued orally.

(2) A crisis could be so time critical, or a single COA so obvious, that the first written directive might be a DEPORD or an EXORD.

(3) Following each of the IPRs described below, OSD will publish a memorandum for record detailing SecDef's guidance for continued planning.

b. **Strategic Guidance.** This function is used to formulate politico-military assessments at the strategic level, develop and evaluate military strategy and objectives, apportion and allocate forces and other resources, formulate concepts and strategic military options, and develop planning guidance leading to the preparation of COAs. The President, SecDef, and CJCS—with appropriate consultation with additional NSC members, other USG departments and agencies, and multinational partners—formulate strategic end states with suitable and feasible national strategic objectives that reflect US national interests.

See Chapter III, "Operational Art and Operational Design," for more details on the development of the commander's approach and operational concept.

(1) The CCDR provides input through a series of IPRs. The CCDR crafts theater and operational objectives that support national strategic objectives with the advice and consent of the CJCS and SecDef. This process begins with an analysis of existing strategic guidance such as the JSCP and GEF for deliberate planning or a CJCS warning order (WARNORD), planning order (PLANORD), or alert order (ALERTORD) in CAP. It includes mission analysis, threat assessment, and development of assumptions, which as a minimum, will be briefed to SecDef during the strategic guidance IPR.

(2) During this initial IPR, referred to as **IPR A,** the CCDR should consider discussing USG SC guidance.

(3) **The primary end products of the strategic guidance function are assumptions, conclusions about the strategic and operational environment (nature of the problem), strategic and military end states, and the supported commander's approved mission statement.**

c. **Concept Development.** During deliberate planning, the supported commander develops several COAs, each containing an initial CONOPS that identifies, at a minimum, major capabilities required and task organization, major operational tasks to be accomplished by components, a concept of employment, and assessment of risk for each COA. Each COA should contain embedded options that describe multiple alternatives to accomplish designated end states as conditions change (e.g., operational environment, problem, strategic direction). In time-sensitive situations, a WARNORD may not be issued, and a PLANORD or ALERTORD might be the first strategic guidance received by the supported commander. Using the strategic guidance and the CCDR's mission statement, planners prepare evaluation request messages to solicit COA input from subordinate units and develop preliminary COAs based upon staff estimates.

See Chapter IV, "Joint Operation Planning Process," for more details on COA development.

(1) During the concept development IPR, referred to as IPR C, the supported commander outlines several COAs and recommends one to SecDef for approval and further development. In a crisis, the supported commander recommends execution of a COA most appropriate for the emerging situation. The commander also requests SecDef's guidance on interorganizational planning and coordination and makes appropriate recommendations based on the interorganizational requirements identified during mission analysis and COA development. Concept development should consider a range of COAs that integrate robust options to provide greater flexibility and speed transition during a crisis.

(2) The main **product from the concept development function is a COA approved for further development. Detailed planning begins upon COA approval in the concept development function.**

d. **Plan Development.** This function is used to fully develop campaign plans, contingency plans, or orders, with applicable supporting annexes, and to refine preliminary feasibility analysis. This function fully integrates mobilization, deployment, employment, sustainment, conflict termination, redeployment, and demobilization activities through the six-phase joint operation construct (Phases 0–V). The CCDR briefs the final plan to SecDef (or a designated representative) during the final plan approval IPR (IPR F). CCDRs may repeat the IPR F, as needed until approval is granted. **The primary product is an approved plan or order.**

See Chapter IV, "Joint Operation Planning Process," for more details on completing the plan.

e. **Plan Assessment (Refine, Adapt, Terminate, Execute—RATE)**

(1) The supported commander continually reviews and assesses the complete plan, resulting in four possible outcomes: refine (R), adapt (A), terminate (T), or execute (E). The

supported commander and the JPEC continue to evaluate the situation for any changes that would trigger RATE. The CCDR will brief SecDef during the plan assessment IPR, referred to as IPR R, of modifications and updates to the plan based on the CCDR's assessment of the situation and the plan's ability to achieve the end states.

(2) **Refine.** During all planning efforts, plan refinement typically is an orderly process that follows plan development and is associated with the *plan assessment* planning function. Refinement then continues on a regular basis as circumstances related to the potential contingency change. In CAP, refinement is almost continuous throughout plans or OPORD development. Planners frequently adjust the plan or order based on evolving commander's guidance, results of force planning, support planning, deployment planning, shortfall identification, adversary or MNF actions, changes to the operational environment, or changes to strategic guidance. Refinement continues even after execution begins, with changes typically transmitted in the form of fragmentary orders (FRAGORDs) rather than revised copies of the plan or order.

(3) **Adapt.** Planners adapt plans when major modifications are required, which may be driven by one or more changes in the following: strategic direction, operational environment, or the problem facing the JFC. Planners continually monitor the situation for changes that would necessitate adapting the plan, to include modifying the commander's operational approach and revising the CONOPS. When this occurs, commanders may need to recommence the IPR process.

(4) **Terminate.** Commanders may recommend termination of a plan when it is no longer relevant or the threat no longer exists. For JSCP tasked plans, SecDef, with advice from the CJCS, is the approving authority to terminate a planning requirement.

(5) **Execute.** See paragraph 13c, "Execution."

15. Deliberate and Crisis Action Planning Products

Joint operation planning encompasses the preparation of a number of planning and execution-related products produced during deliberate planning or products produced during CAP.

a. **Plans Produced During Deliberate Planning.** Deliberate planning encompasses the preparation of plans that occur in non-crisis situations. It is used to develop campaign and contingency plans for a broad range of activities based on requirements identified in the GEF, JSCP, or other planning directives. A representative plans relationship is graphically displayed in Figure II-7. **Theater and global campaign plans** are the centerpiece of DOD's planning construct. They provide the means to translate CCMD theater or functional strategies into executable plans. Theater and global campaign plans provide the vehicle for linking steady-state shaping activities to current operations and contingency plans.

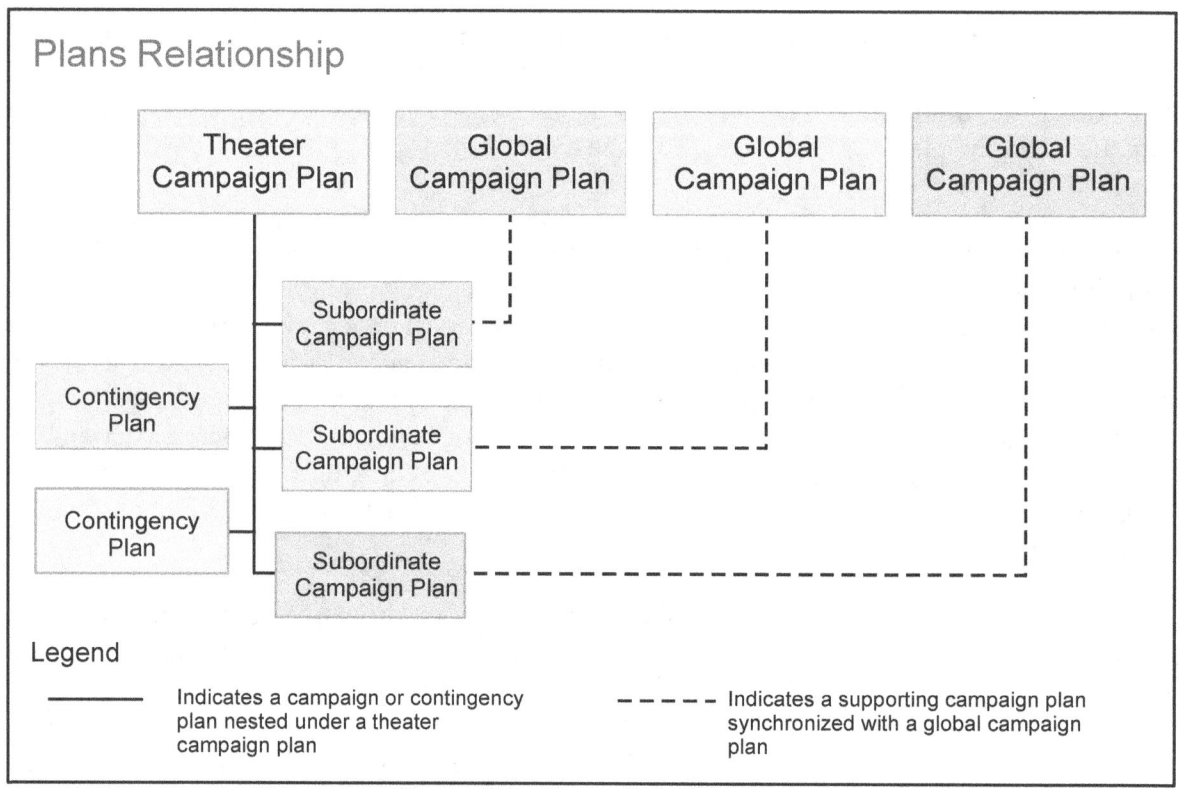

Figure II-7. Plans Relationship

(1) **Campaign Plans.** A campaign is a series of related major operations aimed at accomplishing strategic and operational objectives within a given time and space. Planning for a campaign is appropriate when the contemplated military operations exceed the scope of a single major operation. Thus, campaigns are often the most extensive joint operations in terms of time and other resources. Campaign planning has its greatest application in the conduct of large-scale combat operations, but can be used across the range of military operations.

(a) Joint force headquarters plan and execute campaigns and major operations, while Service and functional components of the joint force conduct subordinate supporting and supported major operations, battles, and engagements, not independent campaigns. GCCs or FCCs can plan and conduct subordinate campaigns as part of a theater or global campaign. While intended primarily to guide the use of military power, campaign plans consider how to coordinate all instruments of national power, as well as the efforts of various interorganizational partners, to attain national strategic objectives.

(b) Campaign plans help achieve a CCDR's strategy by comprehensively and coherently integrating all its directed steady-state activities (actual) and contingency (potential) operations and activities. A CCDR's strategy and resultant campaign plan should be designed to achieve prioritized strategic end states and serve as the integrating framework that informs and synchronizes all subordinate and supporting planning and operations.

(c) Steady-state operations and activities, which encompass shaping activities (including shaping elements of contingency plans), should be designed to support ongoing operations, prepare to defeat potential adversaries, succeed in a wide range of contingencies, build the capacity of partner nations, and, in conjunction with the other instruments of national power, promote stability in key regions and support other broad national goals. The campaign plan is the primary vehicle for designing, organizing, integrating, and executing security cooperation activities.

(d) Under this construct, plans developed to respond to contingencies are best understood as branches to the overarching global campaign plan or TCP. They address scenarios that put one or more US strategic end states in jeopardy and leave the US no recourse other than to address the problem through military actions. Military actions can be in response to many scenarios, including armed aggression, regional instability, a humanitarian crisis, or a natural disaster. Contingency plans should provide a range of military options, to include flexible deterrent options (FDOs) or flexible response operations, and should be coordinated with the total USG response.

(2) Contingency Plans

(a) Contingency plans are developed in anticipation of a potential crisis outside of crisis conditions. A contingency is a situation that likely would involve military forces in response to natural and man-made disasters, terrorists, subversives, military operations by foreign powers, or other situations as directed by the President or SecDef. The JPEC uses deliberate planning to develop plans for a broad range of contingencies based on tasks identified in the GEF, JSCP, or other planning directives. Deliberate planning facilitates the transition to CAP and informs the TCP.

(b) Planners develop plans from the best available information, using forces and resources apportioned and allocated per the GFMIG. Deliberate planning encompasses the activities associated with the development of contingency plans for the deployment, employment, sustainment, and redeployment of apportioned forces and resources in response to potential crises identified in joint strategic planning documents. **Deliberate planning relies heavily on assumptions** regarding the circumstances that will exist when a crisis arises. The transition from deliberate planning to CAP and execution should be as seamless as possible. To accomplish this, planners develop a fully documented CONOPS that details the assumptions, enemy forces, operation phases, prioritized missions, and force requirements, deployment, and positioning. Detailed, war-gamed, refined, and fully documented deliberate planning supports sound force acquisition and training in preparation for the most likely operational requirements. It also enables rapid comparison of the hypothetical conditions, operation phases, missions, and force requirements of the contingency plans to the actual requirements of CAP. Work performed during deliberate planning allows the JPEC to develop the processes and procedures as well as the analytical and planning expertise that are critically needed during CAP.

(c) If a situation develops during the two-year cycle of the GEF/JSCP that warrants a new plan but was not anticipated, SecDef, through the CJCS, tasks the appropriate supported CCDR and applicable supporting CCDRs, Services, and CSAs, out-of-cycle, to begin deliberate planning in response to the new situation. The primary mechanism for tasking deliberate planning for a contingency outside of the GEF/JSCP cycle will be through an SGS from SecDef and a PLANORD from the CJCS to the CCDRs. The SGS (effectively a change to the GEF) provides important strategic and policy guidance on the front end of the planning process.

(d) Plans are produced, reviewed, and updated periodically to ensure relevancy. Deliberate planning most often addresses contingencies where military options focus on combat operations; however, these plans also account for other types of joint military operations. In addition to plans addressing all phases, including those where military action may support other agencies, planning addresses contingencies where the military is in support from the onset. These include homeland security, defense support of civil authorities, and foreign humanitarian assistance.

(e) There are four levels of planning detail for contingency plans, with an associated planning product for each level.

<u>1.</u> **Level 1 Planning Detail—Commander's Estimate.** This level of planning involves the least amount of detail and focuses on producing multiple COAs to address a contingency. The product for this level can be a COA briefing, command directive, commander's estimate, or a memorandum. The commander's estimate provides SecDef with military COAs to meet a potential contingency. The estimate reflects the supported commander's analysis of the various COAs available to accomplish an assigned mission and contains a recommended COA.

<u>2.</u> **Level 2 Planning Detail—Base Plan (BPLAN).** A BPLAN describes the CONOPS, major forces, concepts of support, and anticipated timelines for completing the mission. It normally does not include annexes or a TPFDD.

<u>3.</u> **Level 3 Planning Detail—Concept Plan (CONPLAN).** A CONPLAN is an OPLAN in an abbreviated format that may require considerable expansion or alteration to convert it into an OPLAN or OPORD. It includes a plan summary, a BPLAN, and usually includes the following annexes: A (Task Organization), B (Intelligence), C (Operations), D (Logistics), J (Command Relations), K (Communications), S (Special Technical Operations), V (Interagency Coordination), and Z (Distribution) (see the CJCSM 3122.01 series volumes). It may also produce a TPFDD if applicable. (This is referred to as a level 3-T plan.) A troop list and TPFDD would also require that an annex E (Personnel) be prepared.

<u>4.</u> **Level 4 Planning Detail—OPLAN.** An OPLAN is a complete and detailed joint plan containing a full description of the CONOPS, all annexes applicable to the plan, and a TPFDD. It identifies the specific forces, functional support, and resources required to execute the plan and provide closure estimates for their flow into the theater. OPLANs can be quickly developed into an OPORD. An OPLAN is normally prepared when:

<u>a.</u> The contingency is critical to national security and requires detailed prior planning.

<u>b.</u> The magnitude or timing of the contingency requires detailed planning.

<u>c.</u> Detailed planning is required to support multinational planning.

<u>d.</u> Detailed planning is necessary to determine force deployment, employment, sustainment, and redeployment requirements, determine available resources to fill identified requirements, and validate shortfalls.

(f) Contingency plans are created as part of a collaborative process that engages SecDef, OSD, CJCS, JCS, CCDRs, and staffs of the entire JPEC in the development of relevant plans for all contingencies identified in the GEF, JSCP, and other planning directives. Deliberate planning also includes JPEC concurrent, collaborative, and parallel joint planning activities. The JPEC review those plans tasked in the JSCP for SecDef approval. The Under Secretary of Defense for Policy (USD[P]) also reviews those plans for policy considerations in parallel with their approval by the CJCS. A CCDR can request a JPEC review for any tasked or untasked plans that pertain to the AOR. In addition, the CCDR can request a JPEC review during any planning function in the process, including plan assessment. CCDRs may direct the development of additional plans by their commands to accomplish assigned or implied missions.

(g) When directed by the President or SecDef through the CJCS, CCDRs may convert level 1, 2, and 3 plans into level 4 OPLANs or into fully developed OPORDs for execution.

(3) Global Campaign Plans

(a) When the scope of contemplated military operations exceeds the authority or capabilities of a single CCDR to plan and execute, the President or SecDef directs the CJCS to implement global planning procedures and assist SecDef in the strategic direction and integration of the planning effort. The President or SecDef normally makes the decision to implement global planning procedures as a UCP responsibility delegated to a CCDR or during the assessment of the situation. The commander's assessment supporting this decision could be either the assessments of multiple CCDRs addressing a similar threat in their AORs or a single assessment from a CCDR addressing the threat from a global, cross-AOR, or functional perspective. Situations that may trigger this assessment range from major combat operations to the threat of asymmetric attack that extends across CCMD boundaries and functions and requires the strategic integration of the campaigns and major operations of two or more CCDRs. One example of a persistent threat that is inherently global and poses risk across AOR boundaries is adversary exploitation and attack of DOD computer networks on the global information grid. Another example of a persistent global threat requiring global unity of effort is the threat from transnational terrorists and WMD.

(b) Per Title 10, USC, SecDef may assign the CJCS responsibility for overseeing the activities of the CCMDs. Such assignment by SecDef does not confer any command authority on the CJCS and does not alter CCDRs' responsibilities prescribed in Title 10, USC, Section 164(b)(2). A CCDR delegated that authority will lead the global planning effort for the purposes of planning, integrating, and coordinating a commander's estimate from a global perspective, but does not have the authority to execute the resulting plan.

(c) **When the President or SecDef decides to implement global planning procedures,** the CJCS or delegated CCDR, with the authority of SecDef, issues a planning directive to the JPEC and assigns or assumes the role of a supported commander **for planning purposes only.** The CJCS or delegated CCDR performs a mission analysis; issues initial global planning guidance based on national strategic objectives and priorities; and develops global COAs in coordination with the affected CCMDs, Services, and CSAs. The purpose of this global COA is to mitigate operational gaps, seams, and vulnerabilities from a global perspective. This will be achieved through a recommendation for the optimal allocation, prioritization, or reallocation of forces and capabilities required to develop a cohesive global concept of operation. Global planning procedures will detail how **CCDRs** will employ forces and capabilities in support of another CCDR. The global COA will be based largely on recommendations of the affected CCDRs. These **CCDR** COAs may require reiteration or refinement as initial planning apportionments are adjusted for compliance within the global concept of operation. Planners must be aware of competing requirements for potentially scarce strategic resources such as intelligence, surveillance, and reconnaissance (ISR) capabilities and transportation and ensure global planning is coordinated with GFM procedures.

(d) Global planning procedures are also applicable during CAP. Global crisis conditions exist when CAP procedures address situations that threaten two or more GCCs' AORs and competing demands for forces and capabilities exceed availability. The CJCS or delegated CCDR is required to mitigate operational gaps, seams, and vulnerabilities and resolve the conflict over forces, resources, capabilities, or priorities from a global perspective.

(e) When directing the execution of the contingency plan or OPORD, the President or SecDef will also select a CCDR as supported commander for implementation of the global plan. The supported commander is the commander having primary responsibility for all aspects of a task assigned by the JSCP or other joint operation planning authority. In the context of joint operation planning, this term refers to the commander who prepares OPLANs or OPORDs in response to requirements of the CJCS. The decision to designate a supported commander who is responsible for preparing the joint OPLAN does not mean that the only command relationships option available during execution is "support." Global planning procedures do not absolve GCCs of assigned planning and execution roles and responsibilities within their respective AORs.

(f) **Global Synchronizer**

<u>1</u>. A global synchronizer for planning is the lead CCDR responsible for directing the coordinated planning efforts of CCDRs, Services, CSAs, and applicable DOD agencies and field activities in support of a designated DOD global campaign plan to achieve the integrated, yet decentralized, execution of global activities and operations. The phrase

"synchronizing planning" pertains specifically to planning efforts only and does not, by itself, convey authority to execute operations or direct execution of operations.

a. Unless directed by SecDef, the global synchronizer's role is not to execute specific plans, but to align and harmonize plans and recommend sequencing of actions by CCDRs, Services, CSAs, and applicable DOD agencies and field activities to achieve the DOD global campaign plan's strategic end states and objectives.

b. CCDRs develop **subordinate campaign plans** to satisfy the planning requirements of DOD global campaign plans. While these plans are designated subordinate plans, this designation does not alter current command relationships. GCCs remain the supported commanders for the execution of their plans unless otherwise directed by SecDef.

2. If directed to develop a DOD global campaign plan, the global synchronizer will:

a. Provide a common plan structure and strategic framework to guide and inform development of CCDR subordinate campaign plans, Service, and DOD agency supporting plans and mitigate seams and vulnerabilities from a global perspective.

b. Establish a common process for the development of subordinate and supporting plans.

c. Organize and execute coordination and collaboration conferences in support of the global campaign to enhance development of subordinate and supporting plans consistent with the established strategic framework and to coordinate and conduct synchronization activities.

d. Disseminate "best practices" to CCDRs, Services, and applicable DOD agencies and field activities. This includes the consolidation and standardization of CAP, products, and collaborative tools.

e. Review and synchronize all subordinate and supporting plans to align them with the DOD global campaign plan.

f. Make recommendations for the prioritization of force and capability allocation across CCMDs from a global perspective.

g. Provide advice and recommendations to **CCDRs,** JS, and OSD to enhance integration and synchronization of subordinate and supporting plans with the DOD global campaign plan.

h. Accompany **CCDRs** as they brief their subordinate campaign plans through final approval, as required.

i. Provide global campaign plans to **CCDRs** prior to IPRs with enough time for CCDRs to review and propose modifications.

> > j. In coordination with JS, conduct assessments to measure progress in achieving the campaign plan's strategic end states.

> > k. In coordination with JS, make recommendations for the SC annex.

> 3. CCDRs, Services, applicable DOD agencies, and field activities will:

> > a. Provide detailed planning support to the global synchronizer to assist in development of the DOD global campaign plan.

> > b. Support global synchronizer conferences and planning efforts.

> > c. Develop subordinate or supporting plans consistent with the strategic framework, planning guidance, and process established by the global synchronizer.

> > d. Provide subordinate or supporting plans to the global synchronizer prior to IPRs with enough time for the global synchronizer to review and propose modifications prior to the IPR.

> > e. The global synchronizer and CCDRs will seek to resolve issues prior to SecDef IPRs. As a last option, unresolved issues will be adjudicated during IPRs.

(4) **Supporting Plans.** Supporting CCDRs, subordinate JFCs, component commanders, and CSAs prepare **supporting plans** as tasked by the JSCP or other planning guidance. Commanders and staffs prepare supporting plans in CONPLAN/OPLAN format that follow the supported commander's concept and describe how the supporting commanders intend to achieve their assigned objectives and/or tasks. Supporting commanders and staffs develop these plans responsively in collaboration with the supported commander's planners. As part of this collaborative process, supported commanders specify the level of detail required and review and approve the resulting supporting plans. In almost every case, a supporting plan will not possess a higher level of detail or planning than the directing supported plan. Supporting commanders or agencies may, in turn, assign their subordinates the task of preparing additional supporting plans.

CJCSI 3141.01D, Management and Review of Campaign and Contingency Plans, *governs the formal review and approval process for campaign plans and level 1–4 plans.*

b. **Orders Produced During Crisis Action Planning**

(1) CAP Overview

(a) A crisis is an incident or situation that typically develops rapidly and creates a condition of such diplomatic, economic, or military importance that the President or SecDef considers a commitment of US military forces and resources to achieve national objectives. It may occur with little or no warning. It is fast-breaking and requires accelerated decision making. Sometimes a single crisis may spawn another crisis elsewhere.

(b) CAP provides the CJCS and CCDRs a process for getting vital decision-making information up the chain of command to the President and SecDef. CAP facilitates information sharing among the members of the JPEC and the integration of military advice from the CJCS in the analysis of military options. Additionally, CAP allows the President and SecDef to communicate their decisions rapidly and accurately through the CJCS to the CCDRs, subordinate and supporting commanders, Services, and CSAs to initiate detailed military planning, change deployment posture of the identified force, and execute military options. It also outlines the mechanisms for monitoring the execution of the operation.

(c) CAP encompasses the activities associated with the time-sensitive development of OPORDs for the deployment, employment, and sustainment of assigned, attached, and allocated forces and capabilities in response to a situation that may result in actual military operations. While deliberate planning normally is conducted in anticipation of future events, CAP is based on circumstances that exist at the time planning occurs. CAP can use plans developed in deliberate planning for a similar contingency. If unanticipated circumstances occur, and no plan proves adequate for the operational circumstances, then CAP and execution would begin mission analysis under JOPP in a "no plan" situation. There are always situations arising in the present that might require US military response. Such situations may approximate those previously planned for in deliberate planning, though it is unlikely they would be identical, and sometimes they will be completely unanticipated. The time available to plan responses to such real-time events is short. In as little as a few days, commanders and staffs must develop and approve a feasible COA with TPFDD; publish the plan or order; prepare forces; ensure sufficient communications systems support; develop and execute an all-source ISR planning and directing, collection, processing and exploitation, analysis and production management, and dissemination plan; and arrange sustainment for the employment of US military forces. Figure II-8 provides a comparison of deliberate planning and CAP.

(d) In a crisis, situational awareness is continuously fed by the latest all-source intelligence and operations reports. An adequate and feasible military response in a crisis demands flexible procedures that consider time available, rapid and effective communications, and relevant previous planning products whenever possible.

(e) **In a crisis or time-sensitive situation, the CCDR uses the initial CAP situational awareness phase to review previously prepared contingency plans for suitability.** The CCDR converts these plans to executable OPORDs or develops OPORDs from scratch when no useful contingency plan exists.

(f) CAP activities are similar to deliberate planning activities, but CAP is based on dynamic, real-world conditions. CAP procedures provide for the rapid and effective exchange of information and analysis, the timely preparation of military COAs for consideration by the President or SecDef, and the prompt transmission of their decisions to the JPEC. CAP activities may be performed sequentially or in parallel, with supporting and subordinate plans or OPORDs being developed concurrently. The exact flow of activities is

Deliberate Planning and Crisis Action Planning Comparison

	Deliberate Planning	Crisis Action Planning
Time available	As defined in authoritative directives (normally 6+ months)	Situation dependent (hours, days, up to 12 months)
Environment	Distributed, collaborative planning	Distributed, collaborative planning and execution
JPEC involvement	Full JPEC participation (Note: JPEC participation may be limited for security reasons.)	Full JPEC participation (Note: JPEC participation may be limited for security reasons.)
APEX operational activities	Situational awareness Planning	Situational awareness Planning Execution
APEX functions	Strategic guidance Concept development Plan development Plan assessment	Strategic guidance Concept development Plan development Plan assessment
Document assigning planning task	CJCS issues: 1. JSCP 2. Planning directive 3. WARNORD (for short suspense planning)	CJCS issues: 1. WARNORD 2. PLANORD 3. SecDef-approved ALERTORD
Forces for planning	Apportioned in JSCP	Allocated in WARNORD, PLANORD, or ALERTORD
Planning guidance	CJCS issues JSCP or WARNORD CCDR issues PLANDIR and TPFDD LOI	CJCS issues WARNORD, PLANORD, or ALERTORD CCDR issues WARNORD, PLANORD, or ALERTORD and TPFDD LOI to subordinates, supporting commands, and supporting agencies
COA selection	CCDR selects COA and submits strategic concept to CJCS for review and SecDef approval	CCDR develops commander's estimate with recommended COA
CONOPS approval	SecDef approves CSC, disapproves or approves for further planning	President/SecDef approve COA, disapproves or approves further planning
Final planning product	Campaign plan Level 1–4 contingency plan	OPORD
Final planning product approval	CCDR submits final plan to CJCS for review and SecDef for approval	CCDR submits final plan to President/SecDef for approval
Execution document	Not applicable	CJCS issues SecDef-approved EXORD CCDR issues EXORD

Legend

ALERTORD	alert order	JSCP	Joint Strategic Capabilities Plan
APEX	Adaptive Planning and Execution	LOI	letter of instruction
CCDR	combatant commander	PLANDIR	planning directive
CJCS	Chairman of the Joint Chiefs of Staff	PLANORD	planning order
COA	course of action	OPORD	operations order
CONOPS	concept of operations	SecDef	Secretary of Defense
CSC	commanders' strategic concept	TPFDD	time-phased force and deployment data
EXORD	execution order		
JPEC	joint planning and execution community	WARNORD	warning order

Figure II-8. Deliberate Planning and Crisis Action Planning Comparison

largely determined by the time available to complete the planning and by the significance of the crisis (see Figure II-9). The following paragraphs summarize the activities and interaction that occur during CAP. Refer to the CJCSM 3122 series of publications, which address planning policies and procedures, for detailed procedures.

1. When the President, SecDef, or CJCS decides to develop military options, the CJCS issues a planning directive to the JPEC initiating the development of COAs and requesting that the supported commander submit a commander's estimate of the situation with a recommended COA to resolve the situation. Normally, the directive will be a WARNORD, but a PLANORD or ALERTORD may be used if the nature and timing of the crisis warrant accelerated planning. In a quickly evolving crisis, the initial WARNORD may be communicated vocally with a follow-on record copy to ensure that the JPEC is kept informed. If the directive contains a force deployment preparation order or DEPORD, SecDef approval is required.

2. The WARNORD describes the situation, establishes command relationships, and identifies the mission and any planning constraints. It may identify forces and strategic mobility resources, or it may request that the supported commander develop these factors. It may establish tentative dates and times to commence mobilization,

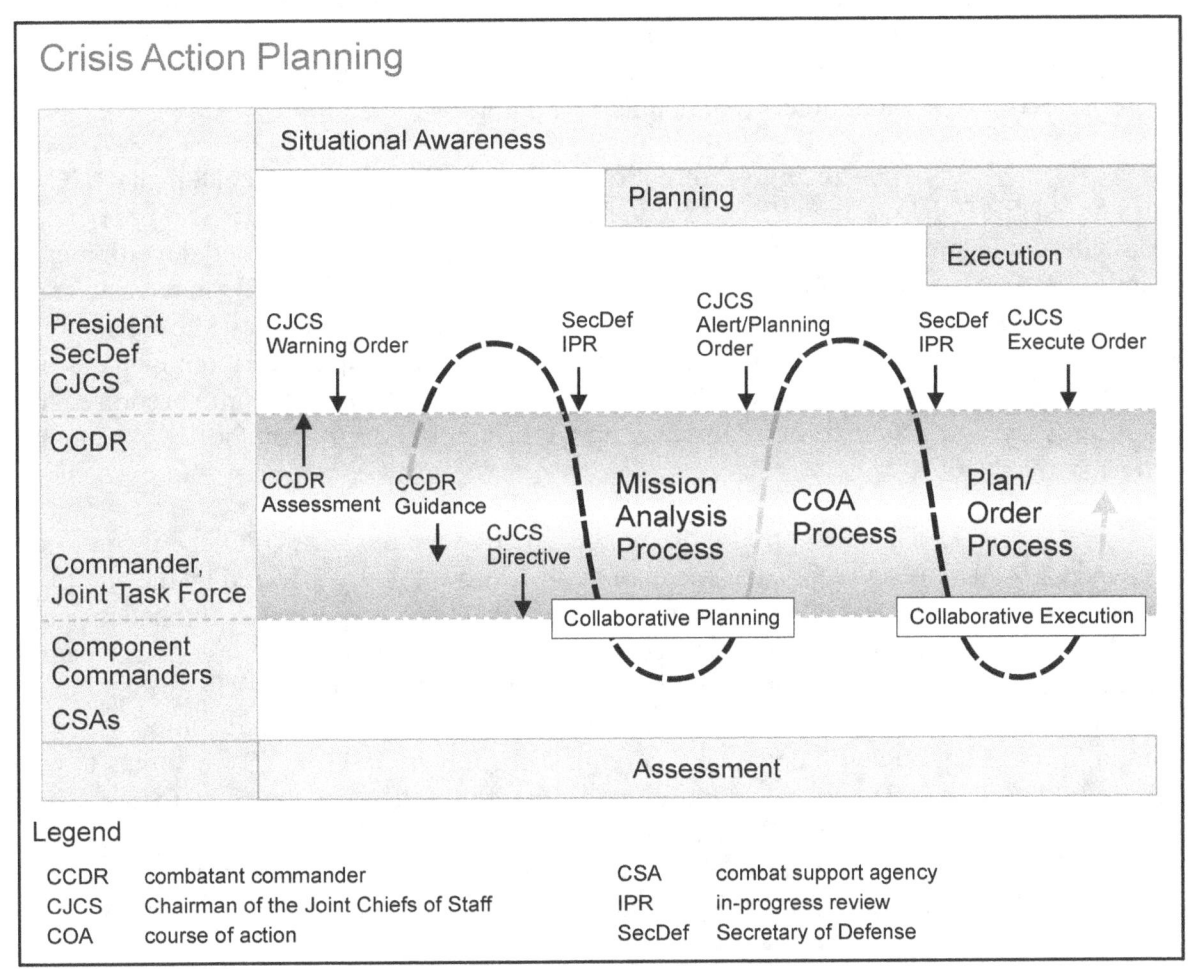

Figure II-9. Crisis Action Planning

deployment, or employment, or it may solicit the recommendations of the supported commander regarding these dates and times. If the President, SecDef, or CJCS directs development of a specific COA, the WARNORD will describe the COA and request the supported commander's assessment. A WARNORD sample is in the CJCSM 3122.01 series volumes.

3. In response to the WARNORD, the supported commander, in collaboration with subordinate and supporting commanders and the rest of the JPEC, reviews existing joint contingency plans for applicability and develops, analyzes, and compares COAs and prepares a commander's estimate that provides recommendations and advice to the President, SecDef, or higher headquarters for COA selection. Based on the supported commander's guidance, supporting commanders begin their planning activities.

4. Although an existing plan almost never completely aligns with an emerging crisis, it can be used to facilitate rapid COA development. An existing OPLAN or CONPLAN can be modified to fit the specific situation. An existing CONPLAN can be fully developed beyond the stage of an approved CONOPS. TPFDDs developed for specific plans are stored in the APEX database and available to the JPEC for review.

5. The CJCS, in consultation with other members of the JCS and CCDRs, reviews and evaluates the supported commander's estimate and provides recommendations and advice to the President and SecDef for COA selection. The supported commander's COAs may be refined or revised, or new COAs may have to be developed. The President or SecDef selects a COA and directs that detailed planning be initiated.

6. Upon receiving directions from the President or SecDef, the CJCS issues an ALERTORD to the JPEC. SecDef approves the ALERTORD. The order is a record communication that the President or SecDef has approved the detailed development of a military plan to help resolve the crisis. The contents of an ALERTORD may vary, and sections may be deleted if the information has already been published, but it should always describe the selected COA in sufficient detail to allow the supported commander, in collaboration with other members of the JPEC, to conduct the detailed planning required to deploy, employ, and sustain forces. However, the ALERTORD does not authorize execution of the approved COA.

7. The supported commander then develops an OPORD using the approved COA. Understandably, the speed of completion is greatly affected by the amount of prior planning and the planning time available. The supported commander and subordinate commanders identify force requirements, contract requirements and management, and mobility resources, and describe the CONOPS in OPORD format. The supported commander reviews available assigned and allocated forces that can be used to respond to the situation and then submits a request for forces (RFF) to JS for forces to be allocated. JS tasks a JFP to provide a sourcing solution for each of the requested forces. The JFPs work collaboratively with the Services (via their assigned Service components) and other CCDRs to provide recommended sourcing solutions to JS. Upon receiving the recommended sourcing solutions, JS recommends the solution to SecDef to authorize

allocation of the force. JS publishes a modification to the GFMAP documenting the force allocation and directing the JFP to publish the GFMAP Annex Schedule as the DEPORD and the JFP publishes a modification to the GFMAP Annex Schedule to deploy forces. Then the supported CCDR, in coordination with the force providers, further refines the TPFDD.

8. The supported CCDR submits the completed OPORD for approval to SecDef or the President via the CJCS. The President or SecDef may decide to begin deployment in anticipation of executing the operation or as a show of resolve, execute the operation, place planning on hold, or cancel planning pending resolution by some other means. Detailed planning may transition to execution as directed or become realigned with continuous situational awareness, which may prompt planning product adjustments and/or updates.

9. **In CAP, plan development continues after the President or SecDef's execution decision.** When the crisis does not lead to execution, the CJCS provides guidance regarding continued planning under either CAP or deliberate planning procedures.

(g) **Abbreviated Procedures.** The preceding discussion describes the activities sequentially. During a crisis, they may be conducted concurrently or considered and eliminated, depending on prevailing conditions. It is also possible that the President or SecDef may decide to commit forces shortly after an event occurs, thereby significantly compressing planning activities. Although the allocation process has standard timelines, these timelines may be accelerated, but the force allocation process is still used and SecDef ultimately allocates forces. No specific length of time can be associated with any particular planning activity. **Severe time constraints may require crisis participants to pass information verbally, including the decision to commit forces.** Verbal orders are followed up with written orders.

(2) Joint Operation Orders (Figure II-10)

(a) **Warning Order.** A WARNORD, issued by the CJCS, is a planning directive that initiates the development and evaluation of military COAs by a supported commander and requests that the supported commander submit a commander's estimate.

(b) **Planning Order.** A PLANORD is a planning directive that provides essential planning guidance and directs the initiation of plan development before the directing authority approves a military COA.

(c) **Alert Order.** An ALERTORD is a planning directive that provides essential planning guidance and directs the initiation of plan development after the directing authority approves a military COA. An ALERTORD does not authorize execution of the approved COA.

(d) **Prepare to Deploy Order.** The CJCS, by the authority of and at the direction of the President or SecDef, issues a prepare to deploy order (PTDO) or DEPORD to increase or decrease the deployability posture of units; to deploy or redeploy forces; or to direct any other action that would signal planned US military action or its termination in response to a particular crisis event or incident.

Types of Orders

	Order Type	Intended Action	SecDef Approval Required
Warning order	WARNORD	Initiates development and evaluation of COAs by supported commander Requests commander's estimate be submitted	No Required when WARNORD includes deployment or deployment preparation actions
Planning order	PLANORD	Begins execution planning for anticipated President or SecDef-selected COA Directs preparation of OPORDs or contingency plan	No Conveys anticipated COA selection by the President or SecDef
Alert order	ALERTORD	Begins execution planning on President or SecDef-selected COA Directs preparation of OPORD or contingency plan	Yes Conveys COA selection by the President or SecDef
Prepare to deploy order	PTDO	Increase/decrease deployability posture of units	Yes Refers to five levels of deployability posture
Deployment/redeployment order	DEPORD	Deploy/redeploy forces Establish C-day/L-hour Increase deployability Establish JTF	Yes Required for movement of unit personnel and equipment into combatant commander's AOR
Execute order	EXORD	Implement President or SecDef decision directing execution of a COA or OPORD	Yes
Operation order	OPORD	Effect coordinated execution of an operation	Specific to the OPORD
Fragmentary order	FRAGORD	Issued as needed after an OPORD to change or modify the OPORD execution	No

Legend

AOR	area of responsibility	L-hour	specific hour on C-day at which a deployment operation commences or is to commence
C-day	unnamed day on which a deployment operation begins		
COA	course of action	OPORD	operation order
JTF	joint task force	SecDef	Secretary of Defense

Figure II-10. Types of Orders

(e) **Deployment/Redeployment Order.** A planning directive from SecDef, issued by the CJCS, that authorizes and directs the transfer of forces between CCMDs by reassignment or attachment. A deployment/redeployment order normally specifies the authority that the gaining CCDR will exercise over the transferred forces.

(f) **Execute Order.** An EXORD is a directive to implement an approved military CONOPS. Only the President and SecDef have the authority to approve and direct the initiation of military operations. The CJCS, by the authority of and at the direction of the President or SecDef, may subsequently issue an EXORD to initiate military operations. Supported and supporting commanders and subordinate JFCs use an EXORD to implement the approved CONOPS.

(g) **Operation Order.** An OPORD is a directive issued by a commander to subordinate commanders for the purpose of effecting the coordinated execution of an operation. Joint OPORDs are prepared under joint procedures in prescribed formats during CAP.

(h) **Fragmentary Order.** A FRAGORD is an abbreviated form of an OPORD (verbal, written, or digital), which eliminates the need for restating information contained in a basic OPORD while enabling dissemination of changes to previous orders. It is usually issued as needed or on a day-to-day basis.

SECTION C. INTERORGANIZATIONAL PLANNING AND COORDINATION

General. Interorganizational planning and coordination is the interaction that occurs among elements of DOD; engaged USG departments and agencies; state, territorial, local, and tribal agencies; foreign military forces and government departments and agencies; IGOs; NGOs; and the private sector for the purpose of accomplishing an objective. Successful interorganizational coordination of plans facilitates unity of effort among multiple organizations by promoting common understanding of the capabilities, limitations, and consequences of military and civilian actions. It also assists with identifying common objectives and the ways in which military and civilian capabilities best complement each other to achieve these objectives.

16. Interagency Planning and Coordination

a. **Interagency Planning and Coordination. Interagency coordination** is the interaction that occurs among USG departments and agencies, including DOD, for the purpose of accomplishing an objective. Interagency coordination forges the vital link between the US military and the other instruments of national power.

b. Through all stages of planning for campaigns, contingencies, and crises, CCDRs and subordinate JFCs should seek to involve relevant USG departments and agencies in the planning process. CCDRs should make an early assessment as to those USG departments and agencies that are the most vital in supporting elements of their plans and coordinate early, through JS and OSD (as per guidance in the GEF), with those interagency partners. Generally, interagency dialogue and coordination will be regulated through the IPR process, with SecDef receiving an update on the scope, scale, and substance of planning exchanges with civilian and multinational counterparts.

c. Effective collaboration and coordination with interagency partners can be a critical component to successful steady-state activities as well as during the stability and enable civil authority phases of an operation when JFCs may also operate in support of other USG departments and agencies. JFCs and their staffs must consider how the capabilities of these departments and agencies and NGOs can assist in accomplishing military missions and the broader national strategic objectives. GCCs should coordinate directly with interagency representatives within their AOR during planning to obtain appropriate agreements that support their plans (such as working with US embassies to secure overflight rights with other nations). Coordination with NGOs should normally be done through the United States Agency for International Development senior development advisor assigned to each CCDR.

d. OSD and JS, in consultation with the Services, National Guard Bureau, and CCMDs, facilitate interagency support and coordination to support DOD plans as required. While supported GCCs are the focal points for interagency coordination in support of operations in their AORs, interagency coordination with supporting commanders is just as important. At the operational level, subordinate commanders should consider and integrate interagency capabilities into their estimates, plans, and operations.

e. The APEX system facilitates interagency review of plans and appropriate annexes approved by the Office of the Under Secretary of Defense for Policy [OUSD(P)] following guidance provided in IPRs. Interagency plan reviews differ from DOD JPEC plan reviews in that inputs from non-DOD agencies are requested but not required. Additionally, non-DOD agency inputs are advisory in nature and, while a valued part of the process, do not carry veto authority. Nevertheless, provision is made for participating agencies to follow up on issues surfaced during the review in accordance with guidance from the OUSD(P).

f. A number of factors can complicate the coordination process, including the agencies' different and sometimes conflicting policies, legal authorities, roles and responsibilities, procedures, decision-making processes, and culture. Operations may be executed by nonmilitary organizations or perhaps even NGOs with the military in support. In such instances, the understanding of military end state and termination requirements may vary among the participants. The JFC must ensure that interagency partners clearly understand military capabilities, requirements, operational limitations, liaison, and legal considerations and that military planners understand the nature of the relationship and the types of support they can provide. The JFC's civil–military operations center can facilitate these relationships. **In the absence of a formal command structure, JFCs may be required to build consensus to achieve unity of effort.** Robust liaison facilitates understanding, coordination, and mission accomplishment.

g. **Planning and Coordination with Other Agencies.** The supported commander is responsible for developing annex V, (Interagency Coordination), for each joint level 3 or 4 plan. Annex V should be collaboratively developed with interagency inputs. CCMDs should seek OSD approval for full releasability of this annex to all affected agencies during development to ensure inputs are considered and incorporated at the earliest stage practicable. Annex V should specify the objectives, tasks, and desired level of shared situational awareness required to resolve the situation, and identify the anticipated capabilities required to accomplish tasks. This common understanding enables interagency planners to more rigorously plan their efforts in concert with the military, to suggest other activities or partners that could contribute to the operation, and to better determine support requirements. The staff considers interagency participation for each phase of the operation (see Chapter III, "Operational Art and Operational Design," for a discussion of phases).

See JP 3-08, Interorganizational Coordination During Joint Operations, *and the CJCSM 3122.01 series volumes, for additional information.*

17. Multinational Planning and Coordination

a. **General.** *Multinational operations* is a collective term to describe military actions conducted by forces of two or more nations. Such operations are usually undertaken within the structure of a coalition or alliance, although other possible arrangements include supervision by an IGO (such as the United Nations or Organization for Security and Cooperation in Europe). A **coalition** is an arrangement between two or more nations for common action. Nations usually form coalitions for a single occasion or for longer cooperation in a narrow area of common interest. An **alliance** is a result of formal agreements between two or more nations for broad, long-term objectives that further the common interests of the members. **Key to any multinational operation is the achievement of unity of effort** among political and military leaders of member nations emphasizing common objectives and shared interests as well as mutual support and respect. Agreement on clearly identified strategic and military end states for the MNF is essential to guide all multinational coordination, planning, and execution. Additionally, the cultivation and maintenance of personal relationships between each counterpart are fundamental to achieving success. At times, it needs to be acknowledged that US national interests may not be in complete agreement with those of the multinational organization or some of its individual nation states. In such situations, additional consultations and coordination will be required at the political and military levels for the establishment of a common set of operational objectives to support unity of effort among nations.

b. Collective security is a strategic goal of the US, and joint operation planning will frequently be accomplished within the context of multinational operation planning. There is no single doctrine for multinational action, and each MNF develops its own protocols and OPLANs/CONPLANs/OPORDs. US planning for joint operations should accommodate and complement such protocols and plans. JFCs must also anticipate and incorporate planning factors such as domestic and international laws, regulations, and operational limitations on the use of contributed forces, various weapons, and tactics.

(1) Joint forces should be prepared for combat and noncombat operations with forces from other nations within the framework of an MNF under US or another nation's leadership. Following, contributing, and supporting are important roles in multinational operations—often as important as leading.

(2) MNF commanders develop multinational strategies and plans in multinational channels. Supporting US JFCs perform operation planning for multinational operations in US national channels. Coordination of these separate planning channels occurs at the national level by established multinational bodies or member nations and at the theater-strategic and operational levels by JFCs, who are responsible within both channels for operation planning matters.

(3) US doctrine and procedures for joint operation planning also are conceptually applicable to multinational challenges, and the general considerations for interaction with IGOs and host-nation organizations are similar to those for interaction with USG departments and agencies. The fundamental issues are much the same for both situations.

c. **Operational-Level Integration.** The commander of US forces dedicated to a multinational military organization is responsible for integrating joint operation planning with multinational planning at the operational level. Normally, this will be the GCC or the subordinate JFC responsible for the geographic area within which multinational operations are to be planned and executed. These commanders always function within two chains of command during any multinational operation—the multinational chain of command and the US national chain of command. Within the multinational organizations, they command or support the designated MNF and plan, as appropriate, for multinational employment in accordance with strategic guidance emanating from multinational leadership. Within the US chain of command, they command joint US forces and prepare joint plans in response to requirements from the President, SecDef, and the CJCS. These tasks include developing joint plans to support each multinational commitment within the GCC's AOR and planning for unilateral US contingencies within the same area. In this dual capacity, the US commander coordinates multinational planning with joint operation planning.

d. Each MNF normally develops its own protocols and plans to guide multinational action.

(1) For example, within the Asia-Pacific region, the Multinational Force Standing Operating Procedures (MNF SOP) developed and administered by the Multinational Planning Augmentation Team, a cadre of military planners from Asia-Pacific Rim nations led by United States Pacific Command, provides a starting point. The intent of this MNF SOP is to increase the speed of response, interoperability, mission effectiveness, and unity of effort in MNF operations during crisis action situations. It is designed to reduce the ad hoc nature of multinational CAP by establishing common "operational start points" for MNF operations and establishing SOPs for the MNF headquarters.

(2) Similarly for NATO operations, US and other NATO countries have developed and ratified an Allied joint doctrine hierarchy of publications that outlines the doctrine and tactics, techniques, and procedures that should be used during NATO operations. JFCs, their staffs, and subordinate forces should have access to and review these publications prior to participating in NATO operations.

18. Review of Multinational Plans

US joint strategic plans or contingency plans prepared in support of multinational plans are developed, reviewed, and approved exclusively within US operational channels. They may or may not be shared in total with multinational partners. Selected portions and/or applicable planning and deployment data may be released in accordance with CJCSI 5714.01, *Policy for the Release of Joint Information*. USG representatives and commanders within each multinational organization participate in multinational planning and exchange information in mutually devised forums, documents, and plans. The formal review and approval of multinational plans is accomplished in accordance with specific procedures adopted by each multinational organization and may or may not include separate US review or approval. Multilateral contingency plans routinely require national-level US approval.

JP 3-16, Multinational Operations, *and JP 4-08,* Logistics Support of Multinational Operations, *provide greater detail. The CJCSM 3122.01 series volumes describe review and approval procedures for plans. Multinational planning augmentation team MNF SOP, available at http://community.apan.org/, provides commonly agreed upon formats and procedures that may assist with planning efforts in a multinational environment.*

Intentionally Blank

CHAPTER III
OPERATIONAL ART AND OPERATIONAL DESIGN

> *"War is an art and as such is not susceptible of explanation by fixed formula"*
>
> **General George S. Patton, Jr., *Success in War*,**
> ***The Infantry Journal Reader*, 1931**

1. Introduction

a. The JFC and staff develop plans and orders through the application of operational art and operational design and by using JOPP. They combine art and science to develop products that describe how (ways) the joint force will employ its capabilities (means) to achieve the military end state (ends). Operational art is the application of creative imagination by commanders and staffs—supported by their skill, knowledge, and experience. Operational design is a process of iterative understanding and problem framing that supports commanders and staffs in their application of operational art with tools and a methodology to conceive of and construct viable approaches to operations and campaigns. Operational design results in the commander's operational approach, which broadly describes the actions the joint force needs to take to reach the end state. Finally, JOPP is an orderly, analytical process through which the JFC and staff translate the broad operational approach into detailed plans and orders. This chapter describes operational art and operational design, while Chapter IV, "Joint Operation Planning Process," discusses the details of JOPP.

b. Commanders who are skilled in the use of operational art provide the vision that links tactical actions to strategic objectives. More specifically, the interaction of operational art and operational design provides a bridge between strategy and tactics, linking national strategic aims to tactical combat and noncombat operations that must be executed to accomplish these aims. Likewise, **operational art promotes unified action** by helping JFCs and staffs understand how to facilitate the integration of other agencies and multinational partners toward achieving strategic and operational objectives.

c. Through operational art, commanders link ends, ways, and means to achieve the desired end state (see Figure III-1). This requires commanders to answer the following questions:

(1) What is the military end state that must be achieved, how is it related to the strategic end state, and what objectives must be achieved to enable that end state? **(Ends)**

(2) What sequence of actions is most likely to achieve those objectives and the end state? **(Ways)**

(3) What resources are required to accomplish that sequence of actions within given or requested resources? **(Means)**

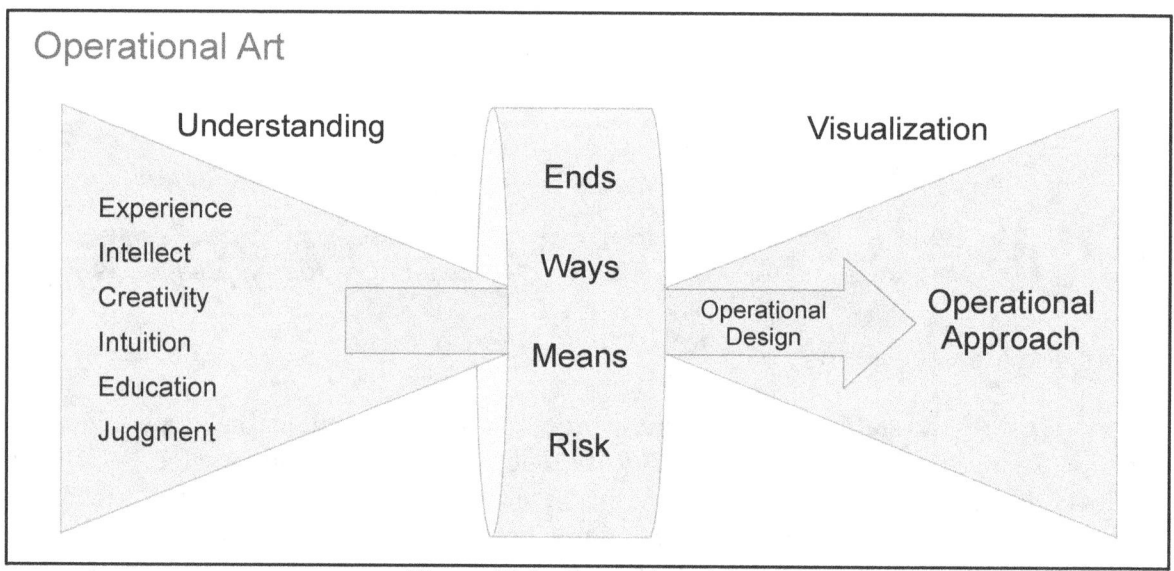

Figure III-1. Operational Art

(4) What is the chance of failure or unacceptable consequences in performing that sequence of actions? **(Risk)**

d. Operational design supports operational art with a general methodology using elements of operational design for understanding the situation and the problem. The methodology helps the JFC and staff to understand conceptually the broad solutions for attaining mission accomplishment and to reduce the uncertainty of a complex operational environment. Additionally, it supports a recursive and ongoing dialogue concerning the nature of the problem and an operational approach to achieve the desired end states (see Figure III-2). The elements of operational design are individual tools, such as center of gravity (COG) and lines of operation (LOOs), which help the JFC and staff visualize and describe the broad operational approach. These operational design elements, described in detail in Section B, "Elements of Operational Design," are also useful throughout JOPP.

2. The Commander's Role

a. **The commander is the central figure in operational design,** due not only to education and experience, but also because the commander's judgment and decisions are required to guide the staff through the process. Generally, the more complex a situation, the more critical is the role of the commander early in planning. Commanders draw on operational design to mitigate the challenges of complexity and uncertainty, leveraging their knowledge, experience, judgment, and intuition to generate a clearer understanding of the conditions needed to focus effort and achieve success. Operational design supports the effective exercise of command, providing a broad perspective that deepens understanding and visualization.

b. Commanders compare similarities of their current situations with their own experiences or history to distinguish the unique features that require innovative or adaptive solutions. They understand that each situation requires a solution tailored to the context of

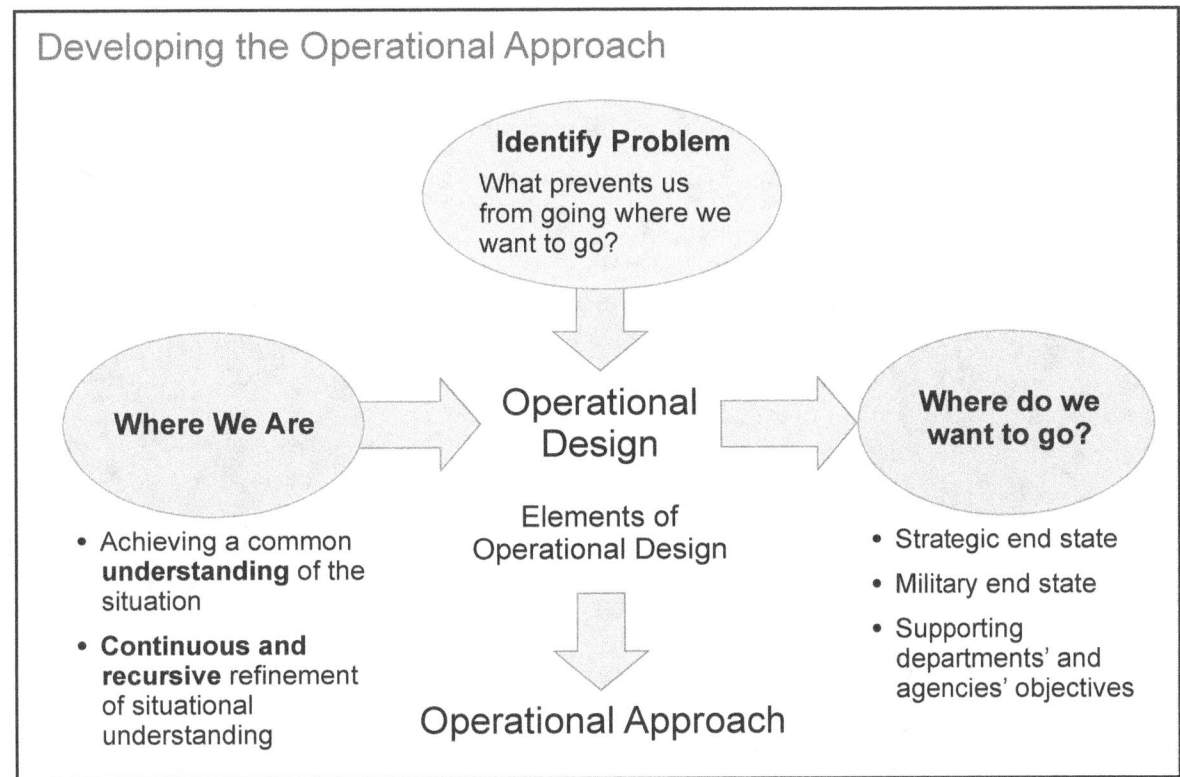

Figure III-2. Developing the Operational Approach

the problem. Through the application of operational design, commanders seek innovative, adaptive options to solve complex challenges.

c. **Operational design requires the commander to encourage discourse and leverage dialogue and collaboration to identify and solve complex, ill-defined problems** (see Figure III-3). To that end, the commander must empower organizational learning and develop methods to determine if modifying the operational approach is necessary during the course of an operation. This requires continuous assessment and reflection that challenge understanding of the existing problem and the relevance of actions addressing that problem.

d. **In particular, commanders collaborate with their higher headquarters to resolve differences of interpretation of higher-level objectives and the ways and means to accomplish these objectives.** Understanding the operational environment, defining the problem, devising a sound approach, and developing a workable solution are rarely achieved the first time. Strategic guidance addressing complex problems can initially be vague, requiring the commander to interpret and filter it for the staff. **While CCDRs and national leaders may have a clear strategic perspective of the problem, operational-level commanders and subordinate leaders often have a better understanding of specific circumstances that comprise the operational situation.** Both perspectives are essential to a sound solution. Subordinate commanders should be aggressive in sharing their perspective with their higher headquarters, and both should resolve differences at the earliest opportunity. While policy and strategic guidance clarify planning, it is equally true that planning offers clarity to policy formulation.

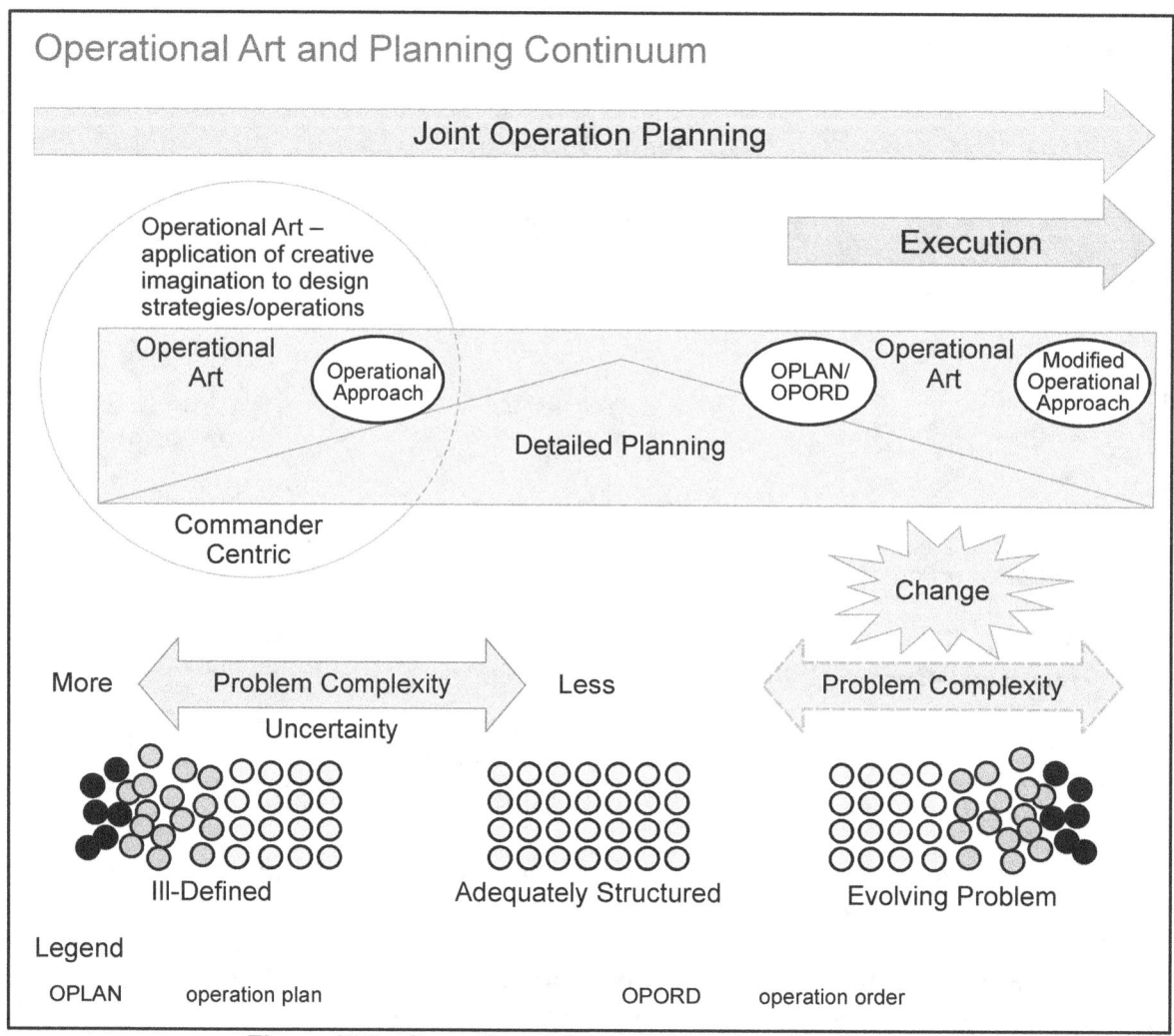

Figure III-3. Operational Art and Planning Continuum

e. Unity of effort is essential to meet the complex challenges facing the US. The need to embrace the participation of interagency and multinational partners in the interest of a comprehensive, unified approach to operations is as important as the commander's effort to build a coherent operational approach. The commander must decide how and when to include other partners early in this effort, and understand that the resulting operational approach may, of necessity, be a consensus-based product.

f. While operational art is generally considered the JFC's responsibility due to advanced experience, education, intuition, and judgment, planners and other staff rely on these attributes as well during planning. This is important because the JFC's typical competing responsibilities, particularly during CAP, usually will not allow full-time participation early in planning. Nonetheless, the JFC must ensure at least the minimum essential interaction with planners during the early design effort as it moves toward the key point when the commander approves an operational approach that will drive detailed planning.

g. Red teaming:

(1) Gathering and analyzing information— along with discerning the perceptions of adversaries, partners and others—is necessary to correctly frame the problem, which enables planning of operations. A red team can aid a commander and the staff to think critically and creatively; to see things from varying perspectives; to challenge their thinking; to avoid false mind-sets, biases, or group thinking; or use inaccurate analogies to frame the problem.

(2) Red teaming provides an independent capability to fully explore alternatives in plans and operations in the context of the operational environment and from the perspective of adversaries and others.

(3) Commanders use red teams to aid them and their staffs to provide insights and alternatives during design, planning, execution, and assessment to:

(a) Broaden the understanding of the operational environment;

(b) Assist the commander and staff in framing problems and defining end state conditions;

(c) Challenge assumptions;

(d) Consider the perspectives of the adversary and others as appropriate;

(e) Aid in identifying friendly and enemy vulnerabilities and opportunities;

(f) Assist in identifying areas for assessment as well as the assessment metrics;

(g) Anticipate the cultural perceptions of partners, adversaries, and others; and

(h) Conduct independent critical reviews and analyses of plans to identify potential weaknesses and vulnerabilities.

(4) In essence, red teams provide the commander and staff with an independent capability to challenge the organization's thinking.

(5) This red team crosses staff functions and time horizons in JOPP. This characteristic makes this red team unlike a red cell, which is composed of members of the staff of the intelligence directorate of a joint staff (J-2) and performs threat emulation, or a joint intelligence operations center red team as an additive element on the J-2 staff to improve the intelligence analysis, products, and processes.

SECTION A. DEVELOPING THE OPERATIONAL APPROACH

3. Overview

a. **The operational approach is a commander's description of the broad actions the force must take to achieve the desired military end state.** It is the commander's visualization of how the operation should transform current conditions into the desired conditions at end state—the way the commander wants the operational environment to look at the conclusion of operations. **The operational approach is based largely on an understanding of the operational environment and the problem facing the JFC.** Once the JFC approves the approach, it provides the basis for beginning, continuing, or completing detailed planning. The JFC and staff should continually review, update, and modify the approach as the operational environment, end states, or the problem change.

b. Commanders and their staffs can use operational design when planning any joint operation. Notwithstanding a commander's judgment, education, and experience, the operational environment often presents situations so complex that understanding them—let alone attempting to change them—exceeds individual capacity. Nor does such complexity lend itself to coherent planning. Bringing adequate order to complex problems to facilitate further detailed planning requires an iterative dialogue between commander and planning staff. Rarely will members of the staff recognize an implicit operational approach during their initial analysis and synthesis of the operational environment. Successful development of the approach requires continuous analysis, learning, dialogue, and collaboration between commander and staff, as well as other subject matter experts. The challenge is even greater when the joint operation involves other agencies and multinational partners (which is typically the case), whose unique considerations can complicate the problem.

c. It is essential that commanders, through a dialogue with their staffs, planning teams, initiative groups, and any other relevant sources of information, first gain an understanding of the operational environment and define the problem facing the joint force prior to conducting detailed planning. From this understanding of the operational environment and definition of the problem, commanders develop their broad operational approach for transforming current conditions into desired conditions at end state. The operational approach will underpin the operation and the detailed planning that follows. As detailed planning occurs, the JFC and staff continue discourse and refine their operational approach.

d. During execution, the JFC will likely have reason to consider updating the operational approach. This could involve significantly refining or discarding the hypotheses or models that form the basis of the operational approach. It could be triggered by significant changes to understanding of the operational environment and/or problem, the conditions of the operational environment, or the end state. The JFC may determine one of three ways ahead:

(1) The current joint OPLAN is adequate, with either no change or minor change (such as execution of a branch)—the current operational approach remains feasible.

(2) The joint OPLAN's mission and objectives are sound, but the operational approach is no longer feasible or acceptable—a new operational approach is required.

(3) The mission and/or objectives are no longer valid, thus a new joint OPLAN is required—a new operational approach is required to support the further detailed planning.

e. Assessment could cause the JFC to shift the focus of the operation, which the JFC would initiate with his new visualization manifested through new planning guidance for an adjusted operation or campaign plan.

For additional information on assessment, see Appendix D, "Assessment."

4. Methodology

a. **Introduction.** Three distinct aspects of a methodology collectively assist with producing an operational approach. Together, they constitute an organizational learning methodology that corresponds to three basic questions that must be answered to produce an actionable operational approach to guide detailed planning:

(1) Understand the strategic direction. (What are the strategic goals to be achieved and the military objectives that support their attainment?)

(2) Understand the operational environment. (What is the larger context that will help me determine our problem?)

(3) Define the problem. (What problem is the design intended to solve?)

(4) The answers to these three questions support the development of an operational approach. (How will the problem be solved?)

b. **Understand the Strategic Direction**

(1) Strategic guidance is essential to operational art and operational design. As discussed in Chapter I, "Role of Joint Operation Planning," the President, SecDef, CJCS, and CCDRs all promulgate strategic guidance. In general, this guidance provides long-term as well as intermediate or ancillary objectives. It should define what constitutes "victory" or success **(ends)** and allocate adequate forces and resources **(means)** to achieve strategic objectives. The operational approach **(ways)** of employing military capabilities to achieve the ends is for the supported JFC to develop and propose. Connecting resources and tactical actions to strategic ends is the responsibility of the operational commander.

(2) For specific situations that require the employment of military capabilities (particularly for anticipated large-scale combat), the President and SecDef typically will establish a set of **strategic objectives;** however, in the absence of coherent guidance or direction, the CCDR/JFC may need to collaborate with policymakers in the development of these objectives. Achievement of strategic objectives should result in attainment of the **strategic end state—the broadly expressed conditions that should exist after the conclusion of a campaign or operation.** Based on the strategic guidance, the CCDR will determine the **military end state** and strategic military objectives, which define the role of military forces. These objectives are the basis for operational design.

(3) The commander and staff must analyze all available sources of guidance. These sources include written documents, such as the GEF and JSCP, written directives, oral instructions from higher headquarters, domestic and international laws, policies of other

organizations that are interested in the situation, SC guidance, and higher headquarters' orders or estimates.

c. **Understand the Operational Environment**

(1) The operational environment is the composite of the conditions, circumstances, and influences that affect the employment of capabilities and bear on the decisions of the commander. It encompasses physical areas and factors of the air, land, maritime, and space domains and the information environment (which includes cyberspace). **Included within these areas are the adversary, friendly, and neutral actors that are relevant to a specific joint operation.** Understanding the operational environment helps the JFC to better identify the problem; anticipate potential outcomes; and understand the results of various friendly, adversary, and neutral actions and how these actions affect achieving the military end state (see Figure III-4).

(2) **The commander must be able to describe both the current state of the operational environment and how the operational environment should look when operations conclude (desired end state) to visualize an approach to solving the problem.** Planners can compare the current conditions of the operational environment with the desired end state conditions. Identifying necessary end state conditions and termination criteria early

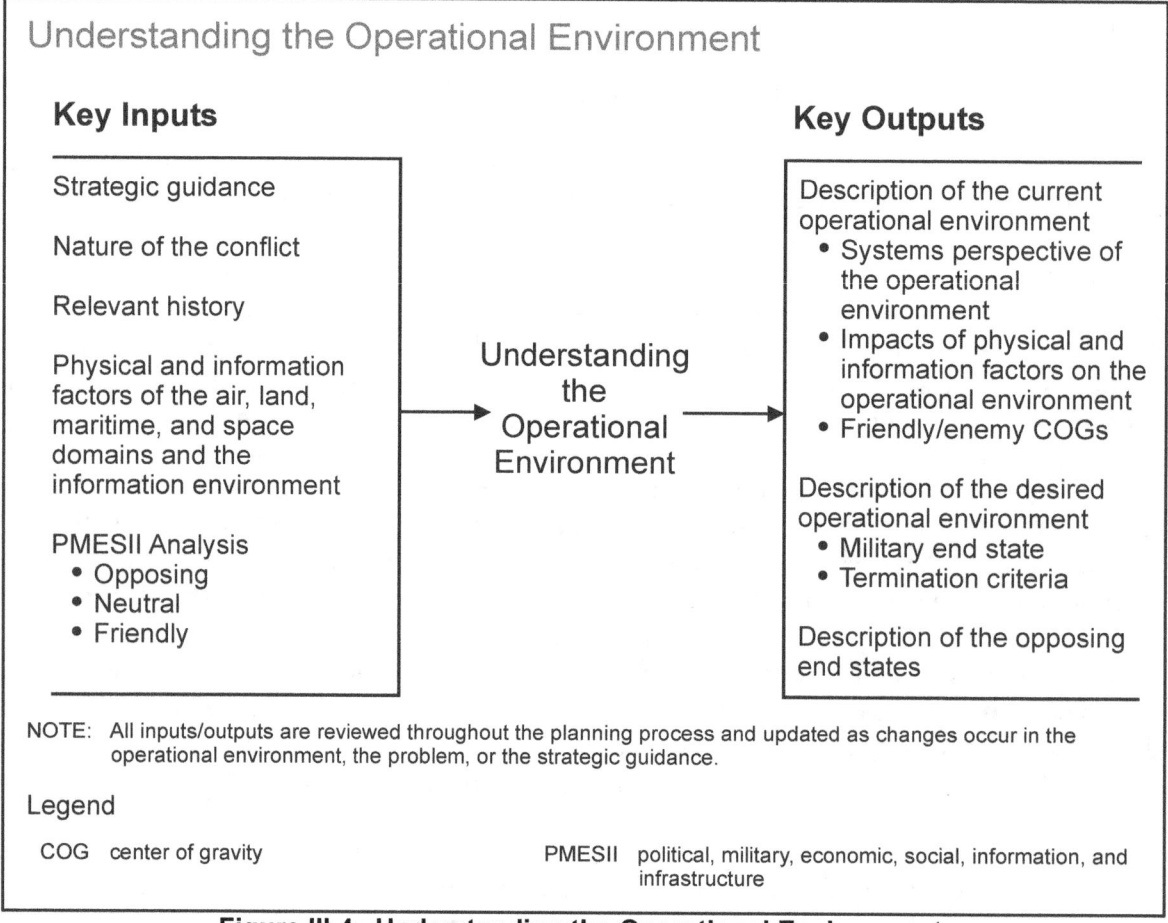

Understanding the Operational Environment

Key Inputs

Strategic guidance

Nature of the conflict

Relevant history

Physical and information factors of the air, land, maritime, and space domains and the information environment

PMESII Analysis
- Opposing
- Neutral
- Friendly

Understanding the Operational Environment

Key Outputs

Description of the current operational environment
- Systems perspective of the operational environment
- Impacts of physical and information factors on the operational environment
- Friendly/enemy COGs

Description of the desired operational environment
- Military end state
- Termination criteria

Description of the opposing end states

NOTE: All inputs/outputs are reviewed throughout the planning process and updated as changes occur in the operational environment, the problem, or the strategic guidance.

Legend

COG   center of gravity

PMESII   political, military, economic, social, information, and infrastructure

Figure III-4. Understanding the Operational Environment

in planning will help the commander and staff devise an ***operational approach*** with lines of effort/operation that link each current condition to a desired end state condition.

(3) Describe the current operational environment. One of the tools that can assist the commander in describing the current operational environment is the joint intelligence preparation of the operational environment (JIPOE) process. JIPOE is the joint process through which J-2 manages the analysis and development of products that help the commander and staff understand the complex and interconnected operational environment— the composite of the conditions, circumstances, and influences that affect the employment of capabilities that bear on the decisions of the commander.

(4) In analyzing the current and future operational environment, the team can use a political, military, economic, social, information, and infrastructure (PMESII) analytical framework to analyze the operational environment and determine relevant and critical relationships between the various actors and aspects of the operational environment (see Figure III-5).

(5) Additional factors that should be considered include:

(a) Geographical features and meteorological and oceanographic characteristics.

(b) Population demographics (ethnic groups, tribes, ideological factions, religious groups and sects, language dialects, age distribution, income groups, public health issues).

(c) Political and socioeconomic factors (economic system, political factions, tribal factions).

(d) Infrastructures, such as transportation, energy, and information systems.

(e) Operational limitations such as rules of engagement (ROE) or legal restrictions on military operations as specified in US law, international law, or host-nation support (HNS) agreements.

(f) All friendly and adversary conventional, irregular, and paramilitary forces and their general capabilities and strategic objectives (including all known and/or suspected chemical, biological, radiological, and nuclear threats and hazards).

(g) Environmental conditions (earthquakes, volcanic activity, pollution, naturally occurring diseases).

(h) Location of toxic industrial materials (TIMs) in the area of interest. TIMs may produce WMD-like effects.

(i) Psychological characteristics of adversary decision making.

(j) All locations of foreign embassies, IGOs, and NGOs.

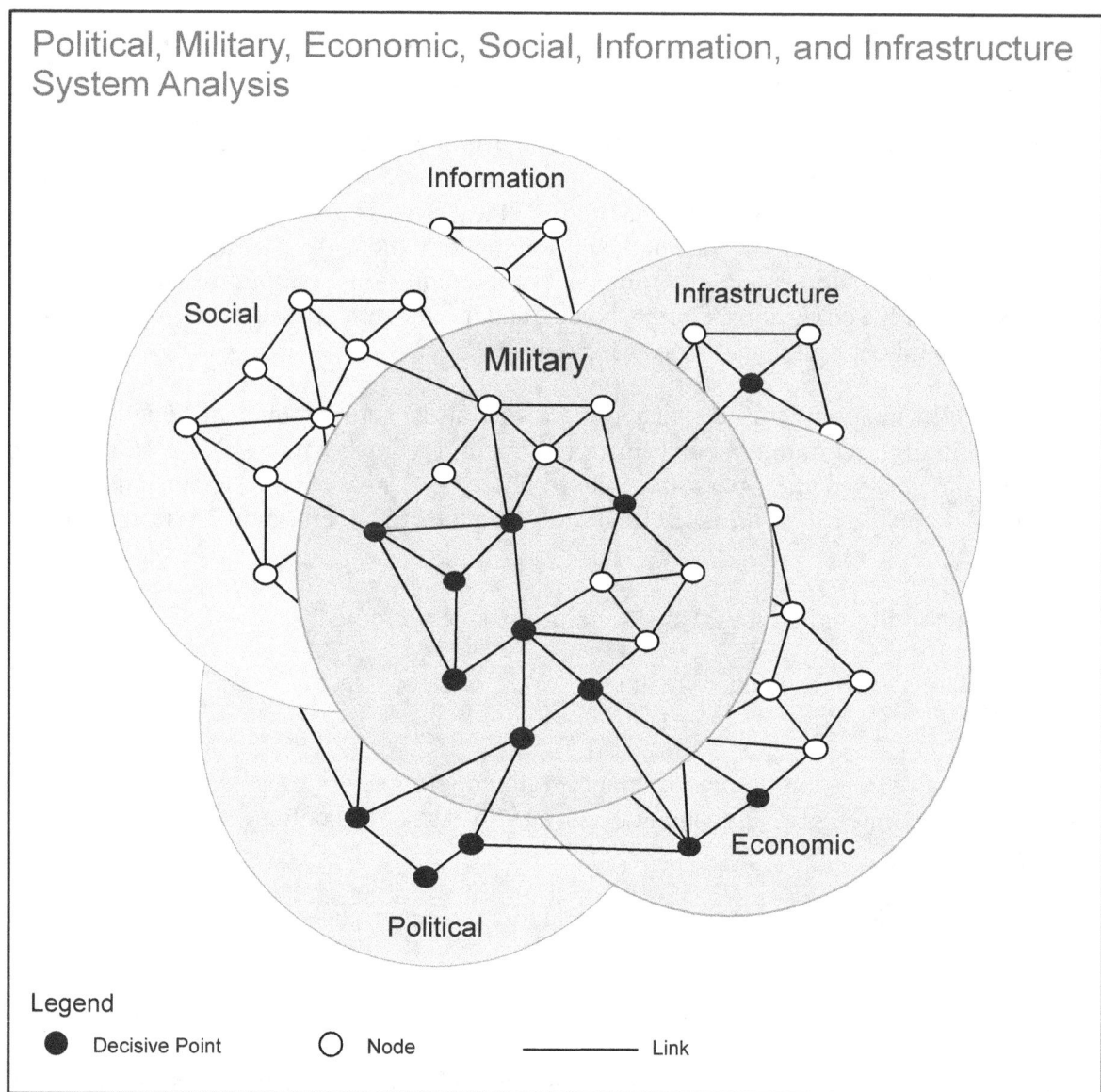

Figure III-5. Political, Military, Economic, Social, Information, and Infrastructure System Analysis

(k) Friendly and adversary military and commercial capabilities provided by assets in space and their current or potential use.

(l) Knowledge of the capabilities and intent of forces, individuals, or organizations conducting cyberspace operations.

(6) To envision developing and employing theater-strategic options for joint, interagency, intergovernmental, and multinational action, the commander must understand the series of complex, interconnected relationships at work within the operational environment. One way of developing solutions is to view these interrelated challenges from a systems perspective. In this systems analysis, it is critical to consider the relationship between all of the aspects of the system.

(7) To produce a holistic view of the relevant enemy, neutral, and friendly systems as a complex whole within a larger system that includes many external influences, analysis should define how these systems interrelate. Most important to this analysis is describing the **relevant relationships** within and between the various systems that directly or indirectly affect the problem at hand. Although the J-2 manages the JIPOE process, other directorates and agencies can contribute valuable expertise to develop and assess the complexities of the operational environment.

For more information on JIPOE, see JP 2-01.3, Joint Intelligence Preparation of the Operational Environment.

(8) **Tendencies and Potentials.** In developing an understanding of the interactions and relationships of relevant actors in the operational environment, commanders and staffs consider natural tendencies and potentials in their analyses. Tendencies reflect the inclination to think or behave in a certain manner. Tendencies are not considered deterministic but as models describing the thoughts or behaviors of relevant actors. Tendencies help identify the range of possibilities that relevant actors may develop with or without external influence. Once identified, commanders and staffs evaluate the potential of these tendencies to manifest within the operational environment. Potential is the inherent ability or capacity for the growth or development of a specific interaction or relationship. Not all interactions and relationships support achieving the desired end state. The desired end state accounts for tendencies and potentials that exist among the relevant actors or other aspects of the operational environment.

Note: Early in JOPP, pertinent lessons learned should be collected and reviewed as part of the analysis. Doing this early allows previously learned lessons to make their way into the plan. Although the Joint Lessons Learned Information System (JLLIS) provides a database of past lessons learned, people experienced in the mission, environment, and functions should also be sought for their knowledge, experience, and lessons. In developing understanding of the interactions and relationships of relevant actors in the operational environment, commanders and staffs consider natural tendencies and potentials in their analyses.

(9) Describe the key conditions that must exist in the future operational environment to achieve the desired end state. Planners should put a temporal aspect to this set of conditions in order to be able to conduct feasibility and acceptability analyses.

(10) Determine opposing desired end states. Other actors will also be affecting the operational environment and may have significantly different desired end states. The enemy/adversary will definitely have a different set of conditions to describe his desired end state. Some other actors may be neutral or friendly, and may not have an opposing mind-set, but some of their desired conditions (or unintended consequences of their actions) may oppose our desired end state conditions.

d. Define the Problem

(1) **Defining the problem is essential to solving the problem.** It involves understanding and isolating the root causes of the issue at hand—defining the essence of a complex, ill-defined problem. Defining the problem begins with a review of the tendencies and potentials of all the concerned actors and identifying tensions among the existing conditions and the desired end state. The problem statement articulates how the operational variables can be expected to resist or facilitate transformation and how inertia in the operational environment can be leveraged to ensure the desired conditions are achieved.

(2) The problem statement identifies the areas for action that will transform existing conditions toward the desired end state. Defining the problem extends beyond analyzing interactions and relationships in the operational environment (see Figure III-6). It identifies areas of tension and competition—as well as opportunities and challenges—that commanders must address to transform current conditions to achieve the desired end state. Tension is the resistance or friction among and between actors. The commander and staff identify the tension by analyzing the context of the relevant actors' tendencies, potentials, and the operational environment.

(3) *Identify the problem.* Critical to defining the problem is determining what needs to be acted on to reconcile the differences between existing and desired conditions.

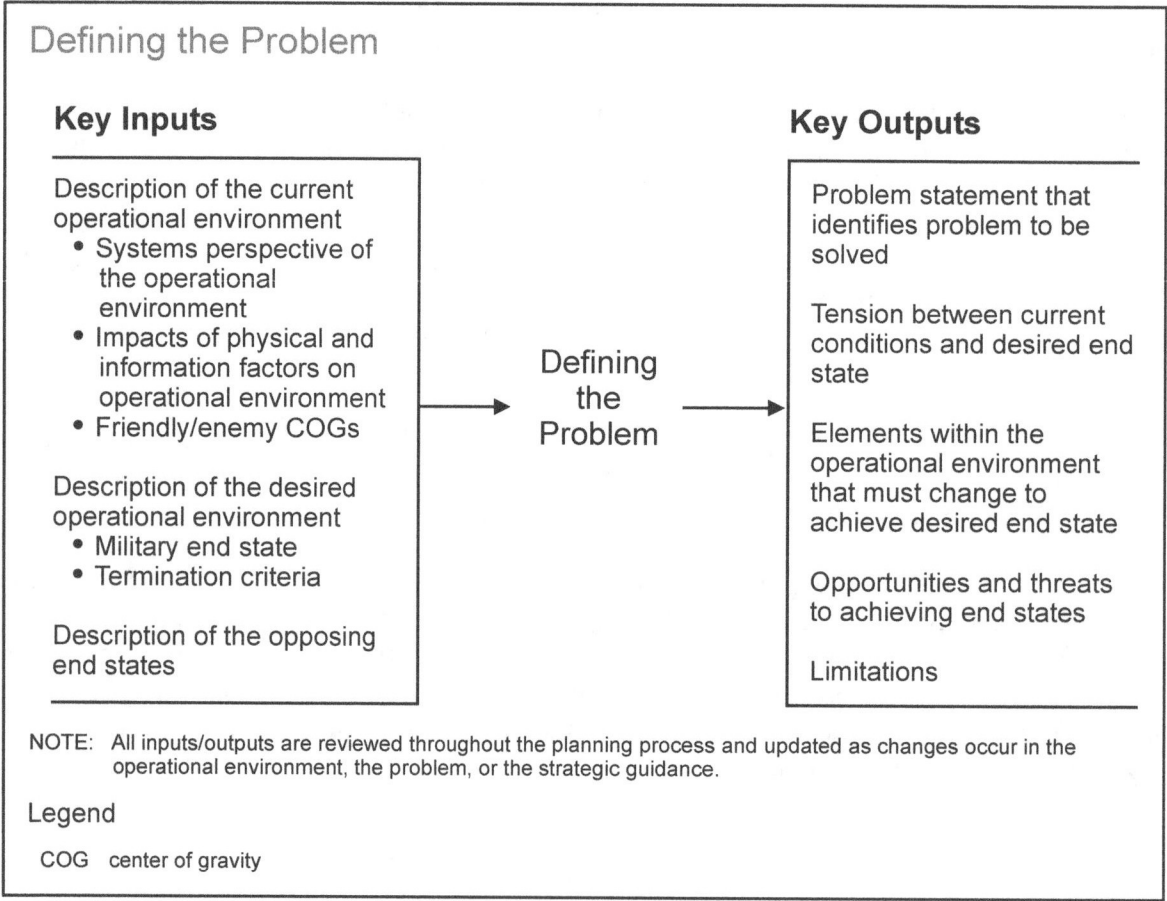

Figure III-6. Defining the Problem

Some of the conditions are critical to success; some are not. Some may be achieved as a secondary or tertiary result of another condition. In identifying the problem, the planning team identifies the tensions between the desired conditions and identifies the areas of tension that merit further consideration as areas of possible intervention.

(4) The JFC and staff must identify and articulate:

(a) Tensions between current conditions and desired conditions at the end state.

(b) Elements within the operational environment which must change or remain the same to achieve desired end states.

(c) Opportunities and threats that either can be exploited or will impede the JFC from achieving the desired end state.

(d) Limitations. An action required or prohibited by higher authority, such as a constraint or a restraint, and other restrictions that limit the commander's freedom of action, such as diplomatic agreements, ROE, political and economic conditions in affected countries, and host-nation issues.

(5) A concise problem statement is used to clearly define the problem or problem set to solve. It considers how tension and competition affect the operational environment by identifying how to transform the current conditions to the desired end state—before adversaries begin to transform current conditions to their desired end state. The statement broadly describes the requirements for transformation, anticipating changes in the operational environment while identifying critical transitions.

e. **Developing an Operational Approach**

(1) The operational approach reflects understanding of the operational environment and the problem while describing the commander's visualization of a broad approach for achieving the desired end state (see Figure III-7). The planning team uses elements of operational design to provide details to the commander's operational approach and to facilitate detailed planning within JOPP. **There are three purposes for developing an operational approach:**

(a) It provides the foundation for the commander's planning guidance to the staff and other partners.

(b) It provides the model for execution of the campaign or operation and development of assessments for that campaign or operation.

(c) It enables a better understanding of the operational environment and of the problem.

(2) In developing an appropriate operational approach, the commander should address the following questions:

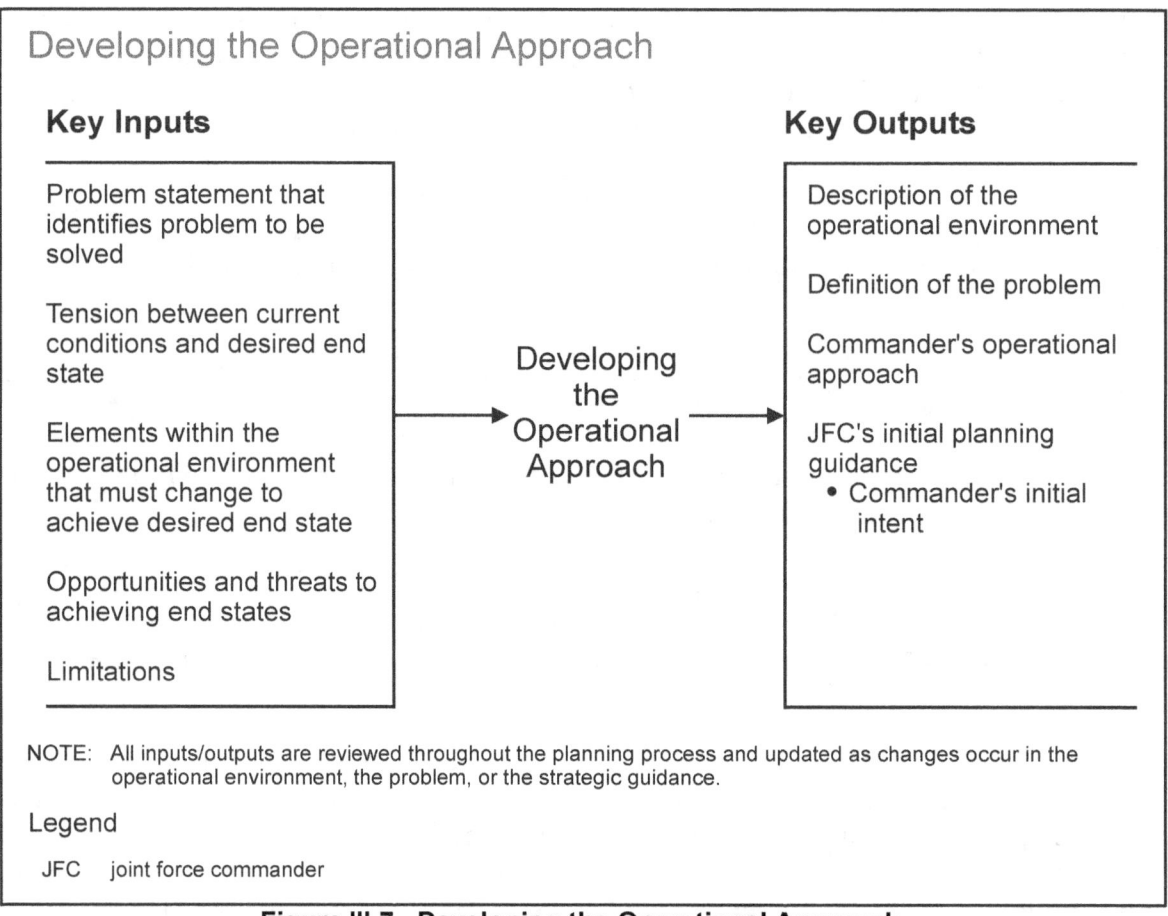

Developing the Operational Approach

Key Inputs

Problem statement that identifies problem to be solved

Tension between current conditions and desired end state

Elements within the operational environment that must change to achieve desired end state

Opportunities and threats to achieving end states

Limitations

Developing the Operational Approach

Key Outputs

Description of the operational environment

Definition of the problem

Commander's operational approach

JFC's initial planning guidance
• Commander's initial intent

NOTE: All inputs/outputs are reviewed throughout the planning process and updated as changes occur in the operational environment, the problem, or the strategic guidance.

Legend

JFC   joint force commander

Figure III-7. Developing the Operational Approach

(a) What are the strengths and weaknesses of the various actors?

(b) What are the opportunities and threats?

(c) How do we go from the existing conditions to the desired conditions?

(d) What will be the likely consequences as we seek to shape the operational environment toward a desired set of conditions?

(3) The *end state, termination, and COG(s)* are relevant to framing the operational environment and problem. The identification of *objectives, COG(s),* and *decisive points* are useful in developing the basis for an operational approach. Depending on the commander's understanding and visualization of the campaign or operation, the commander may also consider *direct or indirect approaches, culmination, operational reach, and arranging operations.* The commander may have a mature enough vision to organize the campaign into *LOOs/lines of effort* and describe how to employ *forces.*

(4) In developing the operational approach, commanders consider the direct or indirect nature of interaction with relevant actors and operational variables in the operational environment. As commanders consider various approaches, they evaluate the types of *defeat and/or stability mechanisms* that may lead to conditions that define the desired end state.

The operational approach enables commanders to begin visualizing and describing possible combinations of actions to reach the desired end state given the understanding of the operational environment and the articulation of the tensions that describe the problem. Thus, the operational approach provides the logic that underpins the unique combinations of tasks that describe the CONOPS required to achieve the desired end state. For an example of an operational approach, see Figure III-8.

(5) The operational approach promotes mutual understanding and unity of effort throughout the echelons of command and partner organizations. Many factors must be considered that can affect the operational approach. For example, the nature of our multinational partners' strategic objectives could influence the approach to achieving the commander's strategic and operational objectives. The availability of HNS, diplomatic

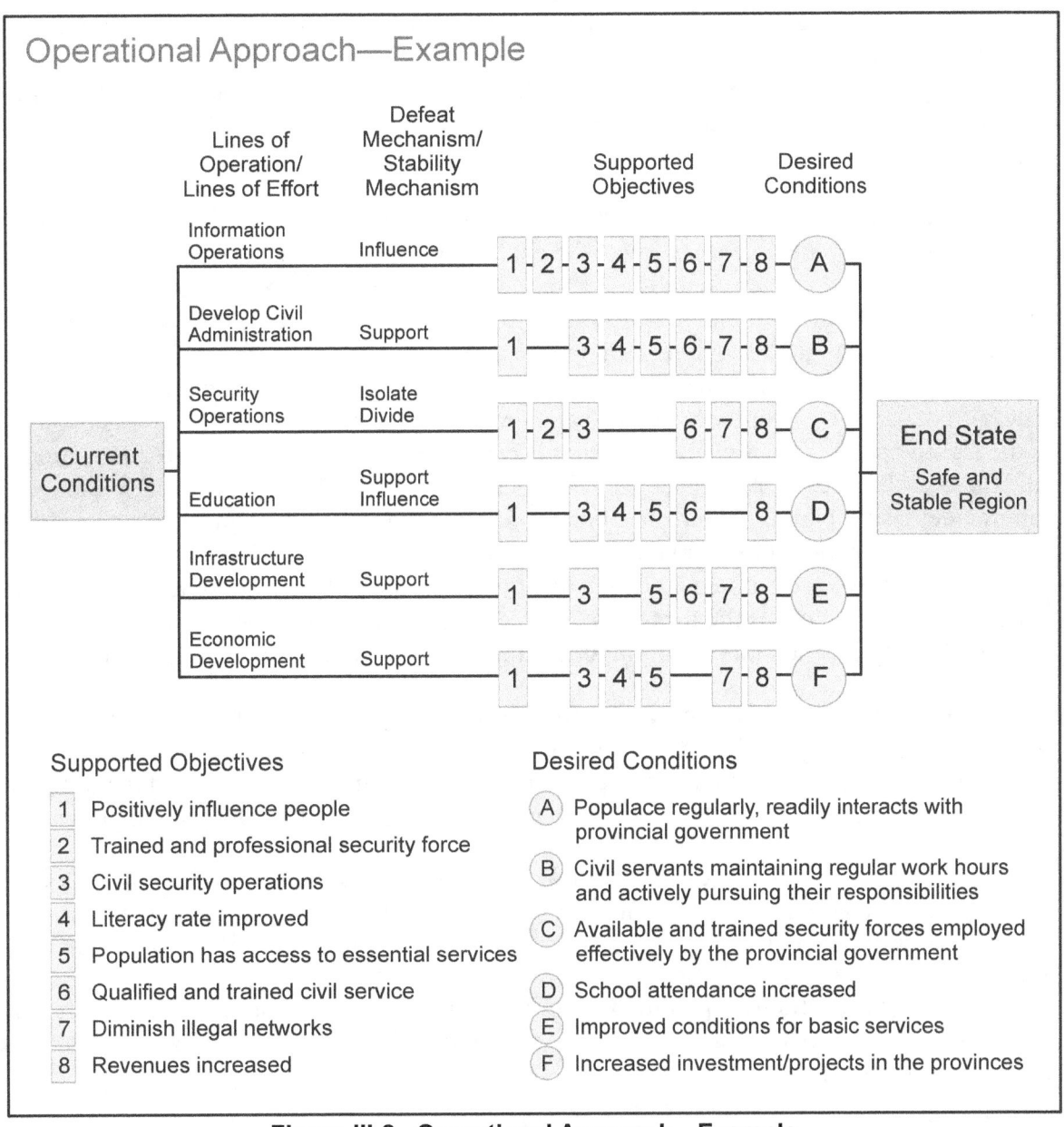

Figure III-8. Operational Approach—Example

permission to overfly nations, access to en route air bases, and the allocation of strategic mobility assets will affect development of a feasible and acceptable operational approach.

(6) The operational approach should describe the operational objectives that will enable achievement of the key conditions of the desired end state. The operational approach may be described using *LOOs/lines of effort* to link *decisive points* to achievement of objectives. It should also include a description of how key adversarial desired conditions will be precluded, and how other non-adversarial desired conditions will be mitigated.

(7) In developing the operational approach, the commander should work within anticipated resource constraints considered in understanding the operational environment.

(8) The commander should reassess his understanding of the operational environment based on the developed operational approach. In doing this, the commander should consider especially any undesired consequences of the operational approach. The purpose of working this iteration is to enable refinement of the operational approach to mitigate undesired effects, and to identify elements of strategic and operational risk inherent to the operational approach.

f. **Developing Commander's Planning Guidance.** The commander provides a summary of his current understanding of the operational environment and the problem, along with his visualization of the operational approach, to the staff and to other partners through commander's planning guidance. The commander may have been able to apply operational design to think through the campaign or operation before the staff begins JOPP. In this case, the commander provides initial planning guidance to help focus the staff in mission analysis. If he has not had such an opportunity, he will be working his understanding and visualization as the staff conducts mission analysis. In this case, the commander will issue his planning guidance, as he sees appropriate, to help focus the staff efforts. At a minimum, the commander issues planning guidance, either initial or refined, at the conclusion of mission analysis, and provides refined planning guidance as his understanding of the operational environment and of the problem and visualization of the operational approach mature. It is critical that he does this as the campaign or operation develops in order to adapt as needed his operational approach to a changing operational environment or changed problem.

(1) The format for the commander's planning guidance varies based on the personality of the commander and the level of command, but should adequately describe the logic to the commander's understanding of the operational environment and of the problem and the description of the operational approach. It may include the following elements:

(a) **Describe the operational environment.** Some combination of graphics showing key relationships and tensions and a narrative describing the operational environment will help convey the commander's understanding to the staff and other partners.

(b) **Define the problem to be solved.** A narrative problem statement that includes the required timing to solve the problem will best convey the commander's understanding of the problem.

(c) **Describe the operational approach.** A combination of a narrative describing objectives, decisive points, and potential LOOs, with a summary of limitations (constraints and restraints) and elements of operational risk (what can be accepted and what cannot be accepted) will help describe the operational approach.

(d) **Provide the commander's initial intent.** The commander should also include his initial intent in his planning guidance. The commander's initial intent describes the purpose of the operations, desired strategic end state, military end state, and operational risks associated with the campaign or operation. It also includes where the commander will and will not accept risk during the operation. It organizes desired conditions and the combinations of potential actions in time, space, and purpose. The JFC should envision and articulate how military power and joint operations, integrated with other applicable instruments of national power, will dominate the adversary in reaching strategic success. It should help staff and subordinate commanders understand the intent for unified action using interorganizational coordination among all partners and other participants. Through his intent, the commander identifies the major unifying efforts during the campaign, the points and events where operations must dominate the enemy and control conditions in the operational environment, and where other instruments of national power will play a central role. The intent must allow for decentralized execution. It provides focus to the staff and helps subordinate and supporting commanders take actions to achieve the military end state without further orders, even when operations do not unfold as planned.

1. The commander develops his intent throughout planning after providing the initial intent to focus the staff. Generally, the commander will write his own intent statement. Frequently the staff will provide substantial input. Note that much of what is covered in the three preceding paragraphs as the essential elements of initial and refined planning guidance may be incorporated into the commander's intent.

2. While there is no specified joint format for the commander's intent, a generally accepted construct includes the purpose, end state, and operational risk.

a. **Purpose.** The reason for the military action with respect to the mission of the next higher echelon. The purpose explains why the military action is being conducted. The purpose helps the force pursue the mission without further orders, even when actions do not unfold as planned. Thus, if an unanticipated situation arises, participating commanders understand the purpose of the forthcoming action well enough to act decisively and within the bounds of the higher commander's intent.

b. **End state.** Describes what the commander desires in military end state conditions that define mission success by friendly forces. Provides the strategic end state and higher command's military end state and describes how reaching the JFC's military end state conditions supports higher headquarters end state guidance.

c. **Operational risk.** Defines aspects of the campaign or operation in which the commander will accept risk in lower or partial achievement or temporary conditions. It also describes areas in which it is not acceptable to accept such lower or intermediate conditions.

    <u>d.</u> The intent may also include operational objectives, method, and effects guidance.

    <u>e.</u> The commander may provide additional planning guidance such as information management, resources, or specific effects that must be created or avoided.

SECTION B. ELEMENTS OF OPERATIONAL DESIGN

5. Overview

  a. **Operational design** employs various *elements* to develop and refine the commander's operational approach. These conceptual tools help commanders and their staffs think through the challenges of understanding the operational environment, defining the problem, and developing this approach, which guides planning and shapes the CONOPS (see Figure III-9).

  b. Section A, "Developing the Operational Approach," mentioned operational design elements, among which *end state, COG,* and *line of effort* are particularly useful in developing the operational approach. However, these elements and the others are useful throughout JOPP and are fundamental to that process. The specific application of each element depends on the operational circumstances. All elements will usually apply to large-scale combat operations, but some, such as *culmination,* may not apply in more benign circumstances such as foreign humanitarian assistance.

6. Elements of Operational Design

  a. **Termination**

    (1) Effective planning cannot occur without a clear understanding of the end state and the conditions that must exist to end military operations. Knowing when to terminate military operations and how to preserve achieved advantages is key to achieving the national strategic end state. To plan effectively for termination, the supported JFC must know how the President and SecDef intend to terminate the joint operation and ensure that its outcomes endure.

Elements of Operational Design

- Termination
- Military end state
- Objectives
- Effects
- Center of gravity
- Decisive points
- Lines of operation and lines of effort
- Direct and indirect approach
- Anticipation
- Operational reach
- Culmination
- Arranging operations
- Forces and functions

Figure III-9. Elements of Operational Design

---

(2) Termination criteria are developed first among the elements of operational design as they enable the development of the military end state and objectives. Termination criteria describe the standards that must be met before conclusion of a joint operation. Commanders and their staffs must think through, in the early stages of planning, the conditions that must exist in order to terminate military operations on terms favorable to the US and its multinational partners. A hasty or ill-defined end to the operation may bring with it the possibility that the adversary will renew hostilities or other actors may interfere, leading to further conflict. Commanders and their staffs must balance the desire for quick victory with termination on truly favorable terms.

(3) Termination criteria should account for a wide variety of operational tasks that the joint force may need to accomplish, to include disengagement, force protection, transition to post-conflict operations, reconstitution, and redeployment.

(4) Termination criteria are briefed to SecDef as part of the IPR process to ensure the criteria support attainment of strategic end states. Once approved, the criteria may change. It is important for commanders and staffs to keep an eye out for potential changes, as they may result in a modification to the military end state as well as the commander's operational approach. As such, it is essential for the military to keep a dialogue between the civilian national leadership, and the leadership of other agencies and partners involved.

EXAMPLES OF TERMINATION CRITERIA

Note the description of condition, not action:

Country X's borders are secure.

Country Y no longer poses an offensive threat to the countries of the region.

Country X's national security force is sufficient to repress internal rebellion.

Percentage of US forces have redeployed with sufficient combat power postured in theater to support Country X's national army.

---

b. **Military End State.** Military end state is the set of required conditions that defines achievement of all military objectives. It normally represents **a point in time and/or circumstances beyond which the President does not require the military instrument of national power as the primary means to achieve remaining national objectives.** While it may mirror many of the conditions of the national strategic end state, the military end state typically will be more specific and contain other supporting conditions. These conditions contribute to developing termination criteria, the specified standards approved by the President and/or SecDef that must be met before a joint operation can be concluded. Aside from its obvious association with strategic or operational objectives, clearly defining the military end state promotes unity of effort, facilitates synchronization, and helps clarify (and may reduce) the risk associated with the campaign or operation. Commanders should include the military end state in their planning guidance and commander's intent statement.

c. **Objectives. An objective is a clearly defined, decisive, and attainable goal toward which every military operation should be directed.** Once the military end state is understood and termination criteria are established, operational design continues with development of strategic and operational military objectives. Joint operation planning integrates military actions and capabilities with those of other instruments of national power in time, space, and purpose in unified action to achieve the JFC's objectives. Objectives and their supporting effects provide the basis for identifying tasks to be accomplished.

(1) **Objectives prescribe friendly goals.** They constitute the aim of military operations and are necessarily linked to national objectives (simply defined as what we want to accomplish). Military objectives are one of the most important considerations in campaign and operational design. **They specify what must be accomplished and provide the basis for describing desired effects.**

(2) A clear and concise end state allows planners to better examine objectives that must be met to attain the desired end state. **Objectives describe what must be achieved to reach the end state.** These are usually expressed in military, diplomatic, economic, and informational terms and help define and clarify what military planners must do to support the national strategic end state. Objectives developed at the national-strategic and theater-strategic levels are the defined, decisive, and attainable goals toward which all operations, not just military operations, and activities are directed within the OA.

(3) Achieving operational objectives ties execution of tactical tasks to reaching the military end state.

(4) There are four primary considerations for an objective.

(a) An objective establishes a single desired result (a goal).

(b) An objective should link directly or indirectly to higher level objectives or to the end state.

(c) An objective is prescriptive, specific, and unambiguous.

(d) An objective does not infer ways and/or means—it is not written as a task.

d. **Effects. An effect is a physical and/or behavioral state of a system that results from an action, a set of actions, or another effect. A desired effect can also be thought of as a condition that can support achieving an associated objective, while an undesired effect is a condition that can inhibit progress toward an objective.** In applying unified action, a JFC synchronizes the diplomatic, informational, military, and economic power of the US to affect an adversary's PMESII systems. **Throughout this publication, the term "effects" is intended to mean both *desired* and *undesired* effects unless otherwise specified.**

(1) The CCDR plans joint operations based on analysis of national strategic objectives and development of theater strategic objectives supported by measurable strategic and operational desired effects and assessment indicators (see Figure III-10). At the

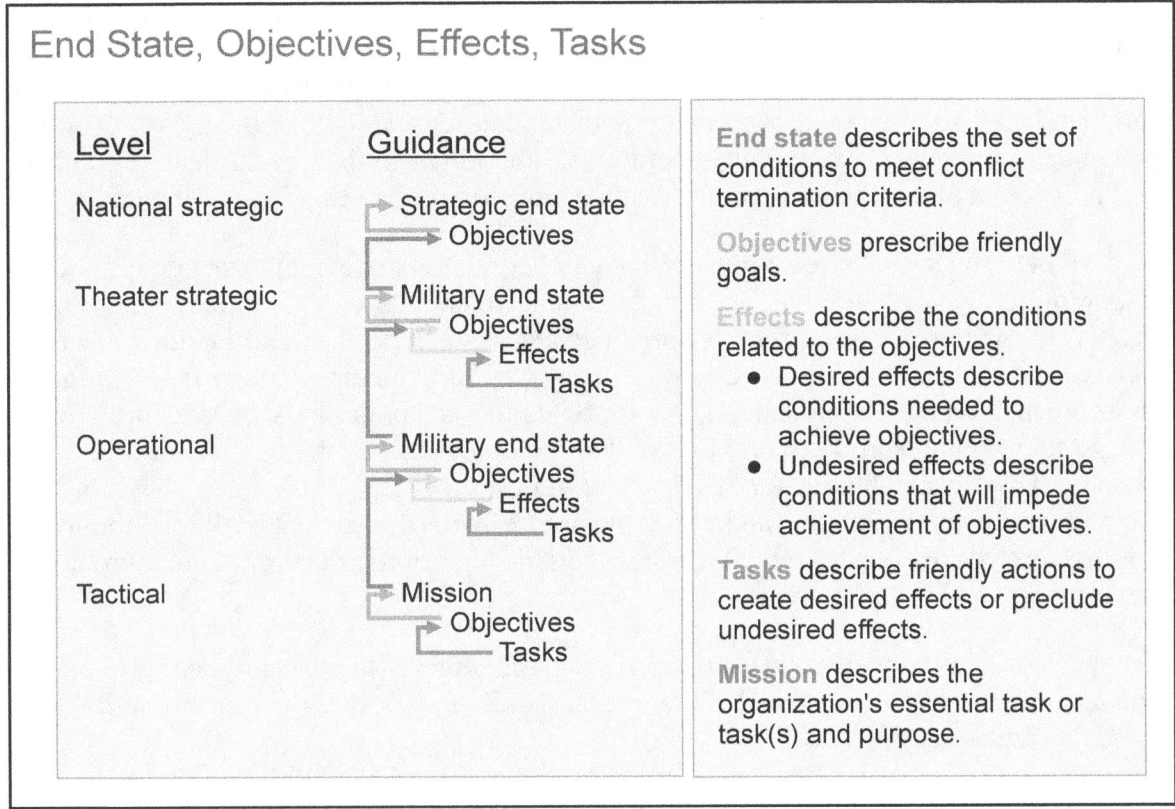

Figure III-10. End State, Objectives, Effects, Tasks

operational level, a subordinate JFC develops supporting plans, which can include objectives supported by measurable operational-level desired effects and assessment indicators. This may increase operational- and tactical-level understanding of the purpose reflected in the higher-level commander's mission and intent. At the same time, commanders consider potential undesired effects and their impact on the tasks assigned to subordinate commands.

(2) There are four primary considerations for writing a desired effect statement.

(a) Each desired effect should link directly to one or more objectives.

(b) The effect should be measurable.

(c) The statement should not specify ways and means for accomplishment.

(d) The effect should be distinguishable from the objective it supports as a condition for success, not as another objective or a task.

(3) The proximate cause of effects in complex situations can be difficult to predict. Even direct effects in these situations can be more difficult to create, predict, and measure, particularly when they relate to moral and cognitive issues (such as religion and the "mind of the adversary," respectively). Indirect effects in these situations often are difficult to foresee. Where there is sufficient intelligence available to predict the direct effects reliably, some of the commander's objectives can also be achieved indirectly. Some military objectives can be

achieved by influencing political, economic, social, and other systems in the operational environment. **However, indirect effects often can be unintended and undesired since there will always be gaps in our understanding of the operational environment.** Commanders and their staffs must appreciate that unpredictable third-party actions, unintended consequences of friendly operations, subordinate initiative and creativity, and the fog and friction of conflict will contribute to an uncertain operational environment.

(4) The use of effects in planning can help commanders and staff determine the tasks required to achieve objectives and use other elements of operational design more effectively by clarifying the relationships between COGs, LOOs, and/or lines of effort, decisive points, and termination criteria. Once a systems perspective of the operational environment has been developed (and appropriate links and nodes have been identified), the linkage and relationship between COGs, LOOs, and decisive points can become more obvious. This linkage allows for efficient use of desired effects in planning. The JFC and planners continue to develop and refine desired effects throughout JOPP. Monitoring progress toward creating desired effects and avoiding undesired effects continues throughout execution.

(5) A mission is a task or set of tasks, together with the purpose, that clearly indicates the action to be taken and the reason for doing so. It is derived primarily from higher headquarters guidance.

e. **Center of Gravity**

(1) One of the most important tasks confronting the JFC's staff during planning is identifying and analyzing friendly and adversary COGs. A COG is a source of power that provides moral or physical strength, freedom of action, or will to act. It is what Clausewitz called "the hub of all power and movement, on which everything depends...the point at which all our energies should be directed." An objective is always linked to a COG. There may also be different COGs at different levels, but they should be nested. At the strategic level, a COG could be a military force, an alliance, political or military leaders, a set of critical capabilities or functions, or national will. At the operational level, a COG often is associated with the adversary's military capabilities—such as a powerful element of the armed forces—but could include other capabilities in the operational environment. In identifying COGs it is important to remember that irregular warfare focuses on legitimacy and influence over a population, unlike traditional warfare, which employs direct military confrontation to defeat an adversary's armed forces, destroy an adversary's war-making capacity, or seize or retain territory to force a change in an adversary's government or policies. Therefore, in an irregular warfare environment, the enemy and friendly COG will most likely be the same population.

(2) **COGs exist in an adversarial context** involving a clash of moral wills and/or physical strengths. They are formed out of the relationships between adversaries, and they do not exist in a strategic or operational vacuum. COGs are framed by each party's view of the threats in the operational environment and the requirements to develop/maintain power and strength relative to their need to be effective in accomplishing their objectives.

Therefore, commanders not only must consider the enemy COGs, but they also must identify and protect their own.

(3) The COG construct is useful as an analytical tool to help JFCs and staffs analyze friendly and adversary sources of strength as well as weaknesses and vulnerabilities. This process cannot be taken lightly, since a faulty conclusion resulting from a poor or hasty analysis can have very serious consequences, such as the inability to achieve strategic and operational objectives at an acceptable cost. The selection of COGs is not solely a static process by the J-2 during JIPOE. Planners must continually analyze and refine COGs due to actions taken by friendly forces and the adversary's reactions to those actions. Figure III-11 shows a number of characteristics that may be associated with a COG.

(4) Analysis of friendly and adversary COGs is a key step in operational design. Joint force intelligence analysts identify adversary COGs, determining from which elements the adversary derives freedom of action, physical strength (means), and the will to fight. The J-2, in conjunction with other operational planners, then attempts to determine if the tentative or candidate COGs truly are critical to the adversary's strategy. This analysis is a linchpin in the planning effort. Others on the joint force staff conduct similar analysis to identify friendly COGs. Once COGs have been identified, JFCs and their staffs determine how to attack enemy COGs while protecting friendly COGs. The protection of friendly strategic

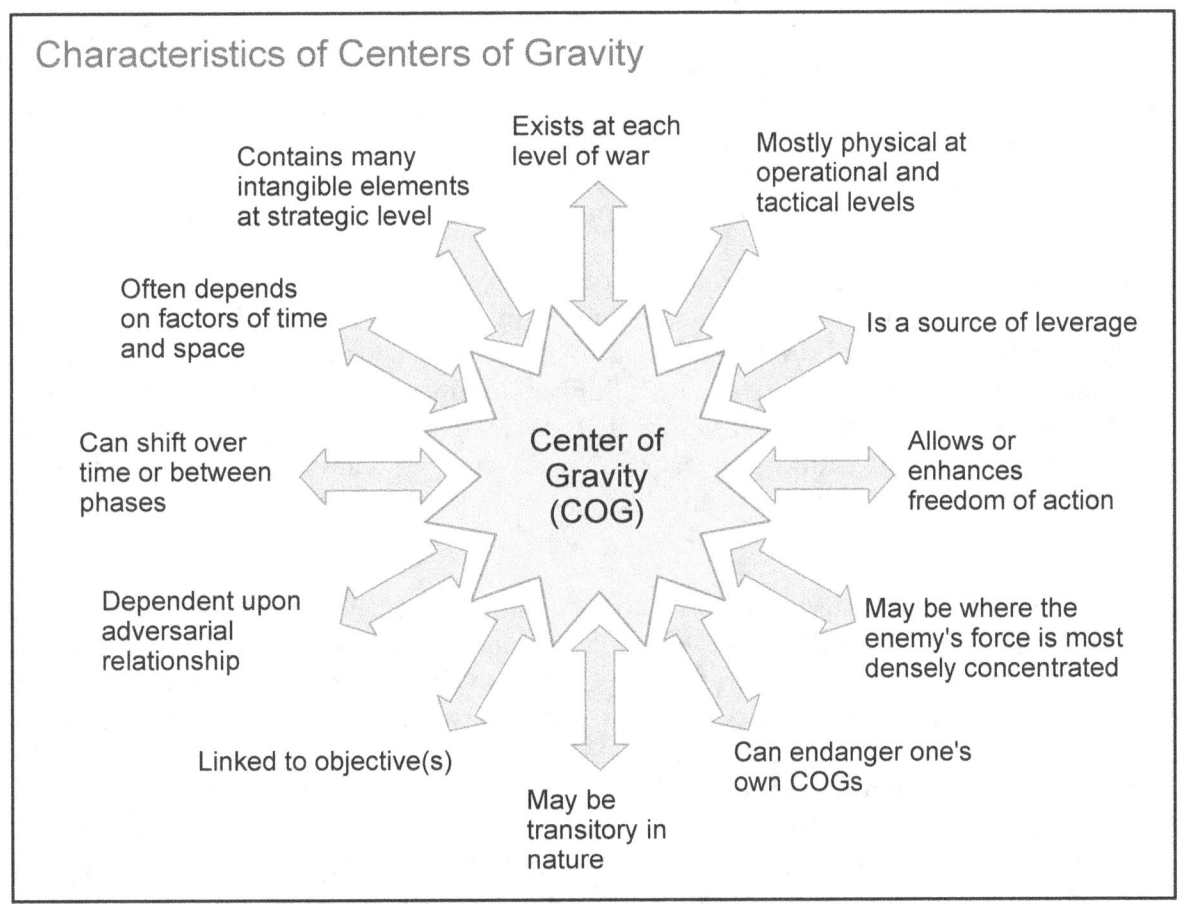

Figure III-11. Characteristics of Centers of Gravity

COGs such as public opinion and US national capabilities typically requires efforts and capabilities beyond those of just the supported CCDR. An analysis of the identified COGs in terms of critical capabilities, requirements, and vulnerabilities is vital to this process.

(5) Understanding the relationship among COGs not only permits but also compels greater precision in thought and expression in operational design. Planners should analyze COGs within a framework of three *critical factors*—capabilities, requirements, and vulnerabilities—to aid in this understanding. **Critical capabilities** are those that are considered crucial enablers for a COG to function as such, and are essential to the accomplishment of the adversary's assumed objective(s). **Critical requirements** are the conditions, resources, and means that enable a critical capability to become fully operational. **Critical vulnerabilities** are those aspects or components of critical requirements that are deficient or vulnerable to direct or indirect attack in a manner achieving decisive or significant results. In general, a JFC must possess sufficient operational reach and combat power or other relevant capabilities to take advantage of an adversary's critical vulnerabilities while protecting friendly critical capabilities within the operational reach of an adversary.

(6) When identifying friendly and adversary critical vulnerabilities, the JFC and staff will understandably want to focus their efforts against the critical vulnerabilities that will do the most decisive damage to an adversary's COG. However, in selecting those critical vulnerabilities, planners must also compare their criticality with their accessibility, vulnerability, redundancy, ability to recuperate, and impact on the civilian populace, and then balance those factors against friendly capabilities to affect those vulnerabilities. The JFC's goal is to seek opportunities aggressively to apply force against an adversary in as vulnerable an aspect as possible, and in as many dimensions as possible. In other words, the JFC seeks to undermine the adversary's strength by exploiting adversary vulnerabilities while protecting friendly vulnerabilities from adversaries attempting to do the same.

(7) A proper analysis of adversary critical factors must be based on the best available knowledge of how adversaries organize, fight, think, and make decisions, and their physical and psychological strengths and weaknesses. JFCs and their staffs must develop an understanding of their adversaries' capabilities and vulnerabilities as well as factors that might influence an adversary to abandon its strategic objectives. They must also envision how friendly forces and actions appear from the adversaries' viewpoints. Otherwise, they may fall into the trap of ascribing to an adversary attitudes, values, and reactions that mirror their own.

(8) Before solidifying COGs into the plan, planners should analyze and test the validity of the COGs. The defeat, destruction, neutralization, or substantial weakening of a valid COG should cause an adversary to change its COA or prevent an adversary from achieving its strategic objectives. If analysis and/or wargaming show that this does not occur, then perhaps planners have misidentified the COG, and they must revise their COG and critical factors analysis. The conclusions, while critically important to the planning process itself, must be tempered with continuous evaluations and reassessments because derived COGs and critical vulnerabilities are subject to change at any time during the campaign or operation. Accordingly, JFCs and their subordinates should be alert to

circumstances during execution that may cause derived COGs and critical vulnerabilities to change and adjust friendly plans and operations accordingly.

(9) Commanders must also analyze friendly COGs and identify critical vulnerabilities (see Figure III-12). For example, long sea and air lines of communications (LOCs) from the continental United States (CONUS) or supporting theaters could be a critical vulnerability for a friendly COG. Through prior planning and coordination, commanders can mitigate the potential impact of challenges such as the failure of foreign governments to provide overflight clearances to US forces or MNFs. A friendly COG could also be something more intangible in nature. During the 1990–1991 Persian Gulf Conflict, for example, the Commander, US Central Command, identified the coalition itself as a friendly operational COG and took appropriate measures to protect it, to include deployment of theater missile defense systems. In conducting the analysis of friendly vulnerabilities, the supported commander must decide how, when, where, and why friendly military forces are (or might become) vulnerable to hostile actions and then plan accordingly. The supported commander must achieve a balance between prosecuting the main effort and protecting critical capabilities and vulnerabilities in the OA to protect friendly COGs.

For more information on COGs and the systems perspective, see JP 2-01.3, Joint Intelligence Preparation of the Operational Environment.

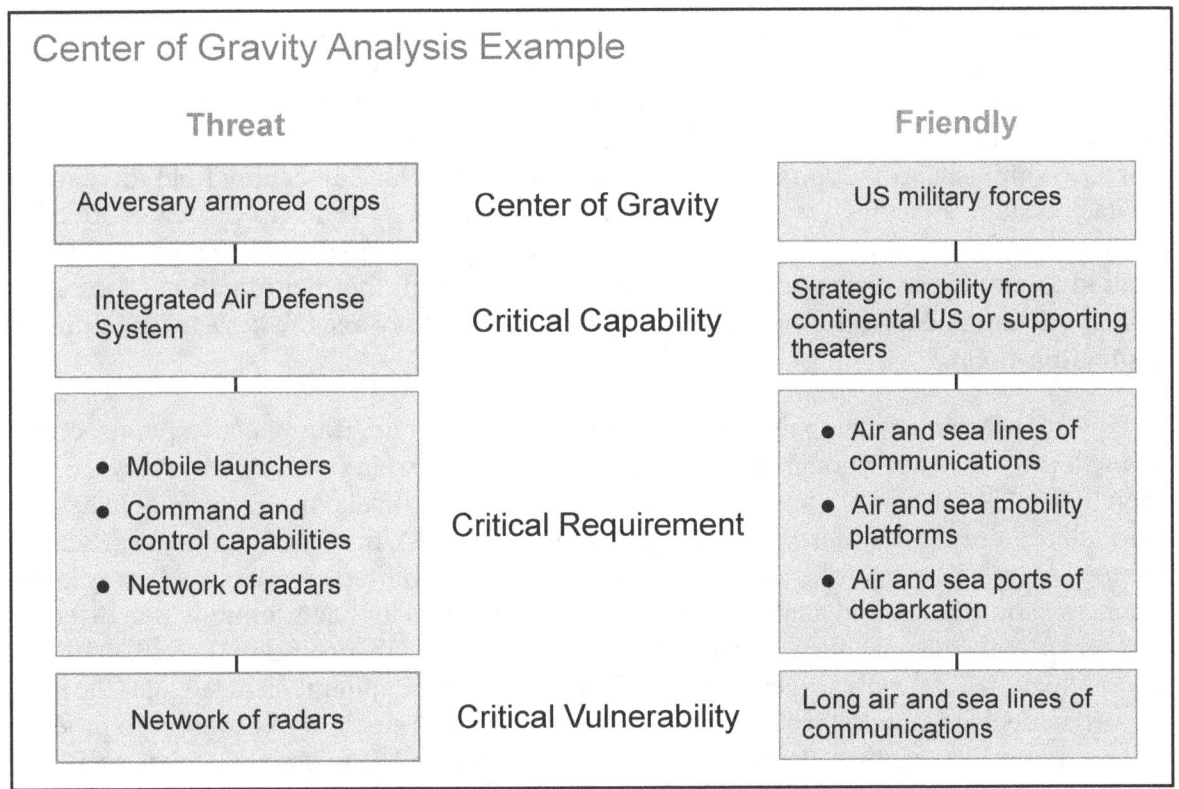

Figure III-12. Center of Gravity Analysis Example

f. **Decisive Points**

(1) **A *decisive point* is a geographic place, specific key event, critical factor, or function that, when acted upon, allows a commander to gain a marked advantage over an adversary or contributes materially to achieving success (e.g., creating a desired effect, achieving an objective).** Decisive points can greatly influence the outcome of an action. Decisive points can be physical in nature, such as a constricted sea lane, a hill, a town, WMD material cache or facility, or an air base; but they could include other elements such as command posts, critical boundaries, airspace, or communications and/or intelligence nodes. In some cases, specific key events also may be decisive points, such as attainment of air or maritime superiority, commitment of the adversary's reserve, opening a supply route during humanitarian operations, or gaining the trust of a key leader. In still other cases, decisive points may have a larger systemic impact and, when acted on, can substantially affect the adversary's information, financial, economic, or social systems. When dealing with an irregular threat, commanders and their staffs should consider how actions against decisive points will affect not only the enemy, but also the relevant population and their behavior and relationships with enemy and friendly forces, and the resultant impact on stability in the area or region of interest.

(2) The most important decisive points can be determined from analysis of critical factors. Understanding the relationship between a COG's critical capabilities, requirements, and vulnerabilities can illuminate direct and indirect approaches to the COG. It is likely that most of these critical factors will be decisive points, which should then be further addressed in the planning process.

(3) There may often be cases where the JFC's combat power and other capabilities will be insufficient to affect the adversary's COGs rapidly with a single action. In this situation, the supported JFC must selectively focus a series of actions against the adversary's critical vulnerabilities until the cumulative effects of these actions lead to mission success. Just as a combined arms approach is often the best way to attack an enemy field force in the military system, attacking several vulnerable points in other systems may offer an effective method to influence an enemy COG. The indirect approach may offer the most effective method to exploit adversary critical vulnerabilities through the identification of decisive points. **Although decisive points are usually not COGs, they are the keys to attacking or protecting them.**

(4) Although campaigns or operations may have numerous decisive points, only a few will truly have operational or even strategic significance relative to an adversary's or our friendly COGs. The art of identifying decisive points is a critical part of operational design. Normally, there are far more decisive points in a given OA than can be attacked, seized, retained, controlled or protected with the forces and capabilities available. Accordingly, planners should study and analyze potential decisive points and determine which offer the best opportunity to attack the adversary's COGs, extend friendly operational reach, or enable the application of friendly forces and capabilities. The commander then designates the most important decisive points for further planning and allocates sufficient resources to produce the desired effects against them. Afterward, the supported JFC should assign sufficient

forces and assets for attacking, seizing, retaining, controlling, or protecting these decisive points.

g. Lines of Operation and Lines of Effort

(1) Lines of Operation

(a) **A *LOO* defines the interior or exterior orientation of the force in relation to the enemy or that connects actions on nodes and/or decisive points related in time and space to an objective(s).** LOOs describe and connect a series of decisive actions that lead to control of a geographic or force-oriented objective (see Figure III-13). Operations designed using LOOs generally consist of a series of actions executed according to a well-defined sequence, although multiple LOOs can exist at the same time (parallel operations). Major combat operations are typically designed using LOOs. These lines tie offensive, defensive, and stability tasks to the geographic and positional references in the OA. Commanders synchronize activities along complementary LOOs to achieve the end state.

(b) **A force operates on *interior lines* when its operations diverge from a central point.** Interior lines usually represent central position, where a friendly force can reinforce or concentrate its elements faster than the enemy force can reposition. With interior lines, friendly forces are closer to separate enemy forces than the enemy forces are to one another. Interior lines allow an isolated force to mass combat power against a specific portion of an enemy force by shifting capabilities more rapidly than the enemy can react.

(c) **A force operates on *exterior lines* when its operations converge on the enemy.** Operations on exterior lines offer opportunities to encircle and annihilate an enemy force. However, these operations typically require a force stronger or more mobile than the enemy.

(d) The relevance of interior and exterior lines depends on the time and space relationship between the opposing forces. Although an enemy force may have interior lines with respect to the friendly force, this advantage disappears if the friendly force is more agile and operates at a higher tempo. Conversely, if a smaller friendly force maneuvers to a

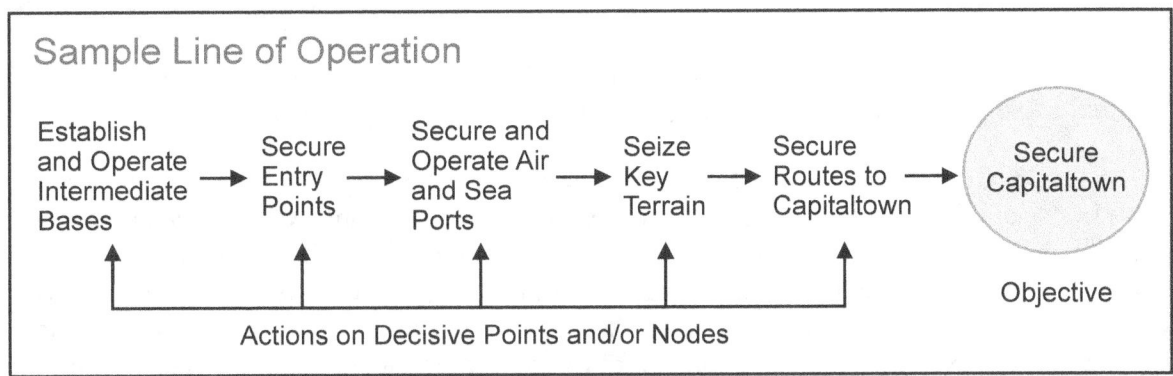

Figure III-13. Sample Line of Operation

position between larger but less agile enemy forces, the friendly force may be able to defeat them in detail before they can react effectively.

(2) **Lines of Effort**

(a) **A *line of effort* links multiple tasks and missions using the logic of purpose—cause and effect—to focus efforts toward establishing operational and strategic conditions.** Lines of effort are essential to operational design when positional references to an enemy or adversary have little relevance, such as in counterinsurgency or stability operations. In operations involving many nonmilitary factors, lines of effort may be the only way to link tasks, effects, conditions, and the desired end state (see Figure III-14). Lines of effort are often essential to helping commanders visualize how military capabilities can support the other instruments of national power. They are a particularly valuable tool when used to achieve unity of effort in operations involving MNFs and civilian organizations, where unity of command is elusive, if not impractical.

(b) Commanders at all levels may use lines of effort to develop missions and tasks and to allocate resources. Commanders synchronize and sequence related actions along multiple lines of effort. Seeing these relationships helps commanders assess progress toward achieving the end state as forces perform tasks and accomplish missions.

(c) Commanders typically visualize stability and civil support operations along lines of effort. For stability operations, commanders may consider linking primary stability tasks to their corresponding DOS post-conflict technical sectors. These stability tasks link military actions with the broader interagency effort across the levels of war. A full array of lines of effort might include offensive and defensive lines, as well as a lines for public affairs, IO, and integrated financial operations (IFO). All typically produce effects across multiple lines of effort.

(d) Commanders and staff should consider cross-cutting lines of effort involving more than one instrument of national power in order to create a more effective system for interagency coordination during execution. Lines of effort designed around functional areas such as diplomacy or economics create unintentional interagency coordination stovepipes during execution, because they are fixed toward the efforts of a single department or agency. Cross-cutting (outcome oriented) lines of effort such as establish essential services or civil security operations create a tendency toward more dynamic and open interagency coordination during execution because they require the synchronization of efforts of multiple departments and agencies. This type of construct brings to bear the capabilities and expertise of multiple elements of the USG, which makes it particularly effective toward achieving more complex objectives or outcomes.

(3) **Combining Lines of Operation and Lines of Effort.** Commanders may use both LOOs and lines of effort to connect objectives to a central, unifying purpose. Lines of effort can also link objectives, decisive points, and COGs. Combining LOOs and lines of effort allows commanders to include nonmilitary activities in their operational design. This combination helps commanders incorporate stability tasks into their operational approach that are necessary to reach the end state. It allows commanders to consider the less tangible

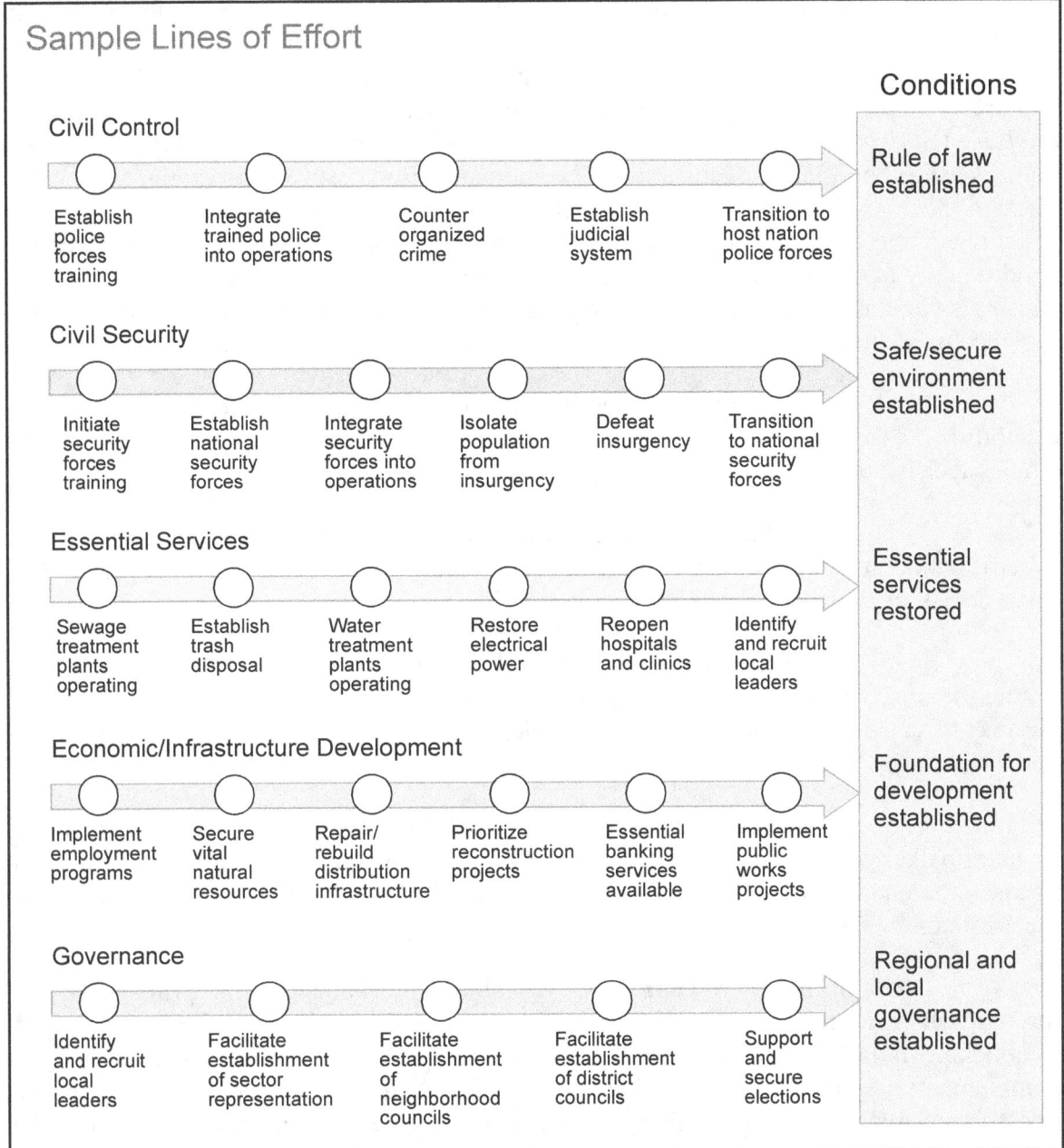

Figure III-14. Sample Lines of Effort

aspects of the operational environment where the other instruments of national power or nontraditional military activities may dominate. Commanders can then visualize concurrent and post-conflict stability activities. Making these connections relates the tasks, effects, and objectives identified in the operation or campaign plan.

(4) **Defeat and stability mechanisms** complement COG analysis. While COG analysis helps us understand a problem, defeat and stability mechanisms suggest means to solve it. They provide a useful tool for describing the main effects a commander wants to create along a LOO or line of effort.

(a) **Defeat Mechanisms.** Defeat mechanisms primarily apply in combat operations against an active enemy force. Combat aims at defeating armed enemies—regular, irregular, or both, through the organized application of force to kill, destroy, or capture by all means available. There are two basic defeat mechanisms to accomplish this: *attrition* and *disruption*. The aim of disruption is to defeat an enemy's ability to fight as a cohesive and coordinated organization. The alternative is to destroy his material capabilities through attrition, which generally is more costly and time-consuming. Although acknowledging that all successful combat involves both mechanisms, joint doctrine conditionally favors disruption because it tends to be a more effective and efficient way of causing an enemy's defeat, and the increasing imperative for restraint in the application of violence may often preclude the alternative. The defeat mechanisms may include:

1. **Destroy.** To identify the most effective way to eliminate enemy capabilities; it may be attained by sequentially applying combat power over time or with a single, decisive attack.

2. **Dislocate.** To compel the enemy to expose forces by reacting to a specific action; it requires enemy commanders to either accept neutralization of part of their force or risk its destruction while repositioning.

3. **Disintegrate.** To exploit the effects of dislocation and destruction to shatter the enemy's coherence; it typically follows destruction and dislocation, coupled with the loss of capabilities that enemy commanders use to develop and maintain situational understanding.

4. **Isolate.** To limit the enemy's ability to conduct operations effectively by marginalizing critical capabilities or limiting the enemy's ability to influence events; it exposes the enemy to continued degradation through the massed effects of other defeat mechanisms.

(b) **Stability Mechanisms.** A stability mechanism is the primary method through which friendly forces affect civilians in order to attain conditions that support establishing a lasting, stable peace. Combinations of stability mechanisms produce complementary and reinforcing effects that help to shape the human dimension of the operational environment more effectively and efficiently than a single mechanism applied in isolation. Stability mechanisms may include compel, control, influence, and support. Proper application of these stability mechanisms is key in an irregular warfare environment where success is dependent on enabling a local partner to maintain or establish legitimacy and influence over relevant populations.

1. **Compel.** To maintain the threat—or actual use—of lethal or nonlethal force to establish control and dominance, effect behavioral change, or enforce cessation of hostilities, peace agreements, or other arrangements. Legitimacy and compliance are interrelated. While legitimacy is vital to achieving host-nation compliance, compliance depends on how the local populace perceives the force's ability to exercise force to accomplish the mission. The appropriate and discriminate use of force often forms a central component to success in stability operations; it closely ties to legitimacy. Depending on the

circumstances, the threat or use of force can reinforce or complement efforts to stabilize a situation, gain consent, and ensure compliance with mandates and agreements. The misuse of force—or even the perceived threat of the misuse of force—can adversely affect the legitimacy of the mission or the military instrument of national power.

2. **Control.** To establish public order and safety, securing borders, routes, sensitive sites, population centers, and individuals and physically occupying key terrain and facilities. As a stability mechanism, control closely relates to the primary stability task, *establish civil control*. However, control is also fundamental to effective, enduring security. When combined with the stability mechanism compel, it is inherent to the activities that comprise disarmament, demobilization, and reintegration, as well as broader security sector reform programs. Without effective control, efforts to establish civil order—including efforts to establish both civil security and control over an area and its population—will not succeed. Establishing control requires time, patience, and coordinated, cooperative efforts across the OA.

3. **Influence.** To alter the opinions and attitudes of the host-nation population through IO, presence, and conduct. It applies nonlethal capabilities to complement and reinforce the compelling and controlling effects of stability mechanisms. Influence aims to effect behavioral change through nonlethal means. It is more a result of public perception than a measure of operational success. It reflects the ability of forces to operate successfully among the people of the host nation, interacting with them consistently and positively while accomplishing the mission. Here, consistency of actions, words, and deeds is vital. Influence requires legitimacy. Military forces earn the trust and confidence of the people through the constructive capabilities inherent to combat power, not through lethal or coercive means. Positive influence is absolutely necessary to achieve lasting control and compliance. It contributes to success across the lines of effort and engenders support among the people. Once attained, influence is best maintained by consistently exhibiting respect for, and operating within, the cultural and societal norms of the local populace.

4. **Support.** To establish, reinforce, or set the conditions necessary for the other instruments of national power to function effectively, coordinating and cooperating closely with host-nation civilian agencies, and assisting aid organizations as necessary to secure humanitarian access to vulnerable populations. Support is vital to a comprehensive approach to stability operations. The military instrument of national power brings unique expeditionary capabilities to stability operations. These capabilities enable the force to quickly address the immediate needs of the host nation and local populace. In extreme circumstances, support may require committing considerable resources for a protracted period. However, easing the burden of support on military forces requires enabling civilian agencies and organizations to fulfill their respective roles. This is typically achieved by combining the effects of the stability mechanisms compel, control, and influence to reestablish security and control; restoring essential civil services to the local populace; and helping to secure humanitarian access necessary for aid organizations to function effectively.

h. **Direct and Indirect Approach. The *approach* is the manner in which a commander contends with a COG. A direct approach attacks the enemy's COG or principal strength by applying combat power directly against it.** However, COGs are generally well protected and not vulnerable to a direct approach. Thus, commanders usually choose an indirect approach. **An indirect approach attacks the enemy's COG by applying combat power against a series of decisive points that lead to the defeat of the COG while avoiding enemy strength.**

(1) Direct attacks against adversary COGs resulting in their neutralization or destruction provide the most direct path to victory. Since direct attacks against adversary COGs mean attacking an opponent's strength, JFCs must determine if friendly forces possess the power to attack with acceptable risk. **In the event that a direct attack is not a reasonable solution, JFCs should seek an indirect approach until conditions are established that permit successful direct attacks** (see Figure III-15). In this manner, the adversary's derived vulnerabilities can offer indirect pathways to gain leverage over its COGs.

(2) At the strategic level, indirect methods of defeating the adversary's COG could include depriving the adversary of allies or friends, emplacing sanctions, weakening the national will to fight by undermining the public support for war, and breaking up cohesion of adversary alliances or coalitions.

(3) At the operational level, the most common indirect method of defeating an adversary's COGs is to conduct a series of attacks against selected aspects of the adversary's combat power. For example, the JFC may sequence combat actions to force an adversary to divide its forces in theater, destroy the adversary's reserves or elements of the adversary's base of operations, or prevent or hinder the deployment of the adversary's major forces or reinforcements into the OA. Indirect methods of attacking the adversary's COGs (through critical vulnerabilities) could entail reducing the adversary's operational reach, isolating the

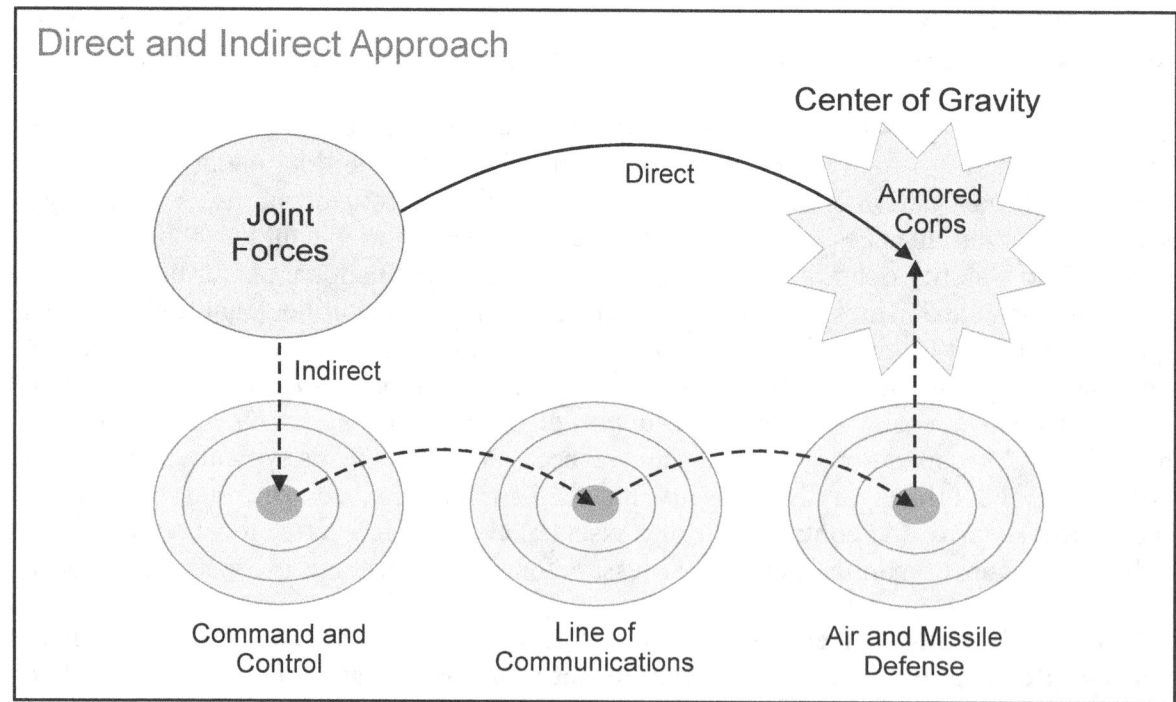

Figure III-15. Direct and Indirect Approach

force from its command and control (C2), and destroying or suppressing key protection functions such as air defense. Additionally, in an irregular warfare environment, a persistent indirect approach will help enable a legitimate and capable local partner to address the conflict's causes and to provide security, good governance, and economic development.

i. **Anticipation**

(1) Anticipation is key to effective planning. JFCs must consider what might happen and look for the signs that may bring the possible event to pass. During execution, JFCs should remain alert for the unexpected and for opportunities to exploit the situation. They continually gather information by personally observing and communicating with higher headquarters, subordinates, partner nations, and other organizations in the OA. JFCs may avoid surprise by gaining and maintaining the initiative at all levels of command and throughout the OA, thus forcing the adversary to react rather than initiate, and by thoroughly and continuously wargaming to identify probable adversary reactions to joint force actions. JFCs also should realize the effects of operations and associated consequences on the adversary, interagency and multinational partners, and civilians, and prepare for their results.

(2) Shared common understanding of the operational environment aids commanders and their staffs in anticipating opportunities and challenges. Knowledge of friendly capabilities; adversary capabilities, intentions, and likely COAs; and the location, activities, and status of dislocated civilians enables commanders to focus joint efforts where they can best, and most directly, contribute to achieving military objectives.

(3) **Anticipation is not without risk.** Commanders and staff officers who tend to lean forward in anticipation of what they expect to encounter are more susceptible to deception efforts by an opponent. Therefore, commanders and their staffs should carefully consider all available information upon which decisions are being based. Where possible, multiple or redundant sources of information should be employed to reduce risk in the decision-making process.

j. **Operational Reach**

(1) **Operational reach is the distance and duration across which a joint force can successfully employ military capabilities.** Although reach may be constrained or limited by the geography in and around the OA, it may be extended through forward positioning of capabilities and resources, increasing the range and effectiveness of weapon systems, leveraging HNS and contract support (system, external, theater) and maximizing the throughput efficiency of the distribution architecture.

(2) **The concept of operational reach is inextricably tied to the concept of LOOs.** The geography surrounding and separating adversaries influences operational reach. Locating forces, reserves, bases, pre-positioned equipment sets, and logistics forward extends operational reach. Operational reach is also affected by increasing the range of weapons, and by improving transportation availability and the effectiveness of LOCs and throughput capability. Some assets—such as air, space, and cyberspace—maintain a responsive global capability that significantly extends operational reach. Nevertheless, **for**

any given campaign or major operation, there is a finite range beyond which predominant elements of the joint force cannot prudently operate or maintain effective operations.

(3) Basing, in the broadest sense, is an indispensable part of operational art, since it is tied to the concept of LOOs and directly affects operational reach. Whether from overseas locations, sea-based platforms, or CONUS, basing directly affects the combat power and other capabilities that a joint force can generate. In particular, the arrangement and positioning of advanced bases (often in austere, rapidly emplaced configurations) underwrites the ability of the joint force to shield its components from adversary action and deliver symmetric and asymmetric blows. It also directly influences the combat power and other capabilities the joint force can generate because of its impact on such critical factors as sortie or resupply rates. Political and diplomatic considerations can often affect basing decisions.

(4) US force basing options span the range from permanently based forces to temporary sea basing during crisis response in littoral areas of instability. Bases are typically selected to be within operational reach of the adversary. To that end, theater assessments must determine whether sufficient infrastructure and diplomatic support exist or can be obtained to support the operational and sustainment requirements of deployed forces, and where they can be assured of some degree of security from attack. Determining where to locate bases poses certain challenges for planners. Recognizing the critical role basing plays in campaigns and operations, **potential adversaries may try to develop anti-access or area denial strategies designed to prevent the build up and sustainment of forces.** One such strategy could be a preemptive attack against US forces located outside the adversary's national boundaries, so planners must also consider the risk of placing US combat capabilities within the adversary's operational reach. Planners must determine how to mitigate an adversary's efforts to deny access to the theater and its infrastructure.

k. **Culmination**

(1) *Culmination* **is that point in time and/or space at which the operation can no longer maintain momentum.** In the offense, the culminating point is the point at which effectively continuing the attack is no longer possible and the force must consider reverting to a defensive posture or attempting an operational pause. Here the attacker greatly risks counterattack and defeat and continues the attack only at great peril. Success in the attack at all levels is to secure the objective before reaching culmination. A defender reaches culmination when the defending force no longer has the capability to go on the counteroffensive or defend successfully. Success in the defense is to draw the attacker to offensive culmination, then conduct an offensive to expedite the adversary's defensive culmination. During **stability operations,** culmination may result from the erosion of national will, decline of popular support, questions concerning legitimacy or restraint, or lapses in protection leading to excessive casualties.

(2) The JFC must ensure that forces and assets arrive at the right times and places to support the campaign and that sufficient resources will be available when needed in the later stages of the campaign. This is a key point, because sustainment is a significant aspect

of the campaign. Integration and synchronization of sustainment with combat operations can forestall culmination and help commanders control the tempo of their operations. At both tactical and operational levels, theater logistic planners forecast the drain on resources associated with conducting operations over extended distance and time. They respond by generating enough military resources at the right times and places to enable their commanders to achieve military strategic and operational objectives before reaching their culminating points. If commanders cannot generate these resources, they should revise their CONOPS.

l. **Arranging Operations**

(1) Commanders must determine the best arrangement of joint force and component operations to conduct the assigned tasks and joint force mission. This arrangement often will be a combination of simultaneous and sequential operations to reach the end state conditions with the least cost in personnel and other resources. Commanders consider a variety of factors when determining this arrangement, including geography of the OA, available strategic lift, changes in command structure, force protection, distribution and sustainment capabilities, adversary reinforcement capabilities, and public opinion. Thinking about the best arrangement helps determine the tempo of activities in time, space, and purpose. Planners should consider factors such as simultaneity, depth, timing, and tempo when arranging operations.

(a) *Simultaneity* **refers to the simultaneous application of military and nonmilitary power against the enemy's key capabilities and sources of strength.** Simultaneity in joint force operations contributes directly to an enemy's collapse by placing more demands on enemy forces and functions than can be handled. This does not mean that all elements of the joint force are employed with equal priority or that even all elements of the joint force will be employed. It refers specifically to the concept of attacking appropriate enemy forces and functions throughout the OA (across the physical domains and the information environment [which includes cyberspace]) in such a manner as to cause failure of their moral and physical cohesion.

(b) **Simultaneity also refers to the concurrent conduct of operations at the tactical, operational, and strategic levels.** Tactical commanders fight engagements and battles, understanding their relevance to the contingency plan. JFCs set the conditions for battles within a major operation or campaign to achieve military strategic and operational objectives. GCCs integrate theater strategy and operational art. At the same time, they remain acutely aware of the impact of tactical events. Because of the inherent interrelationships between the various levels of war, commanders cannot be concerned only with events at their respective echelon, but also must understand how their actions contribute to the military end state.

(c) The evolution of warfare and advances in technology have continuously expanded the depth of operations. US joint forces can rapidly maneuver over great distances and strike with precision. Joint force operations should be conducted across the full breadth and depth of the OA, creating competing and simultaneous demands on adversary commanders and resources. **The concept of *depth* seeks to overwhelm the enemy**

throughout the OA, creating competing and simultaneous demands on enemy commanders and resources and contributing to the enemy's speedy defeat. Depth applies to time as well as geography. Operations extended in depth shape future conditions and can disrupt an opponent's decision cycle. Strategic attack, interdiction, and some IO are examples of the applications of depth in joint operations. Operations in depth contribute to protection of the force by destroying adversary potential before its capabilities can be realized or employed.

(d) The joint force should conduct operations at a tempo and point in time that best exploits friendly capabilities and inhibits the adversary. **With proper *timing*, JFCs can dominate the action, remain unpredictable, and operate beyond the adversary's ability to react.**

(e) The *tempo* of warfare has increased over time as technological advancements and innovative doctrines have been applied to military requirements. While in many situations JFCs may elect to maintain an operational tempo that stretches the capabilities of both friendly and adversary forces, on other occasions JFCs may elect to conduct operations at a reduced pace. During selected phases of a campaign, JFCs could reduce the pace of operations, frustrating adversary commanders while buying time to build a decisive force or tend to other priorities in the OA such as relief to displaced persons. During other phases, JFCs could conduct high-tempo operations designed specifically to overwhelm adversary defensive capabilities. Assuring strategic mobility preserves the JFC's ability to control tempo by allowing freedom of theater access.

(2) Several tools are available to planners to assist with arranging operations. Phases, branches and sequels, operational pauses, and the development of a TPFDD all improve the ability of the planner to arrange, manage, and execute complex operations.

(a) **Phases.** Phasing is a way to view and conduct a complex joint operation in manageable parts. The main purpose of phasing is to integrate and synchronize related activities, thereby enhancing flexibility and unity of effort during execution. Reaching the end state often requires arranging a major operation or campaign in several phases. Phases in a contingency plan are sequential, but during execution there will often be some simultaneous and overlapping execution of the activities within the phases. In a campaign, each phase can represent a single major operation, while in a major operation a phase normally consists of several subordinate operations or a series of related activities. See Section C, "Phasing," for a more detailed discussion.

(b) **Branches and Sequels.** Many contingency plans require adjustment beyond the initial stages of the operation. Consequently, JFCs build flexibility into their plans by developing branches and sequels to preserve freedom of action in rapidly changing conditions. They are primarily used for changing deployments or direction of movement and accepting or declining combat. Branches and sequels directly relate to the phasing construct.

<u>1.</u> *Branches* **provide a range of options often built into the basic plan.** Branches add flexibility to plans by anticipating situations that could alter the basic plan.

Such situations could be a result of adversary action, availability of friendly capabilities or resources, or even a change in the weather or season within the OA.

2. ***Sequels* anticipate and plan for subsequent operations based on the possible outcomes of the current operation—victory, defeat, or stalemate.** For every action or major operation that does not accomplish a strategic or operational objective, there should be a sequel for each possible outcome, such as win, lose, draw, or win big.

3. Once the commander and staff have determined possible branches and sequels as far in advance as practicable, they should determine what or where the **decision points** (not to be confused with decisive points) should be. Such decision points capture in space and/or time decisions a commander must make. To aid the commander, planners develop a decision support matrix (DSM) to link those decision points with the earliest and latest timing of the decision and the appropriate priority intelligence requirements (PIRs) (things the commander must know about the enemy to make the decision) and friendly force information requirements (FFIRs) (things the commander must know about his forces to make the decision). **Each branch from a decision point requires different actions, and each action demands various follow-up actions, such as sequels or potential sequels.**

(c) **Operational Pause**

1. The supported JFC should aggressively conduct operations to obtain and maintain the initiative. However, there may be certain circumstances when this is not feasible because of logistic constraints or force shortfalls. Therefore, ***operational pauses* may be required when a major operation may be reaching the end of its sustainability.** As such, operational pauses can provide a safety valve to avoid potential culmination, while the JFC retains the initiative in other ways. However, if an operational pause is properly executed in relation to one's own culminating point, the adversary will not have sufficient combat power to threaten the joint force or regain the initiative during the pause.

2. **Operational pauses are also useful tools for obtaining the proper synchronization of sustainment and operations.** Normally, operational pauses are planned to regenerate combat power or augment sustainment and forces for the next phase, although this will result in extending the duration of a major operation or campaign. Moreover, **properly planned and sequenced operational pauses will ensure that the JFC has sufficient forces and assets to accomplish strategic or operational objectives.** However, planners must guard against cutting the margin of sustainment and combat effectiveness too thin. Executing a pause before it is necessary provides for flexibility in the timing of the pause and allows for its early termination under urgent conditions without unduly endangering the future effectiveness of the force.

3. **The primary drawback to operational pauses is that they risk forfeiture of strategic or operational initiative.** It is therefore incumbent upon the JFC to plan on as few operational pauses as possible, if any, and consistent with the CONOPS, to alternate pauses and tempo between components of the force. In this manner, a major portion of the joint force can maintain pressure on the adversary through offensive actions while other components pause.

(d) Realistic plans, branches, sequels, orders, and an accurate TPFDD are important to enable the proper sequencing of operations. Further, the dynamic nature of modern military operations requires adaptability concerning the arrangement of military capabilities in time, space, and purpose. For example, a rapidly changing adversary situation or other aspects of the operational environment may cause the commander to alter the planned arrangement of operations even as forces are deploying. Therefore, maintaining overall force visibility, to include both in-transit visibility and asset visibility, are critical to maintaining flexibility. The arrangement that the commander chooses should not foreclose future options.

m. **Forces and Functions**

(1) **Commanders and planners can design campaigns and operations that focus on defeating either *adversary forces, functions, or a combination of both*.** Typically, JFCs structure operations to attack both adversary forces and functions concurrently to create the greatest possible friction between friendly and adversary forces and capabilities. These types of operations are especially appropriate when friendly forces enjoy technological and/or numerical superiority over an opponent.

(2) JFCs can focus on destroying and disrupting critical adversary functions such as C2, sustainment, and protection. Attack of an adversary's functions normally is intended to destroy the adversary's balance, thereby creating vulnerabilities to be exploited. The direct effect of destroying or disrupting critical adversary functions can create the indirect effects of uncertainty, confusion, and even panic in adversary leadership and forces and may contribute directly to the collapse of adversary capability and will. When assessing whether functional attack should be the principal operational approach, JFCs should evaluate several variables, such as time required to cripple the adversary's critical functions, time available to the JFC, the adversary's current actions, and likely responses to such actions.

SECTION C. PHASING

7. Application

a. **A phase can be characterized by the "focus" that is placed on it.** Phases are distinct in time, space, and/or purpose from one another, but must be planned in support of each other and should represent a natural progression and subdivision of the campaign or operation, as shown in Figure III-16. Each phase should have a set of starting conditions (that define the start of the phase) and ending conditions (that define the end of the phase). The ending conditions of one phase are the starting conditions for the next phase.

b. Phases are necessarily linked and gain significance in the larger context of the campaign. As such, it is imperative the campaign or operation not be broken down into numerous arbitrary components that may inhibit tempo and lead to a plodding, incremental approach. Since a campaign is required whenever pursuit of a strategic objective is not attainable through a single major operation, the theater operational design includes provision for related phases that may or may not be executed.

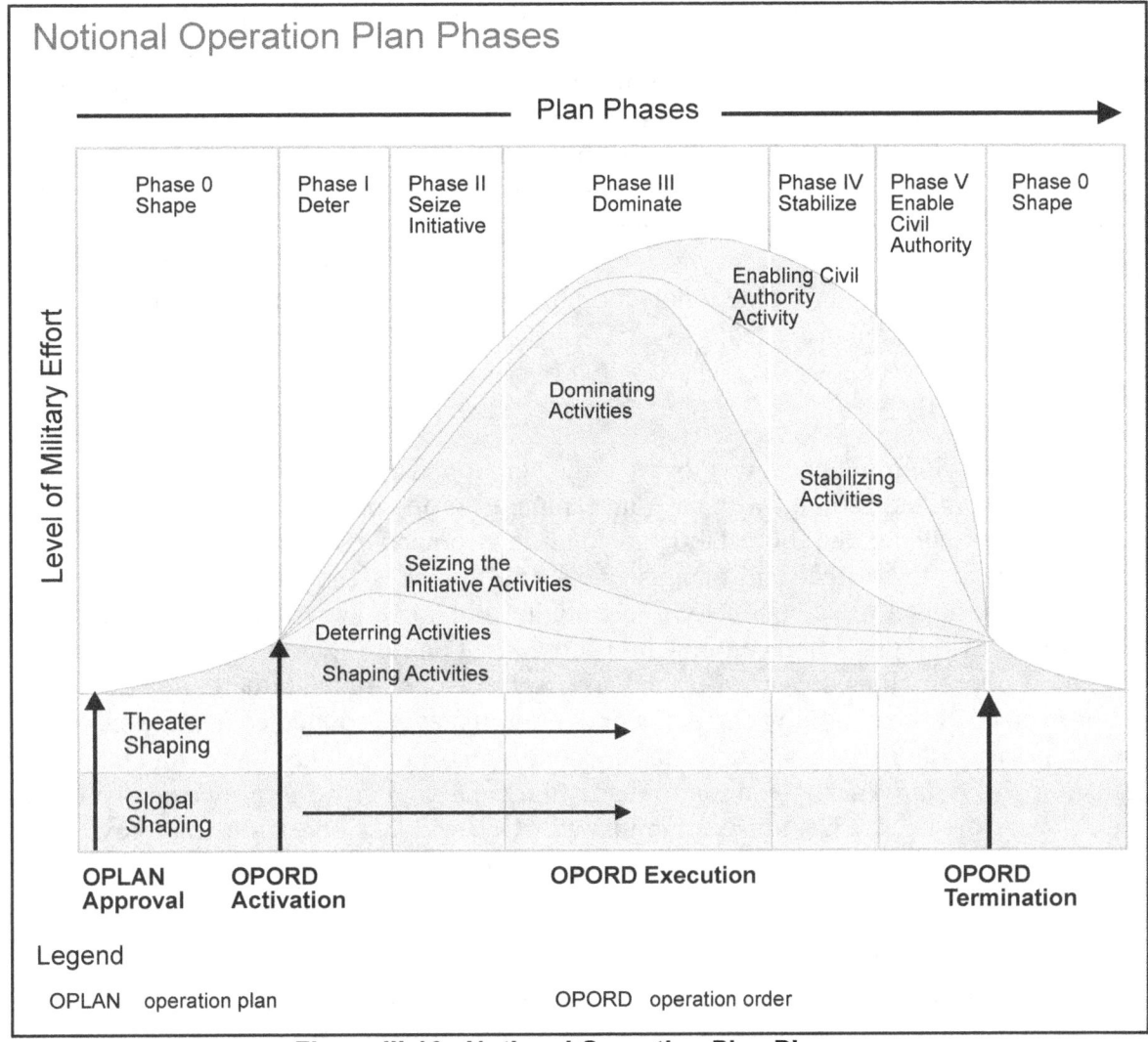

Figure III-16. Notional Operation Plan Phases

c. Activities in phases may overlap. The commander's vision of how a campaign or operation should unfold drives subsequent decisions regarding phasing. Phasing, in turn, assists with synchronizing the CONOPS and aids in organizing the assignment of tasks to subordinate commanders. By arranging operations and activities into phases, the JFC can better integrate and synchronize subordinate operations in time, space, and purpose. Each phase should represent a natural subdivision of the campaign or operation's intermediate objectives. As such, a phase represents a definitive stage during which a large portion of the forces and joint/multinational capabilities are involved in similar or mutually supporting activities.

d. As a general rule, **the phasing of the campaign or operation should be conceived in condition-driven rather than time-driven terms.** However, resource availability depends in large part on time-constrained activities and factors—such as sustainment or deployment rates—rather than the events associated with the operation. **The challenge for planners, then, is to reconcile the reality of time-oriented deployment of forces and sustainment with the event-driven phasing of operations.**

e. Effective phasing must address how the joint force will avoid reaching a culminating point. If resources are insufficient to sustain the force until achieving the end state, planners should consider phasing the campaign or operation to account for necessary operational pauses between phases. Such phasing enables the reconstitution of the joint force during joint operations, but the JFC must understand that this may provide the adversary an opportunity to reconstitute as well. In some cases, sustainment requirements, diplomatic factors, and political factors within the host nation may even dictate the purpose of certain phases as well as the sequence of those phases. For example, phases may shift the main effort among Service and functional components to maintain momentum while one component is being reconstituted.

8. Number, Sequence, and Overlap

Working within the phasing construct, the actual phases used will vary (compressed, expanded, or omitted entirely) with the joint campaign or operation and be determined by the JFC. During planning, the JFC establishes conditions, objectives, or events for transitioning from one phase to another and plans sequels and branches for potential contingencies. Phases are designed to be conducted sequentially, but some activities from a phase may begin in a previous phase and continue into subsequent phases. The JFC adjusts the phases to exploit opportunities presented by the adversary or operational situation or to react to unforeseen conditions. A joint campaign or operation may be conducted in multiple phases simultaneously if the OA has widely varying conditions. For instance, the commander may transition to the *stabilize* phase in some areas while remaining in the *dominate* phase in those areas where the enemy has not yet capitulated. Occasionally operations may revert to a previous phase in an area where a resurgent or new enemy reengages friendly forces.

9. Transitions

Transitions between phases are designed to be distinct shifts in focus by the joint force, often accompanied by changes in command or support relationships. The activities that predominate during a given phase, however, rarely align with neatly definable breakpoints. The need to move into another phase normally is identified by assessing that a set of objectives are achieved or that the enemy has acted in a manner that requires a major change in focus for the joint force and is therefore usually event driven, not time driven. Changing the focus of the operation takes time and may require changing commander's objectives, desired effects, measures of effectiveness (MOEs), priorities, command relationships, force allocation, or even the design of the OA. An example is the shift of focus from sustained combat operations in the *dominate* phase to a preponderance of stability operations in the *stabilize* and *enable civil authority* phases. Hostilities gradually lessen as the joint force begins to reestablish order, commerce, and local government and deters adversaries from resuming hostile actions while the US and international community take steps to establish or restore the conditions necessary for long-term stability. This challenge demands an agile shift in joint force skill sets, actions, organizational behaviors, and mental outlooks, and interorganizational coordination with a wider range of interagency and multinational partners and other participants to provide the capabilities necessary to address the mission-specific factors.

10. Phasing Model

a. Although the commander will determine the number and actual phases used during a campaign or operation, use of the phases shown in Figure III-17 and described below provides a flexible model to arrange combat and stability operations. **Within the context of these phases established by a higher-level JFC, subordinate JFCs and component commanders may establish additional phases that fit their CONOPS.** For example, the joint force land component commander (JFLCC) or a subordinate joint task force (JTF) might have the following four phases inside the GCC's *seize initiative* phase: deploy, forcible entry, defense, and offense. The JFLCC could use the offense phase as a transition to the GCC's *dominate* phase.

b. The six-phase model is not intended to be a universally prescriptive template for all conceivable joint operations and may be tailored to the character and duration of the operation to which it applies.

c. The general phasing construct can be applied to various campaigns and operations. Operations and activities in the *shape* phase normally are outlined in TCPs and those in the remaining phases are outlined in JSCP-directed contingency plans. While most shaping

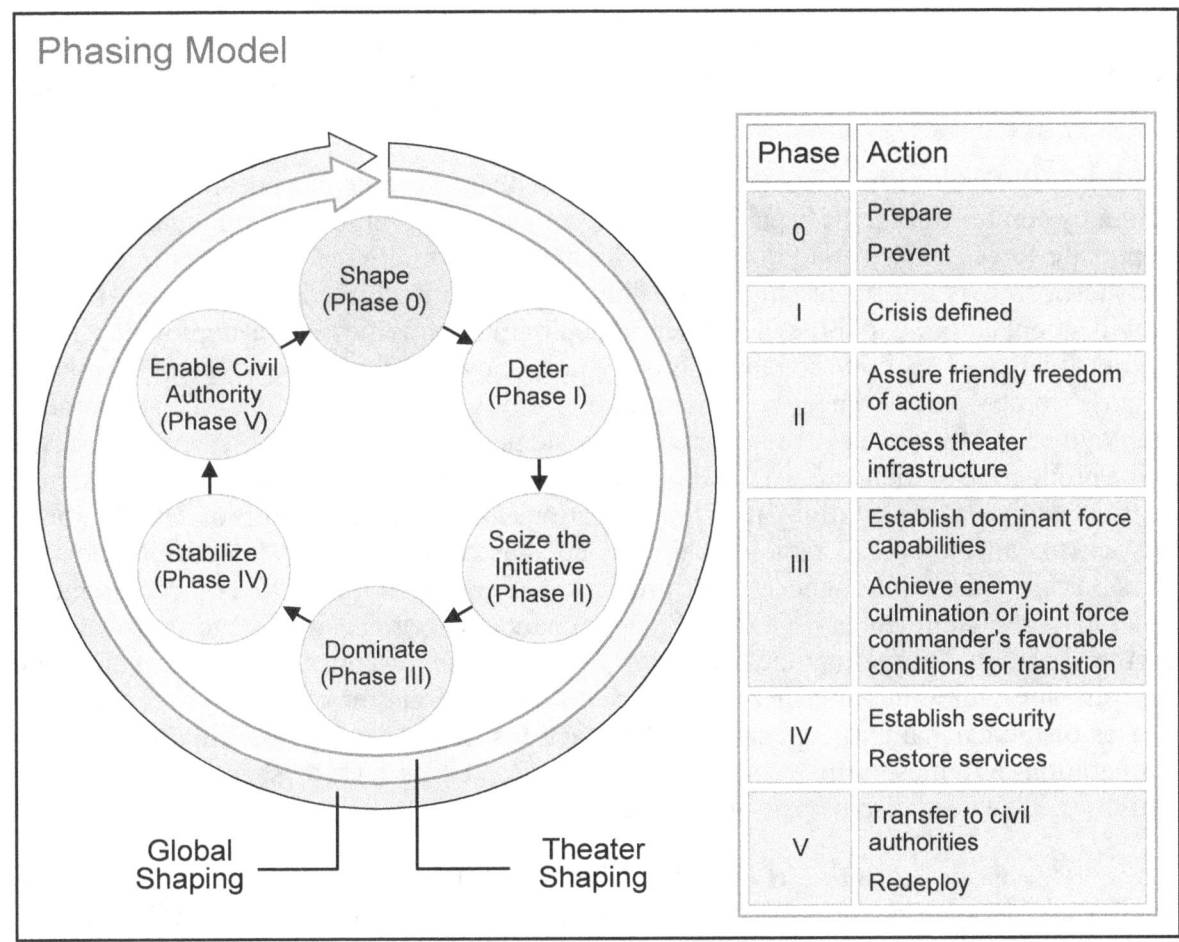

Figure III-17. Phasing Model

activities are contained in the TCP, contingency plans may include shaping activities that must be accomplished to support an operation. GCCs generally use the phasing model to link the pertinent TCP and OPLAN operations and activities.

(1) **Shape (Phase 0).** Joint and multinational operations—inclusive of normal and routine military activities—and various interagency activities are performed to dissuade or deter potential adversaries and to assure or solidify relationships with friends and allies. They are executed continuously with the intent to enhance international legitimacy and gain multinational cooperation in support of defined national strategic and strategic military objectives. They are designed to ensure success by shaping perceptions and influencing the behavior of both adversaries and partner nations, developing partner nation and friendly military capabilities for self-defense and multinational operations, improving information exchange and intelligence sharing, and providing US forces with peacetime and contingency access. *Shape* phase activities must adapt to a particular theater environment and may be executed in one theater in order to create effects and/or achieve objectives in another. Planning that supports most "shaping" requirements typically occurs in the context of day-to-day security cooperation, and CCMDs will nest phase 0 activities and tasks into the TCP. Planners developing contingency plans must identify shaping requirements that can be accomplished within the scope of the TCP's steady-state activities; however, planners may also identify shaping requirements specific to their plan that would only be implemented in the event of crisis. Other activities can also be performed during phase 0, such as establishing logistics capabilities needed to support phase 1 activities. For example, time and distance challenges may require taking actions or setting the conditions during the shape phase for sustainment to be available should use of military force become necessary.

(2) **Deter (Phase I).** The intent of this phase is to deter undesirable adversary action by demonstrating the capabilities and resolve of the joint force. It includes activities to prepare forces and set conditions for deployment and employment of forces in the event that deterrence is not successful. Once the crisis is defined, these actions may include mobilization; tailoring of forces and other predeployment activities; initial deployment into a theater; increased security cooperation activities; shows of force; deployment of missile defense forces; development and maturation of joint or multinational C2 structures; employment of ISR assets to provide real-time and near-real-time situational awareness; the surge production of foundational intelligence required to employ advanced weapon systems; setting up of transfer operations at en route locations to support aerial ports of debarkation in post-chemical, biological, radiological, and nuclear environments; and development of mission-tailored C2, intelligence, force protection, transportation, and logistic requirements to support the commanders' CONOPS. Commanders continue to engage multinational partners, thereby providing the basis for further crisis response. Liaison teams and coordination with other agencies assist in setting conditions for execution of subsequent phases of the campaign or operation. Many actions in the *deter* phase build on security cooperation activities from phase 0 and are conducted as part of security cooperation activities. They can also be part of stand-alone operations.

(3) **Seize Initiative (Phase II).** JFCs seek to seize the initiative through the application of appropriate joint force capabilities. In combat operations, this involves executing offensive operations at the earliest possible time, forcing the adversary to offensive

culmination, and setting the conditions for decisive operations. Rapid application of joint combat power may be required to delay, impede, or halt the adversary's initial aggression and to deny the initial objectives. If an adversary has achieved its initial objectives, the early and rapid application of offensive combat power can dislodge adversary forces from their position, creating conditions for the exploitation, pursuit, and ultimate destruction of both those forces and their will to fight during the *dominate* phase. During this phase, operations to gain access to theater infrastructure and to expand friendly freedom of action continue while the JFC seeks to degrade adversary capabilities with the intent of resolving the crisis at the earliest opportunity. In all operations, the JFC establishes conditions for stability by providing immediate assistance to relieve conditions that precipitated the crisis.

(4) **Dominate (Phase III).** The *dominate* phase focuses on breaking the enemy's will for organized resistance or, in noncombat situations, control of the operational environment. Success in this phase depends upon overmatching joint force capability at the critical time and place. This phase includes full employment of joint force capabilities and continues the appropriate sequencing of forces into the OA as quickly as possible. When a campaign or operation is focused on conventional enemy forces, the *dominate* phase normally concludes with decisive operations that drive an adversary to culmination and achieve the JFC's operational objectives. Against irregular threats, decisive operations are characterized by dominating and controlling the operational environment through a combination of traditional warfare, irregular warfare (with counterinsurgency, foreign internal defense, stability operations, and counterterrorism as subsets), and IO. Stability operations are conducted as needed to ensure a smooth transition to the next phase and relieve suffering. In noncombat situations, the joint force's activities seek to control the situation or operational environment. *Dominate* phase activities may establish the conditions for an early favorable conclusion of operations or set the conditions for transition to the next phase.

(5) **Stabilize (Phase IV).** The *stabilize* phase is required when there is no fully functional, legitimate civil governing authority present. The joint force may be required to perform limited local governance, integrating the efforts of other supporting/contributing multinational, IGO, NGO, or USG department and agency participants until legitimate local entities are functioning. This includes providing or assisting in the provision of basic services to the population. A significant proportion of this support may require contracted goods and services. IFO support this by synchronization and deconfliction to avoid contractor inefficiency, duplicative spending, and inadvertent funding of adversaries. The *stabilize* phase is typically characterized by a change from sustained combat operations to stability operations. The purpose of stability operations is to help move a host nation from instability (and particularly the violent conflict that often accompanies increased instability) to increased stability (and reduced violent conflict). This involves comprehensive efforts by the US and its partners to stabilize states in crisis and to build the capacity of fragile states. Planning for rotational deployments and redeployment operations should begin as early as possible and continue through all phases of the operation. Throughout this segment, the JFC continuously assesses the impact of current operations on the ability to transfer overall regional authority to a legitimate civil entity, which marks the end of the phase.

(6) **Enable Civil Authority (Phase V).** This phase is predominantly characterized by joint force support to legitimate civil governance in theater. Depending upon the level of indigenous state capacity, joint force activities during phase V may be at the behest of that authority or they may be under its direction. The goal is for the joint force to enable the viability of the civil authority and its provision of essential services to the largest number of people in the region. This includes coordination of joint force actions with supporting or supported multinational, agency, and other organization participants, and continuing integrated finance operations and security cooperation activities to influence the attitude of the population favorably regarding the US and local civil authority's objectives. DOD policy is to support indigenous persons or groups promoting freedom, rule of law, and an entrepreneurial economy and opposing extremism and the murder of civilians. The joint force will be in a supporting role to the legitimate civil authority in the region throughout the *enable civil authority* phase. Redeployment operations, particularly for combat units, will often begin during this phase, and deployments, including force rotations, may occur to support and enable civil authorities. CCMD involvement with other nations and agencies, beyond the termination of the joint operation, may be required to achieve the national strategic end state.

SECTION D. ASSESSMENT

11. Overview

Assessment is the continuous monitoring and evaluation of the current situation and progress of a joint operation toward mission accomplishment. It involves deliberately comparing forecasted outcomes to actual events to determine the overall effectiveness of force employment. In general, assessments should answer two questions: Is the JFC doing things right? Is the JFC doing the right things? More specifically, assessment helps JFCs determine progress toward achieving objectives and whether the current tasks and objectives are relevant to reaching the end state. It helps identify opportunities, counter threats, and any needs for course correction, thus resulting in modifications to plans and orders. This process of continuous assessment occurs throughout the joint planning process. It is an essential tool that allows planners to monitor performance of tactical actions (measures of performance [MOPs]) and to determine whether the desired effects are created (MOE) to support achievement of the objectives.

12. Application

a. Assessment and learning enable incremental improvements to the commander's operational approach and the campaign or contingency plan. The aim is to understand the problem and develop effective actions to address it. These actions may be a military activity—or may involve military actions in support of nonmilitary activities. Once JFCs understand the problem and what needs to be accomplished to succeed, they identify the means to assess effectiveness and the related information requirements that support assessment. This feedback becomes the basis for learning, adaptation, and subsequent adjustment.

b. Not all joint operations proceed smoothly toward the desired end state. JFCs examine instances of unexpected success or failure, unanticipated adversary actions, or operations that simply do not progress as planned. They assess the causes of success, friction, and failure and their overall impact on the force and the operation. JFCs and staffs continuously assess an operation's progress to determine if the current order is still valid or if there are better ways to achieve the end state. Assessments by staff sections form the foundation of running estimates. Assessments by JFCs allow them to maintain accurate situational understanding and revise their visualization or operational approach appropriately.

c. **Commanders must also be attuned to a change in the operational environment (to include the political environment) that may cause the mission to be in question.** Is the current desired end state still the desired end state, or have circumstances changed to the point that the desired end state may need to be revised?

d. Assessment precedes and guides every activity within the JOPP and concludes each operation or phase of an operation. Assessment entails two distinct tasks: continuously monitoring the situation and the progress of the operations and evaluating the operation against MOEs and MOPs to determine progress relative to the mission, objectives, and end states. Effective assessment requires criteria for evaluating the degree of success in accomplishing the mission. Criteria can be expressed as MOEs and MOPs.

(1) **A *MOE* is a criterion used to assess changes in system behavior, capability, or operational environment that is tied to measuring the attainment of an end state, an objective, or the creation of an effect. It measures the relevance of actions being performed.**

(2) **A *MOP* is a criterion used to assess friendly actions that is tied to measuring task accomplishment.**

e. Many aspects of operations are quantifiable. Examples include movement rates, fuel consumption, and weapons effects. While not easy, assessing physical aspects of joint operations can be straightforward. However, the dynamic interaction among friendly forces, adaptable adversaries, and populations makes assessing many aspects of operations difficult. For example, assessing the results of planned actions to convince a group of people to support their central government is very challenging. As planners assess complex human behaviors like this, they draw on multiple sources across the operational environment, including both analytical and subjective measures that support a more informed assessment.

f. Just as JFCs devote time and staff resources to planning, they must also provide guidance on *what to assess and to what level of detail*. Depending on the situation and the echelon of command, assessment may be a detailed process (formal assessment plan with dedicated assessment cell or element). Alternatively, it may be an informal process that relies more on the intuition of the JFC, subordinate commanders, and staffs.

g. As a general rule, the level at which a specific operation, task, or action occurs should be the level at which such activity is assessed. This focuses assessment at each level and enhances the efficiency of the overall assessment process.

For an expanded discussion of assessment, see Appendix D, "Assessment."

CHAPTER IV
JOINT OPERATION PLANNING PROCESS

> *"In forming the plan of a campaign, it is requisite to foresee everything the enemy may do, and be prepared with the necessary means to counteract it. Plans of the campaign may be modified ad infinitum according to the circumstances, the genius of the general, the character of the troops, and the features of the country."*
>
> **Napoleon**
> ***Maxims of War, 1831***

1. Introduction

a. **JOPP** is an orderly, analytical process, which consists of a set of logical steps to examine a mission; develop, analyze, and compare alternative COAs; select the best COA; and produce a plan or order. Operational art and the application of operational design provide the conceptual basis for structuring campaigns and operations discussed in Chapter III, "Operational Art and Operational Design." **JOPP** provides a proven process to organize the work of the commander, staff, subordinate commanders, and other partners, to develop plans that will appropriately address the problem to be solved. It focuses on defining the military mission and development and synchronization of detailed plans to accomplish that mission. Commanders and staffs can apply the thinking methodology introduced in the previous chapter to discern the correct mission, develop creative and adaptive CONOPS to accomplish the mission, and synchronize those CONOPS so that they can be executed. It applies to both supported and supporting JFCs and to joint force component commands when the components participate in joint planning. Together with operational design, JOPP facilitates interaction between the commander, staff, and subordinate and supporting headquarters throughout planning. JOPP helps commanders and their staffs organize their planning activities, share a common understanding of the mission and commander's intent, and develop effective plans and orders. Figure IV-1 shows the primary steps of JOPP.

b. In common application, JOPP proceeds according to planning milestones and other requirements established by commanders at various levels. However, the CJCSM 3122 series specifies JPEC milestones, deliverables, and interaction points for plans developed using APEX.

2. Operational Art and Operational Design Interface with the Joint Operation Planning Process

a. Operational design and JOPP are complementary elements of the overall planning process. Operational design provides an iterative process that allows for the commander's vision and mastery of operational art to help planners answer ends–ways–means–risk questions and appropriately structure campaigns and operations. The commander, supported by the staff, gains an understanding of the operational environment, defines the problem, and develops an operational approach for the campaign or operation through the application of operational design during the initiation step of JOPP. Commanders communicate their

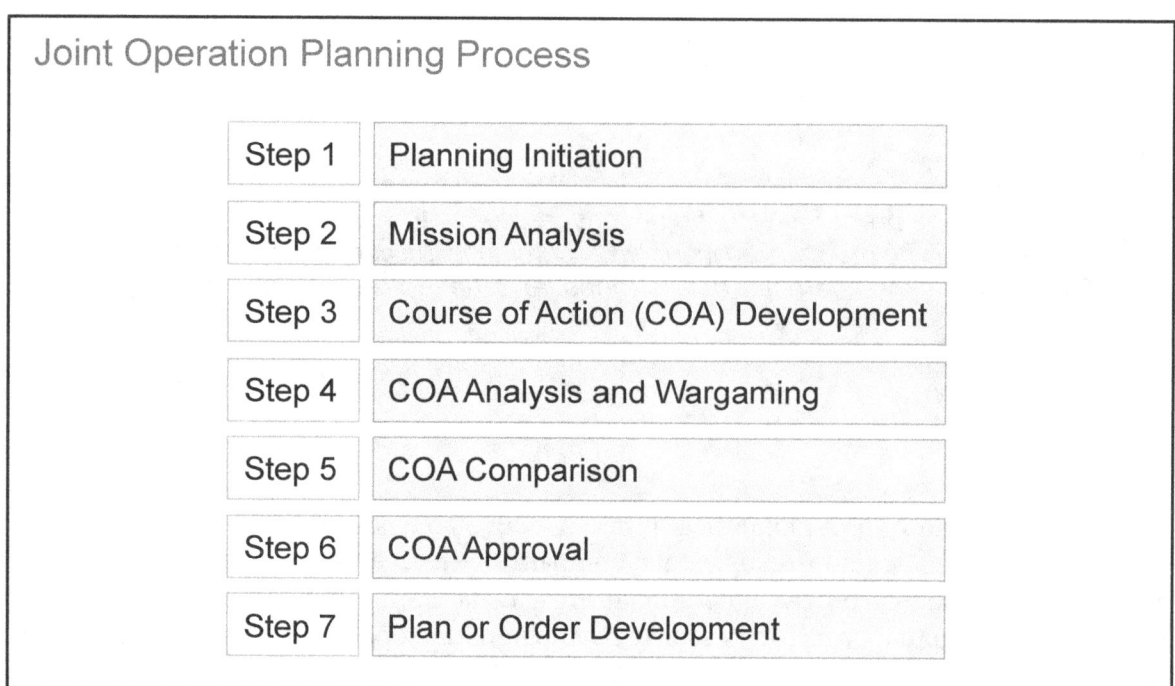

Figure IV-1. Joint Operation Planning Process

operational approach to their staff, subordinates, supporting commands, agencies, and multinational/nongovernmental entities as required in their initial planning guidance so that their approach can be translated into executable plans. As JOPP is executed, commanders learn more about the operational environment and the problem and refine their initial operational approach. Commanders provide their updated approach to the staff to guide detailed planning. This iterative process between the commander's maturing operational approach and the development of the mission and CONOPS through JOPP facilitates the continuing development of possible COAs and their refinement into eventual CONOPS and executable plans.

b. This relationship between the application of operational art, operational design, and JOPP continues throughout execution of the campaign or operation. By applying the operational design methodology in combination with the procedural rigor of JOPP, the command can help keep its aperture as wide as possible to always question the mission's continuing relevance and suitability while executing operations in accordance with the current approach and revising plans as needed. By combining the best aspects of both of these approaches, the friendly force can maintain the greatest possible flexibility and do so in a proactive vice reactive manner (see Figure IV-2).

3. **Planning Initiation**

a. Joint operation planning begins when an appropriate authority recognizes potential for military capability to be employed in response to a potential or actual crisis. **At the strategic level, that authority—the President, SecDef, or CJCS—initiates planning by deciding to develop military options.** The GEF, JSCP, and related strategic guidance documents (when applicable) serve as the primary guidance to begin deliberate planning.

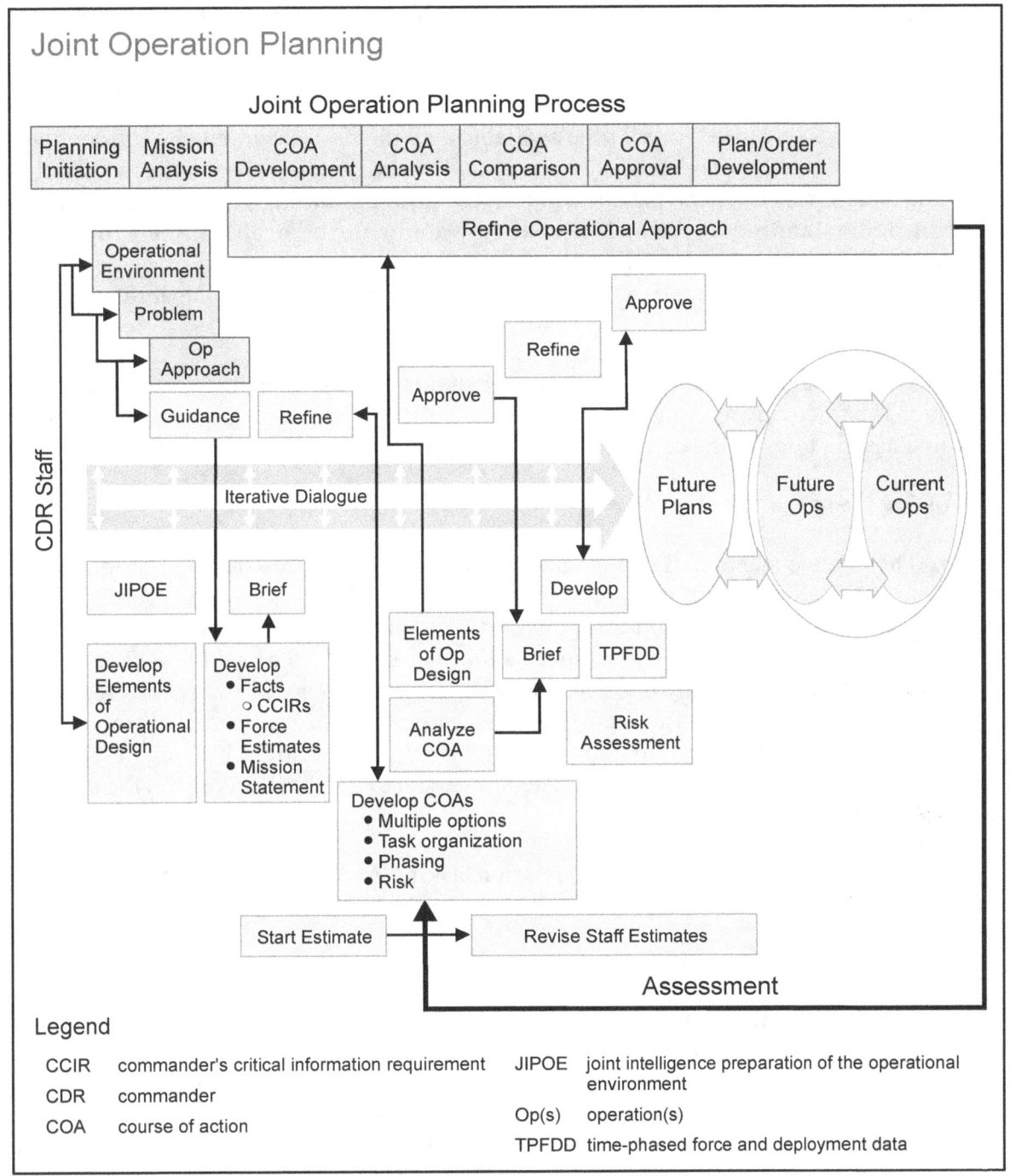

Figure IV-2. Joint Operation Planning

CCDRs and other commanders also initiate planning on their own authority when they identify a planning requirement not directed by higher authority. Additionally, analyses of developing or immediate crises may result in the President, SecDef, or CJCS initiating military planning through a WARNORD or other planning directive. Military options normally are developed in combination with other nonmilitary options so that the President can respond with all the appropriate instruments of national power. Whether or not planning begins as described here, the commander may act within approved authorities and ROE in an immediate crisis.

b. Particularly when planning for crises, the JFC and staff will perform an assessment of the initiating directive to determine time available until mission execution, the current status of intelligence products and staff estimates, and other factors relevant to the specific planning situation. The JFC typically will provide **initial planning guidance based upon current understanding of the operational environment, the problem, and the initial operational approach for the campaign or operation.** It could specify time constraints, outline initial coordination requirements, or authorize movement of key capabilities within the JFC's authority.

c. While planning is continuous once execution begins, planning initiation during execution is particularly relevant when there are significant changes to the current mission or planning assumptions or the commander receives a mission for follow-on operations.

4. Mission Analysis

a. The commander's staff is responsible for analyzing the mission and proposing, if required, the restated mission for the commander's approval, thus allowing subordinate and supporting commanders to begin their own estimate and planning efforts and for higher headquarters' concurrence. **The joint force's mission is the task or set of tasks, together with the purpose, that clearly indicates the action to be taken and the reason for doing so.** Mission analysis is used to study the assigned tasks and to identify all other tasks necessary to accomplish the mission. Mission analysis is critical because it provides direction to the commander and the staff, enabling them to focus effectively on the problem at hand.

b. When the commander receives a mission tasking, analysis begins with the following questions:

(1) What tasks must my command do for the mission to be accomplished?

(2) What is the purpose of the mission received?

(3) What limitations have been placed on my own forces' actions?

(4) What forces/assets are needed to support my operation?

c. **The primary inputs to mission analysis** are the higher headquarters' planning directive, other strategic guidance, and the commander's initial planning guidance, which may include a description of the operational environment, a definition of the problem, the operational approach, initial intent, and the JIPOE (see Figure IV-3). **The primary products of mission analysis** are staff estimates, the mission statement, a refined operational approach, the commander's intent statement, updated planning guidance, and commander's critical information requirements (CCIRs).

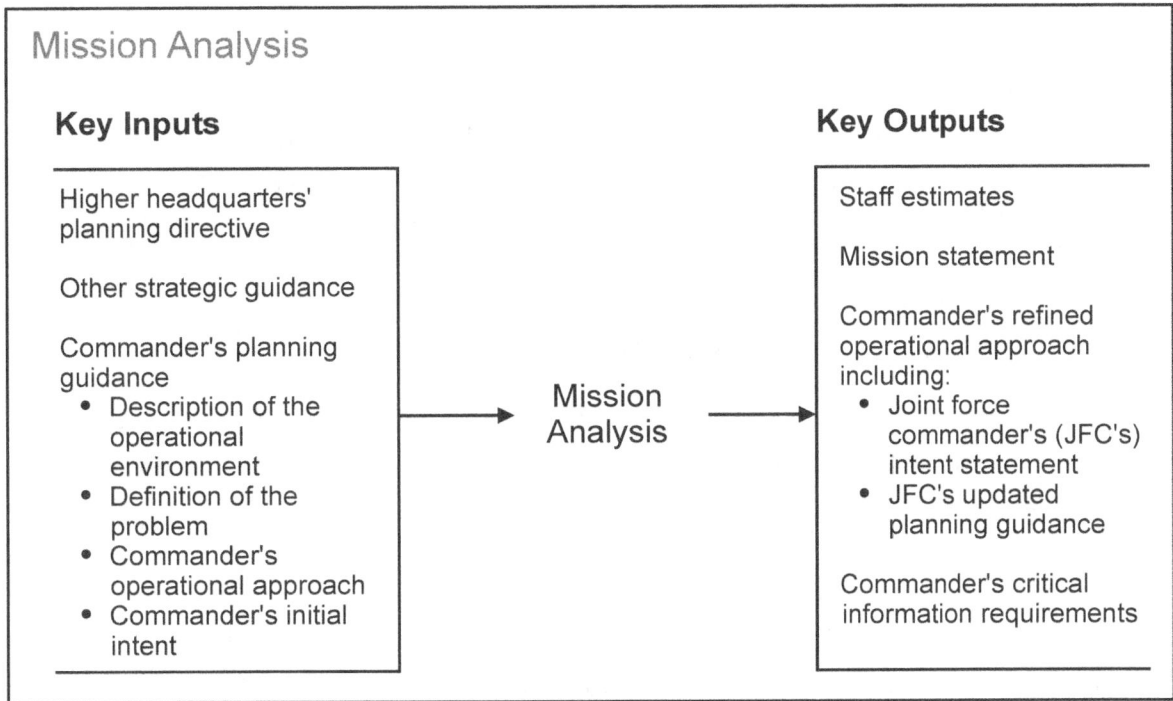

Figure IV-3. Mission Analysis

d. Mission analysis helps the JFC understand the problem and purpose of the operation and issue appropriate guidance to drive the rest of the planning process. The JFC and staff can accomplish mission analysis through a number of logical activities, such as those shown in Figure IV-4.

(1) Although some activities occur before others, mission analysis typically involves substantial parallel processing of information by the commander and staff, particularly in a CAP situation.

(2) During mission analysis, it is essential that the tasks (specified and implied) and their purposes are clearly stated to ensure planning encompasses all requirements; limitations (restraints—cannot do, or constraints—must do) on actions that the commander or subordinate forces may take are understood; and the correlation between the commander's mission and intent and those of higher and other commanders is understood.

e. **Analyze Higher Headquarters' Planning Directives and Strategic Guidance**

(1) Strategic guidance is essential to joint operation planning and operational design. The President, SecDef, CJCS, and CCDRs promulgate strategic guidance that covers a broad range of situations. Documents such as the NDS, NMS, and the CCDR's theater strategy provide long-term as well as intermediate or ancillary objectives.

(2) For a specific crisis, a planning directive such as a CJCS PLANORD, ALERTORD, or WARNORD provides specific guidance, typically including a description of the situation, purpose of military operations, objectives, anticipated mission or tasks, pertinent constraints, and forces available to the commander for planning and strategic lift

---

Mission Analysis Activities

- Analyze higher headquarters planning activities and strategic guidance

- Review commander's initial planning guidance, including his initial understanding of the operational environment, of the problem, and description of the operational approach

- Determine known facts and develop planning assumptions

- Determine and analyze operational limitations

- Determine specified, implied, and essential tasks

- Develop mission statement

- Conduct initial force allocation review

- Develop risk assesment

- Develop mission success criteria

- Develop commander's critical information requirements

- Prepare staff estimates

- Prepare and deliver mission analysis brief

- Publish commander's updated planning guidance, intent statement, and refined operational approach

Steps are not necessarily sequential.

Figure IV-4. Mission Analysis Activities

allocations. The apportionment tables provide a quantity of forces that the planner can reasonably expect to be available, but not necessarily allocated when a plan transitions to execution. The CJCS orders may amplify the guidance from the apportionment tables for the specific crisis. This guidance can confirm or modify the guidance in an existing contingency plan. This might simplify the analysis step, since consensus should already exist between the supported command and higher authority on the nature of the operational environment in the potential joint operations area (JOA)—such as the political, economic, social, and military circumstances—and potential US or multinational responses to various situations described in the existing plan. But even with a preexisting contingency plan, planners should not assume that the current operational environment is as the plan and higher headquarters describe. The specific nature of the emerging crisis can change many key aspects of the environment compared with earlier estimates. These changes can greatly affect the plan's original operational approach upon which the commander and staff based decisions about COA alternatives and tasks to potential subordinate and supporting commands. In particular, planners must reconfirm strategic and operational objectives and the criteria that comprise the military end state. Differences between the commander's perspective and that of higher headquarters must be resolved at the earliest opportunity.

---

(3) In time-compressed, crisis situations with no preexisting plan, planners may be inclined to trust the higher headquarters' assessment of the operational environment and objectives associated with a desired end state. However, this circumstance is one that can benefit the most from the commander's and staff's independent assessment of circumstances to ensure they agree with higher headquarters on the operational environment, the description of strategic objectives, and the tasks or mission assigned to achieve these objectives.

(4) **Multinational Strategic Guidance.** In multinational settings, military committee directives provide the strategic guidance and direction for joint operation planning. The JFC and staff, as well as component and supporting commanders and their staffs, must clearly understand the strategic and military end states, objectives, and conditions that the national or multinational political leadership want the multinational military force to attain in terms of the internal and external balance of power, regional security, and geopolitics. When multinational strategic objectives are unclear, the senior US military commander must seek clarification and convey the positive or negative impact of continued ambiguity to the President and SecDef.

For additional information on multinational operations, see JP 3-16, Multinational Operations, *and for specific information on NATO operations, see Allied Joint Publication (AJP)-01,* Allied Joint Doctrine; *AJP-3,* Allied Joint Operations; *and AJP-5,* Operational Planning for Joint Operations.

f. **Review Commander's Initial Planning Guidance**

(1) Staffs should analyze the operational approach to gain an appreciation for the commander's understanding and visualization. This provides a basis for continued detailed analysis of the operational environment and of the tasks that may describe the mission and its parameters. The staff should not take the commander's perspective as the final answer, but should analyze his understanding and visualization, so that the intent and planning guidance provided during the latter stages of mission analysis provide a strong basis for development of appropriate COAs.

(2) Staff members and representatives from supporting organizations should maintain an open dialogue with the commander to better develop an appropriate solution to the problem, and be able to adapt solutions to match the evolving operational environment and any potentially changing problems.

g. **Determine Known Facts and Develop Planning Assumptions.** The staff assembles both facts and assumptions to support the planning process and planning guidance.

(1) A fact is a statement of information known to be true (such as verified locations of friendly and adversary force dispositions).

(2) An assumption provides a supposition about the current situation or future course of events, assumed to be true in the absence of facts. Assumptions that address gaps in knowledge are critical for the planning process to continue. For planning purposes, subordinate commanders can treat assumptions made by higher headquarters as true in the

absence of proof to the contrary. However, they should challenge those assumptions if they appear unrealistic. **Assumptions must be continually reviewed to ensure validity.** A valid assumption has three characteristics: logical, realistic, and essential for the planning to continue. Assumptions are made for both friendly and adversary situations.

(3) Commanders and staffs should anticipate changes to the plan that may become necessary should an assumption prove to be incorrect. Because of assumptions' influence on planning, planners must either validate the assumptions (turn them into facts) or invalidate the assumptions (alter the plan accordingly) as quickly as possible. Commanders and staffs should never assume away adversary capabilities or assume that unrealistic friendly capabilities would be available.

(4) Plans developed during deliberate planning may contain assumptions that cannot be resolved until a potential crisis develops. In CAP, however, assumptions should be replaced with facts as soon as possible. The staff accomplishes this by identifying the information needed to convert assumptions to facts and submitting an information request to an appropriate agency as an information requirement. If the commander needs the information to make a key decision, the information requirement can be designated a CCIR. Although there may be exceptions, the staff should strive to resolve all assumptions before issuing the OPORD.

h. **Determine and Analyze Operational Limitations.** Operational limitations are actions required or prohibited by higher authority and other restrictions that limit the commander's freedom of action, such as diplomatic agreements, political and economic conditions in affected countries, and host-nation issues. A **constraint** is a requirement placed on the command by a higher command that **dictates an action,** thus restricting freedom of action. For example, General Eisenhower was required to liberate Paris instead of bypassing it during the 1944 campaign in France. A **restraint** is a requirement placed on the command by a higher command that **prohibits an action,** thus restricting freedom of action. For example, General MacArthur was prohibited from striking Chinese targets north of the Yalu River during the Korean War. Many operational limitations are commonly expressed as ROE. Operational limitations may restrict or bind COA selection or may even impede implementation of the chosen COA. Commanders must examine the operational limitations imposed on them, understand their impacts, and develop options that minimize these impacts to promote maximum freedom of action during execution.

i. **Determine Specified, Implied, and Essential Tasks.** The commander and staff typically will review the planning directive's specified tasks and discuss implied tasks even as early as planning initiation to resolve unclear or incorrectly assigned tasks with higher headquarters. If there is no immediate disconnect, the JFC and staff will confirm the tasks later in mission analysis before developing the initial mission statement.

(1) *Specified tasks* are those that the higher commander assigns to a subordinate commander in a WARNORD, OPORD, or other planning directive. These are tasks the higher commander wants the subordinate command to accomplish during execution of the operation, usually because they are important to the higher command's mission and/or

objectives. One or more specified tasks often become essential tasks for the subordinate commander. Following are examples of specified tasks:

(a) Ensure freedom of navigation for US forces through the Strait of Gibraltar.

(b) Defend Country Green against attack from Country Red.

(2) *Implied tasks* are additional tasks the commander must accomplish, typically in order to accomplish the specified and essential tasks, support another command, or otherwise accomplish activities relevant to the operation. In addition to the higher headquarters' planning directive, the commander and staff will review other sources of guidance for implied tasks, such as multinational planning documents and the GCC's TCP, enemy and friendly COG analysis products, JIPOE products, relevant doctrinal publications, interviews with subject matter experts, and the commander's operational approach. The commander can also deduce implied tasks from knowledge of the operational environment, such as the enemy situation and political conditions in the assigned OA. However, implied tasks do not include routine tasks or SOPs that are inherent in most operations, such as conducting reconnaissance and protecting a flank. The following are examples of implied tasks:

(a) Establish maritime superiority out to 50 miles from the Strait of Gibraltar.

(b) Be prepared to conduct foreign internal defense and security force assistance operations to enhance the capacity and capability of Country Green security forces to provide stability and security if a regime change occurs in Country Red.

(3) *Essential tasks* are those that the joint force must execute successfully to achieve the desired end state. The commander and staff determine essential tasks from the lists of both specified and implied tasks. The mission statement contains only essential tasks. Depending on the scope of the operation and its purpose, the commander may synthesize certain specified and implied task statements into an essential task statement. See the example mission statement below for examples of essential tasks.

j. **Develop Mission Statement.** The mission statement contains the elements of who, what, when, where, and why. **The commander's operational approach informs the mission statement** and helps form the basis for planning. The commander includes the

---

EXAMPLE MISSION STATEMENT

When directed, United States X Command (USXCOM) employs joint forces in concert with coalition partners to deter Country X from coercing its neighbors and proliferating weapons of mass destruction (WMD). If deterrence fails, the coalition will defeat Country X's armed forces; destroy known WMD production, storage, and delivery capabilities; and destroy its ability to project offensive force across its borders. On order, USXCOM will then stabilize the theater, transition control to an international peacekeeping force, and redeploy.

---

mission statement in the planning guidance, planning directive, staff estimates, commander's estimate, CONOPS, and completed plan.

   k. **Conduct Initial Force Analysis**

      (1) **Analysis of Available Forces and Assets**

         (a) Review forces that have been provided for planning and their locations (if known).

         (b) Determine the status of reserve forces and the time they will be available.

         (c) Refer to specified and implied tasks and determine what broad force structure and capabilities are necessary to accomplish these tasks (e.g., is a show of force or a forcible entry capability required?).

         (d) Identify shortfalls between the two.

      (2) **Availability of Forces for Joint Operations.** Staffs should analyze the actual availability of joint forces and other capabilities that may be required. Forces that are apportioned for planning may not actually be available for allocation for execution. Other capabilities may be more appropriate or acceptable as a substitute. Such analyses will provide some of the parameters under which feasible COAs can be built.

   l. **Develop Mission Success Criteria**

      (1) **Mission success criteria** describe the standards for determining mission accomplishment. The JFC includes these criteria in the initial planning guidance so that the joint force staff and components better understand what constitutes mission success. Mission success criteria can apply to any joint operation, phase, and joint force component operation. These criteria help the JFC determine if and when to move to the next major operation or phase. The initial set of criteria determined during mission analysis becomes the basis for **assessment.**

      (2) If the mission is unambiguous and limited in time and scope, mission success criteria could be readily identifiable and linked directly to the mission statement. For example, if the JFC's mission is to *evacuate all US personnel from the US Embassy in Grayland*, then mission analysis could identify two primary success criteria: all US personnel are evacuated and established ROE are not violated.

      (3) However, more complex operations will require MOEs and MOPs for each task, effect, and phase of the operation. For example, if the JFC's specified tasks are to *ensure friendly transit through the Straits of Gray, eject Redland forces from Grayland, and restore stability along the Grayland–Redland border*, then mission analysis should indicate many potential success criteria—measured by MOEs and MOPs—some for each desired effect and task.

(4) Measuring the status of tasks, effects, and objectives becomes the basis for reports to senior commanders and civilian leaders on the progress of the operation. The CCDR can then advise the President and SecDef accordingly and adjust operations as required. Whether in a supported or supporting role, JFCs at all levels must develop their mission success criteria with a clear understanding of termination criteria established by the CJCS and SecDef.

m. **Develop Risk Assessment**

(1) Planners conducting a preliminary risk assessment must identify the obstacles or actions that may preclude mission accomplishment and then assess the impact of these hazards to the mission. Once planners identify the obstacles or actions, they assess the probability and severity of loss linked to an obstacle or action, the risk and its potential impact on the joint force, and the success of the joint force mission.

(2) Probability may be ranked as frequent: occurs often, continuously experienced; likely: occurs several times; occasional: occurs sporadically; seldom: unlikely, but could occur at some time; or unlikely: can assume it will not occur. Severity may be catastrophic: mission is made impossible; critical: severe mission impact; marginal: mission possible using alternate options; or negligible: minor disruptions to mission.

(3) Determining the risk is more an art than a science. Planners use historical data, intuitive analysis, and judgment to estimate the risk of each threat. Probability and severity levels are estimated based on the user's knowledge of probability of occurrence and the severity of consequences once the occurrence happens. The level of risk is assigned by assessing the hazards'/obstacles' probability of occurring and their degree of severity. The levels of risk are:

(a) Extremely high: loss of ability to accomplish mission;

(b) High: significantly degrades mission capabilities in terms of required mission standards;

(c) Moderate: degrades mission capabilities in terms of required mission standards; and

(d) Low: little or no impact on accomplishment of the mission.

n. **Determine Commander's Critical Information Requirements**

(1) **CCIRs are elements of information that the commander identifies as being critical to timely decision making.** CCIRs help focus information management and help the commander assess the operational environment and identify decision points during operations. **CCIRs belong exclusively to the commander. They are situation-dependent, focused on predictable events or activities, time-sensitive, and always established by an order or plan.** The CCIR list is normally short so that the staff can focus its efforts and allocate scarce resources. The CCIR list is not static; JFCs add, delete, adjust, and update CCIRs throughout an operation based on the information they need for decision making.

(2) **Categories.** PIRs and FFIRs constitute the total list of CCIRs (see Figure IV-5).

(a) **PIRs** focus on the adversary and the operational environment and drive ISR requirements. All staff sections can recommend potential PIRs they believe meet the commander's guidance. However, the joint force J-2 has overall staff responsibility for consolidating PIR nominations and for providing the staff recommendation to the commander. **JFC-approved PIRs are automatically CCIRs.**

For more information on PIRs, see JP 2-0, Joint Intelligence.

(b) FFIRs focus on information the JFC must have to assess the status of the friendly force and supporting capabilities. All staff sections can recommend potential FFIRs that they believe meet the commander's guidance. However, the joint force J-5 has overall staff responsibility for consolidating FFIR nominations and for providing the staff recommendation to the commander during planning prior to execution. During execution, the joint force J-3 is responsible for consolidating these nominations and providing the recommendation for FFIRs that relate to current operations. However, the J-5 remains responsible for consolidating nominations and recommending FFIRs related to the future plans effort (e.g., planned sequels to the current operation). Commander-approved FFIRs are automatically CCIRs.

(3) **General CCIR criteria that planners must consider when proposing them to the commander for approval include the following:** answering a CCIR must be a decision required of the commander, and not of the staff, and answering a CCIR must be critical to the success of the mission.

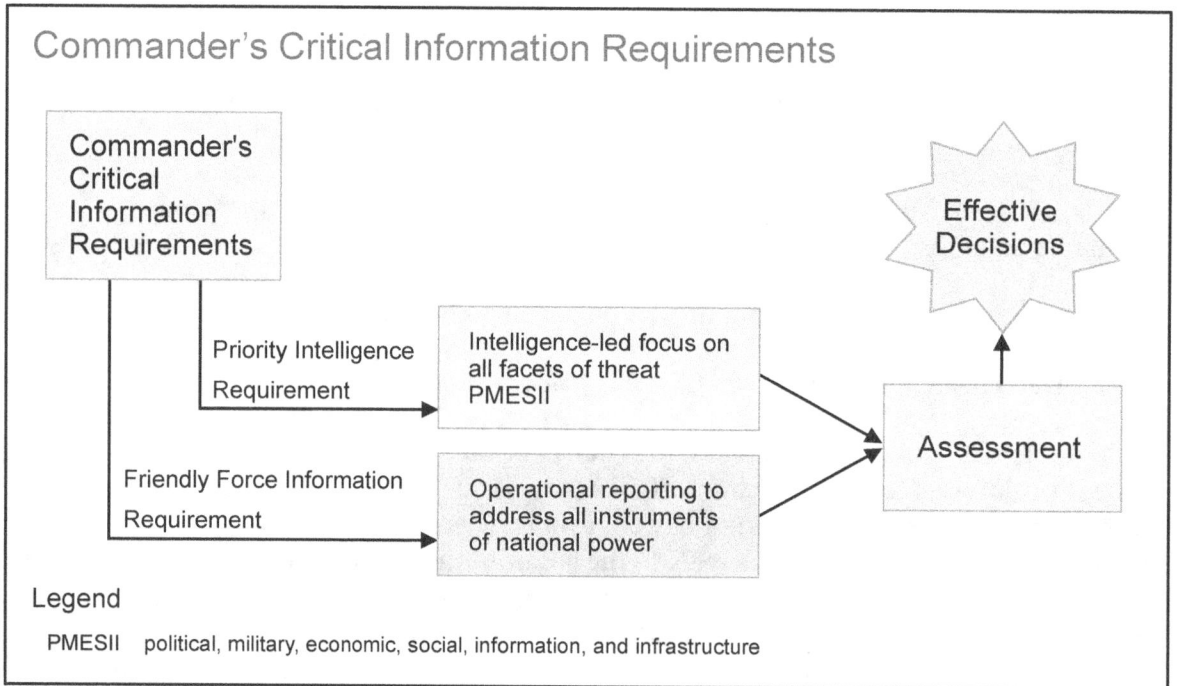

Figure IV-5. Commander's Critical Information Requirements

(4) **Decision Support.** CCIRs support the commander's future decision requirements and are often related to MOEs and MOPs. PIRs are often expressed in terms of the elements of PMESII while FFIRs are often expressed in terms of the diplomatic, informational, military, and economic instruments of national power. All are developed to support specific decisions the commander must make.

o. **Prepare Staff Estimates**

(1) A staff estimate is an evaluation of how factors in a staff section's functional area support and impact the mission. The purpose of the staff estimate is to inform the commander, staff, and subordinate commands how the functional area supports mission accomplishment and to support COA development and selection.

(2) Staff estimates are initiated during mission analysis, at which point functional planners are focused on collecting information from their functional areas to help the commander and staff understand the situation and conduct mission analysis. Later, during COA development and selection, functional planners fully develop their estimates providing functional analysis of the COAs as well as recommendations on which COAs are supportable. They should also identify critical shortfalls or obstacles that impact mission accomplishment. Staff estimates are continually updated based on changes in the situation.

(3) Not every situation will require or permit a lengthy and formal staff estimate process. During CAP, staff estimates may be given orally to support the rapid development of plans. However, deliberate planning will demand a more formal and thorough process. Staff estimates should be shared with subordinate and supporting commanders to help them prepare their supporting estimates, plans, and orders. This will improve parallel planning and collaboration efforts of subordinate and supporting elements and help reduce the planning times for the entire process.

(4) **Intelligence Support to Joint Operation Planning.** Intelligence support to joint operation planning includes intelligence product delivery/dissemination of the intelligence estimate, which feeds the commander's estimate and continuously updates the DTA. Production of the intelligence task list and intelligence synchronization matrix addresses how the intelligence community plans to satisfy the commander's intelligence requirements. These are baseline information and finished intelligence products that inform the situational awareness activity of APEX and continuously drive changes to the DTA and the JFC's JIPOE-based intelligence estimate.

(5) **Planning Intelligence Operations.** The J-2 staff estimate addresses the ability to produce annex B and the intelligence support plan developed during the strategic guidance and concept development steps within APEX. Intelligence planners plan the entirety of the integrated intelligence operation (collect, exploit, analyze, produce, and disseminate intelligence) for the JFC and his planning staff to ultimately deliver the right product at the right time. To facilitate planning, intelligence planners must continuously assess or estimate and deliver these products. The intelligence task list and the JFC's J-2 staff estimate are foundations for the intelligence planning effort and the basis for federated analysis and production.

(6) **Logistics Staff Estimate.** The staff of the JFC's logistics directorate of a joint staff and Service component logisticians should develop a logistics overview, which includes but is not restricted to critical logistics assumptions and information requirements that must be incorporated into the CCIRs; current or anticipated HNS and status; identification of aerial and sea port of debarkation plus any other distribution infrastructure and associated capacity; inventory (on-hand, prepositioned, theater reserve, etc.); combat support and combat service support capabilities; known or potential capability shortfalls. From this theater logistics overview, a logistics estimate can be produced that identifies and addresses known and anticipated factors that may influence the feasibility of providing required logistics support.

For more information on estimates, see Appendix C, "Staff Estimates."

The CJCSM 3122.01 series volumes contain sample formats for staff estimates.

p. **Prepare and Deliver Mission Analysis Brief**

(1) Upon conclusion of the mission analysis and JIPOE, the staff will present a mission analysis brief to the JFC. The purpose of this brief is to provide the commander with the results of the staff's analysis of the mission, offer a forum to surface issues that have been identified, and provide an opportunity for the commander to synthesize the staff's mission analysis with his initial visualization of the campaign as described in the operational approach for the campaign or operation. The commander approves or disapproves the staff's analysis and provides refined planning guidance as well as his intent to guide subsequent planning. Figure IV-6 shows an example mission analysis briefing.

(2) The mission analysis briefing may be the only time the entire staff is present and the only opportunity to ensure that all staff members are starting from a common reference point. The briefing focuses on relevant conclusions reached as a result of the mission analysis.

(3) Immediately after the mission analysis briefing, the commander approves a restated mission. This can be the staff's recommended mission statement, a modified version of the staff's recommendation, or one that the commander has developed personally. **Once approved, the restated mission becomes the unit mission.**

(4) At the mission analysis brief, the commander will likely describe his updated understanding of the operational environment, the problem, and his vision of the operational approach to the entire assemblage, which should include representatives from subordinate commands and other partner organizations. This provides the ideal venue for facilitating unity of understanding and vision, which is essential to unity of effort.

q. **Publish Commander's Refined Planning Guidance**

(1) After approving the mission statement and issuing the intent, the commander provides the staff (and subordinates in a collaborative environment) with enough additional guidance (including preliminary decisions) to focus the staff and subordinate planning

---

Example Mission Analysis Briefing

- Introduction
- Situation overview
  - Operational environment (including joint operations area) and threat overview
  - Political, military, economic, social, information, and infrastructure strengths and weaknesses
  - Red threat (including center of gravity)

- Friendly assessment
  - Facts and assumptions
  - Limitations—constraints/restraints
  - Capabilities allocated
  - Legal considerations

- Communications strategy
- Objectives, effects, and task analysis
  - United States Government interagency objectives
  - Higher commander's objectives/mission/guidance
  - Objectives and effects
  - Specified/implied/essential tasks
  - Centers of gravity

- Operational protection
  - Operational risk
  - Mitigation

- Proposed initial commander's critical information requirements
- Mission
  - Proposed mission statement
  - Proposed commander's intent

- Command relationships
- Conclusion—potential resource shortfalls
- Mission analysis approval and commander's course of action planning guidance

Figure IV-6. Example Mission Analysis Briefing

activities during COA development. At a minimum, this refined planning guidance should include the following elements:

(a) An approved mission statement.

(b) Key elements of the operational environment.

(c) A clear statement of the problem to be solved.

(d) Key assumptions.

(e) Key operational limitations.

(f) A discussion of the national strategic end state.

(g) Termination criteria.

(h) Military end state and its relation to the national strategic end state.

(i) Military objectives.

(j) The JFC's initial thoughts on the conditions necessary to achieve objectives.

(k) Acceptable or unacceptable levels of risk in key areas.

(l) The JFCs visualization of the operational approach to achieve the objectives in broad terms. This operational approach sets the basis for development of COAs. The commander should provide as much detail as appropriate to provide the right level of freedom to the staff in developing COAs. Planning guidance should also address the role of interorganizational partners in the pending operation and any related special considerations as required.

(2) Commanders describe their visualization of the forthcoming campaign or operations to help build a shared understanding among the staff. Enough guidance (preliminary decisions) must be provided to allow the subordinates to plan the action necessary to accomplish the mission consistent with commander's intent. The commander's guidance must focus on the *essential tasks* and associated objectives that support the accomplishment of the assigned national objectives. It emphasizes in broad terms when, where, and how the commander intends to employ *military capabilities integrated with other instruments of national power* to accomplish the mission within the higher JFC's intent.

(3) The JFC may provide the planning guidance to the entire staff and/or subordinate JFCs or meet each staff officer or subordinate unit individually as the situation and information dictates. The guidance can be given in a written form or orally. No format for the planning guidance is prescribed. However, the guidance should be sufficiently detailed to provide a clear direction and to avoid unnecessary efforts by the staff or subordinate and supporting commands.

(4) Planning guidance can be very explicit and detailed, or it can be very broad, allowing the staff and/or subordinate commands wide latitude in developing subsequent COAs. However, no matter its scope, the content of planning guidance must be arranged in a logical sequence to reduce the chances of misunderstanding and to enhance clarity. Moreover, one must recognize that all the elements of planning guidance are *tentative only*. The JFC may issue successive planning guidance during the decision-making process; yet the focus of the JFC's staff should remain upon the framework provided in the initial planning guidance. The JFC should continue to provide refined planning guidance during the rest of the plan development process as his understanding of the problem continues to develop.

5. Course of Action Development

a. Introduction

(1) **A COA is a potential way (solution, method) to accomplish the assigned mission.** The staff develops COAs to provide unique choices to the commander, all oriented on accomplishing the military end state. A good COA accomplishes the mission within the commander's guidance, provides flexibility to meet unforeseen events during execution, and positions the joint force for future operations. It also gives components the maximum latitude for initiative.

(2) Figure IV-7 shows the key inputs and outputs of COA development. The products of *mission analysis* drive COA development. Since the *operational approach* contains the JFC's broad approach to solve the problem at hand, each COA will expand this concept with the additional details that describe **who** will take the action, **what type** of military action will occur, **when** the action will begin, **where** the action will occur, **why** the action is required (purpose), and **how** the action will occur (method of employment of forces). Likewise, **the *essential tasks* identified during mission analysis (and embedded in the draft mission statement) must be common to all potential COAs.**

(3) Planners can vary COAs by adjusting the use of joint force capabilities throughout the OA by physical domain, through the information environment, and through cyberspace and by varying the combinations of these elements.

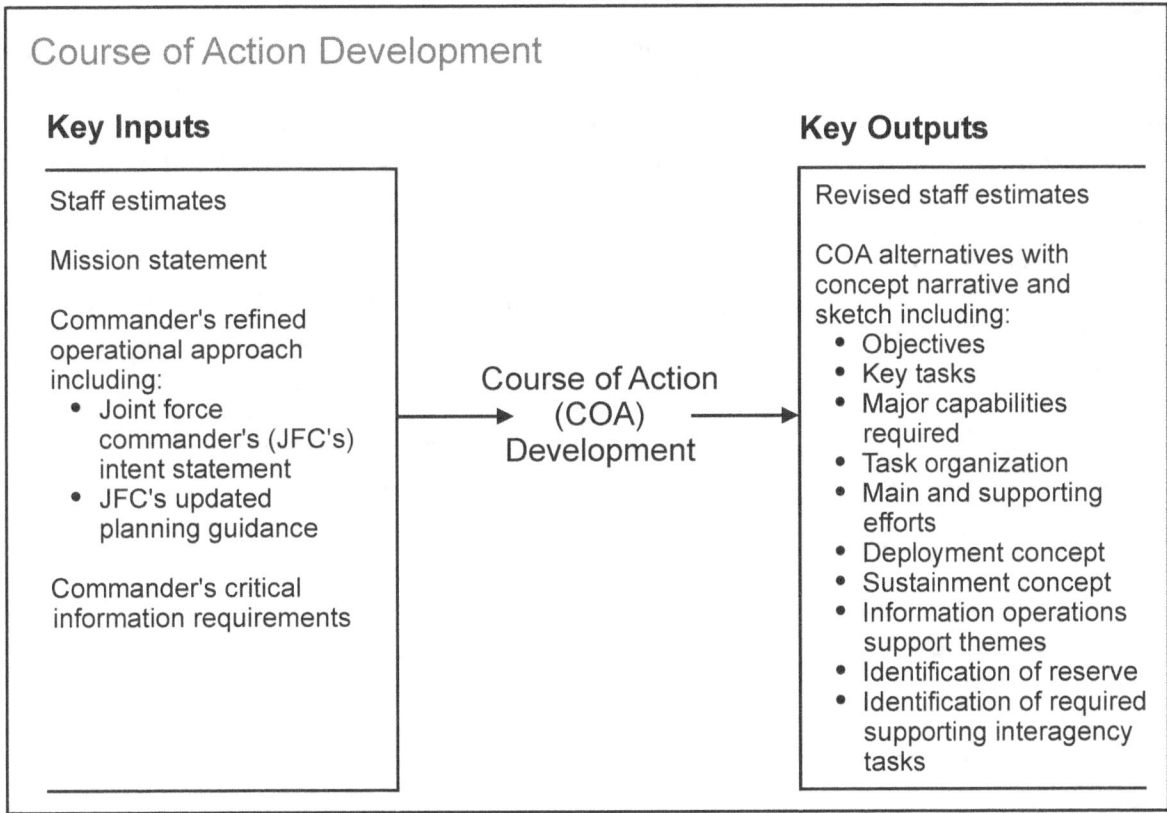

Figure IV-7. Course of Action Development

b. COA Development Considerations

(1) The products of COA development are **tentative COAs,** with a sketch for each if possible. Each COA describes, in broad but clear terms, what is to be done throughout the campaign or operation, the size of forces deemed necessary, and time in which joint force capabilities need to be brought to bear. These COAs will undergo additional validity testing, analysis and wargaming, and comparison, and they could be eliminated at any point during this process. These COAs provide conceptualization and broad descriptions of potential concepts of operation for the conduct of operations that will accomplish the desired end state.

(2) Available planning time is always a key consideration, particularly during CAP. The JFC gives the staff additional considerations early in COA development to focus the staff's efforts, helping the staff concentrate on developing COAs that are the most appropriate. There should always be more than one way to accomplish the mission, which suggests that commanders and planners should give due consideration to the pros and cons of valid COA alternatives. However, developing several COAs could violate time constraints. Usually, the staff develops two or three COAs to focus their efforts and concentrate valuable resources on the most likely scenarios. However, COAs must be substantially distinguishable from each other. Commanders should not unnecessarily overburden staffs by developing similar solutions to the problem. The commander's involvement in the early operational design process can help ensure that only value-added options are considered. If time and personnel resources permit, different COAs could be developed by different teams to ensure they are unique.

(3) For each COA, the commander must envision the employment of all participants in the operation as a whole—US military forces, MNFs, and interagency partners—taking into account operational limitations, political considerations, the OA, existing FDOs, and the conclusions previously drawn during the mission analysis and the commander's guidance.

(4) During COA development, the commander and staff consider all feasible adversary COAs. Other actors may also create difficult conditions that must be considered during COA development. It is best to consider all opposing actors' actions likely to challenge the achievement of the desired end states when exploring adversary COAs.

(5) Each COA typically will constitute an operational concept and provide a narrative and sketch that include the following:

    (a) Objectives.

    (b) Key tasks.

    (c) Major capabilities required.

    (d) Task organization.

    (e) Main and supporting efforts.

(f) Sustainment concept.

(g) Deployment concept.

(h) SC supporting themes.

(i) Identification of reserve.

(j) Identification of required supporting interagency tasks.

(6) **Options.** An option is an activity within a COA that may be executed to enable achieving an objective. Options, and groups of options comprising branches, allow the commander to act rapidly and transition as conditions change through the campaign or operation. Options, and more broadly branches, should enable the commander to progress sequentially or skip ahead based on success or other changes to the conditions or strategic direction from dialogue with higher commanders, SecDef, and/or the President. They should also enable the commander to transition rapidly, exploit success, and control escalation and tempo while denying the same to the enemy. The development of options within COAs empowers the commander and translates up and down the chain of command and enables strategic flexibility for SecDef and the President.

(7) A *tentative COA* should be simple and brief, yet complete. Individual COAs should have descriptive titles. Distinguishing factors of the COA may suggest titles that are descriptive in nature.

c. **COA Development Techniques and Procedures**

(1) **Review information** contained in the mission analysis and commander's operational approach, planning guidance, and intent statement. All staff members must understand the mission and the tasks that must be accomplished within the commander's intent to achieve mission success.

(2) **Determine the COA Development Technique**

(a) A critical first decision in COA development is whether to conduct simultaneous or sequential development of the COAs. Each approach has distinct advantages and disadvantages. The advantage of simultaneous development of COAs is potential time savings. Separate groups are simultaneously working on different COAs. The disadvantage of this approach is that the synergy of the JPG may be disrupted by breaking up the team. The approach is manpower intensive and requires component and directorate representation in each COA group, and there is an increased likelihood that the COAs will not be distinctive. While there is potential time to be saved, experience has demonstrated that it is not an automatic result. The simultaneous COA development approach can work, but its inherent disadvantages must be addressed and some risk accepted up front. The recommended approach if time and resources allows is the sequential method.

(b) There are several *planning sequence techniques* available to facilitate COA development. One option is the step-by-step approach (see Figure IV-8), which uses the *backward-planning* technique (also known as *reverse planning*).

(3) **Review operational objectives and tasks and develop ways to accomplish tasks.** Planners must review and refine theater and supporting operational objectives from the initial work done during the development of the operational approach. These objectives establish the conditions necessary to reach the desired end state and achieve the national strategic objectives. Tasks are shaped by the CONOPS—intended sequencing and integration of air, land, sea, special operations, and space forces. Tasks are prioritized in order of criticality while considering the enemy's objectives and the need to gain advantage.

Step-by-Step Approach to Course of Action Development

Step Action

1   Determine how much force will be needed in the theater at the end of the campaign, what those forces will be doing, and how those forces will be postured geographically. Use troop-to-task analysis. Draw a sketch to help visualize the forces and their locations.

2   Looking at the sketch and working backwards, determine the best way to get the forces postured in Step 1 from their ultimate positions at the end of the campaign to a base in friendly territory. This will help formulate the desired basing plan.

3   Using the mission statement as a guide, determine the tasks the force must accomplish en route to their locations/positions at the end of the campaign. Draw a sketch of the maneuver plan. Make sure the force does everything the Secretary of Defense (SecDef) has directed the commander to do (refer to specified tasks from the mission analysis).

4   Determine the basing required to posture the force in friendly territory, and the tasks the force must accomplish to get to those bases. Sketch this as part of the deployment plan.

5   Determine if the planned force is enough to accomplish all the tasks SecDef has given the commander. Adjust the force strength to fit the tasks. This should provide the answer to the first question.

6   Given the tasks to be performed, determine in what order the forces should be deployed into theater. Consider the force categories such as combat, protection, sustainment, theater enablers, and theater opening. This should answer the second question.

7   The information developed should now answer the remaining questions regarding force employment, major tasks and their sequencing, sustainment, and command relationships.

Figure IV-8. Step-By-Step Approach to Course of Action Development

---

(a) Regardless of the eventual COA, the staff should plan to accomplish the higher commander's intent by understanding its essential task(s) and purpose and the intended contribution to the higher commander's mission success.

(b) The staff must ensure that all the COAs developed will fulfill the command mission and the purpose of the operation by conducting a review of all essential tasks developed during mission analysis. They should then consider ways to accomplish the other tasks.

(4) Once the staff has begun to visualize a *tentative* COA, it should see how it can best synchronize (arrange in terms of time, space, and purpose) the actions of all the elements of the force. The staff should estimate the anticipated duration of the operation. One method of synchronizing actions is the use of phasing as discussed earlier. Phasing assists the commander and staff to visualize and think through the entire operation or campaign and to define requirements in terms of forces, resources, time, space, and purpose. Planners should then **integrate and synchronize** these requirements by using the joint functions of C2, intelligence, fires, movement and maneuver, protection, and sustainment. At a minimum, planners should ensure the synchronized actions answer the following questions:

(a) How do land forces, maritime forces, air forces, and special operations forces (SOF) integrate across the joint functions to accomplish their assigned tasks?

(b) What are the major ways that space operations can support operations across the joint functions?

(c) How can the joint forces integrate IO and cyberspace operations to support joint operations?

(5) The *tentative* COAs should focus on **COGs** and **decisive points.** The commander and the staff review and refine their COG analysis begun during mission analysis based on updated intelligence, JIPOE products, and initial staff estimates. The refined enemy and friendly COG analysis, particularly the critical vulnerabilities, is considered in the development of the initial COAs. The COG analysis helps the commander become oriented to the enemy and compare his strengths and weakness with those of the enemy. By looking at friendly COGs and vulnerabilities, the staff understands the capabilities of their own force and critical vulnerabilities that will require protection. Protection resource limitations will probably mean that the staff cannot plan to protect every capability, but rather will look at prioritizing protection for critical capabilities and developing overlapping protection techniques. The strength of one asset or capability may provide protection from the weakness of another.

(6) **Identify the sequencing** (simultaneous, sequential, or a combination) of the actions for each COA. Consider the use of defeat and stability mechanisms as appropriate to create the desired effects (and preclude undesired effects).

(7) **Identify main and supporting efforts,** by phase, the purposes of these efforts, and key supporting/supported relationships within phases.

(8) **Identify component-level missions/tasks** (who, what, and where) that will accomplish the stated purposes of main and supporting efforts. Think of component and joint function tasks such as movement and maneuver, intelligence, fires, protection, sustainment, and C2. Display them with graphic control measures as much as possible. A designated LOO will help identify these tasks.

(9) **Develop the IO support items.** Since the results of deception operations may influence the positioning of units, planners should conceive major elements of the story before developing any COAs.

(10) **Task Organization**

(a) The staff should develop **an outline** task organization to execute the COA. The commander and staff determine appropriate command relationships and appropriate missions and tasks.

(b) **Determine command relationships and organizational options.** Joint force organization and command relationships are based on the operation or campaign CONOPS, complexity, and degree of control required. Establishing **command relationships** includes determining the types of subordinate commands and the degree of authority to be delegated to each. Clear definition of command relationships further clarifies the intent of the commander and contributes to decentralized execution and unity of effort. The commander has the authority to determine the types of subordinate commands from several doctrinal options, including Service components, functional components, and subordinate joint commands. **Regardless of the command relationships selected, it is the JFC's responsibility to ensure that these relationships are understood and clear to all subordinate, adjacent, and supporting headquarters.** The following are considerations for establishing joint force organizations:

1. Joint forces will normally be organized with a combination of Service and functional components with operational responsibilities.

2. Functional component staffs should be joint with Service representation in approximate proportion to the mix of subordinate forces. These staffs should be organized and trained prior to employment in order to be efficient and effective, which will require advanced planning.

3. Commanders may establish support relationships between components to facilitate operations.

4. Commanders define the authority and responsibilities of functional component commanders based on the strategic CONOPS and may alter their authority and responsibility during the course of an operation.

5. Commanders must balance the need for centralized direction with decentralized execution.

        <u>6.</u> Major changes in the joint force organization are normally conducted at phase changes.

        (11) **Sustainment Concept. No COA is complete without a plan to sustain it properly.** The sustainment and personnel services concept is more than just gathering information on various logistic functions. It entails identifying the requirements for classes of supply, creating distribution, transportation, and disposition plans to support the commander's execution, and organizing capabilities and resources into an overall theater campaign or operation sustainment concept. It concentrates forces and material resources strategically so the right force is available at the designated times and places to conduct decisive operations. It requires thinking through a cohesive sustainment for joint, single Service, and supporting forces relationships in conjunction with CSAs, multinational, interagency, nongovernmental, or international organizations.

        (12) **Deployment Concept.** A COA must consider the deployment concept in order to describe the general flow of forces into theater. There is no way to determine the feasibility of the COA without including the deployment concept. While the detailed deployment concept will be developed during plan synchronization, enough of the concept must be described in the COA to visualize force buildup, sustainment requirements, and military–political considerations.

        (13) **Define the Operational Area**

        (a) The OA is normally established by a legally/politically binding document. It will provide flexibility/options and/or limitations to the commander. The OA must be precisely defined because the specific geographic area will impact planning factors such as basing, overflight, and sustainment.

        (b) OAs include, but are not limited to, such descriptors as AOR, theater of war, theater of operations, JOA, amphibious objective area, joint special operations area, and area of operations. Except for AOR, which is assigned in the UCP, GCCs and their subordinate JFCs designate smaller OAs on a temporary basis. OAs have physical dimensions composed of some combination of air, land, and maritime domains. JFCs define these areas with geographical boundaries, which facilitate the coordination, integration, and deconfliction of joint operations among joint force components and supporting commands. The size of these OAs and the types of forces employed within them depend on the scope and nature of the crisis and the projected duration of operations.

See JP 3-0, Joint Operations, *for additional information on OAs.*

        (14) **Develop initial COA sketches and statements.** Each tentative COA should answer the following questions:

        (a) Who (type of forces) will execute the tasks?

        (b) What are the tasks?

(c) Where will the tasks occur? (Start adding graphic control measures, e.g., areas of operation, amphibious objective areas).

(d) When will the tasks begin?

(e) How (but do not usurp the components' prerogatives) the commander should provide "operational direction" so the components can accomplish "tactical actions."

(f) Why (for what purpose) will each force conduct its part of the operation?

(g) Develop an initial ISR support concept.

(15) **Test the validity of each *tentative* COA.** All COAs selected for analysis must be valid, and the **staff should reject *tentative* COAs that do not meet all five of the following validity criteria:**

(a) **Adequate**—Can accomplish the mission within the commander's guidance. Preliminary tests include:

<u>1.</u> Does it accomplish the mission?

<u>2.</u> Does it meet the commander's intent?

<u>3.</u> Does it accomplish all the essential tasks?

<u>4.</u> Does it meet the conditions for the end state?

<u>5.</u> Does it take into consideration the enemy and friendly COGs?

(b) **Feasible**—Can accomplish the mission within the established time, space, and resource limitations.

<u>1.</u> Does the commander have the force structure and lift assets (means) to execute it? The COA is feasible if it can be executed with the forces, support, and technology available within the constraints of the physical environment and against expected enemy opposition.

<u>2.</u> Although this process occurs during COA analysis and the test at this time is preliminary, it may be possible to declare a COA infeasible (for example, resources are obviously insufficient). However, it may be possible to fill shortfalls by requesting support from the commander or other means.

(c) **Acceptable**—Must balance cost and risk with the advantage gained.

<u>1.</u> Does it contain unacceptable risks? (Is it worth the possible cost?) A COA is considered acceptable if the estimated results justify the risks. The basis of this test consists of an estimation of friendly losses in forces, time, position, and opportunity.

2. Does it take into account the limitations placed on the commander (must do, cannot do, other physical limitations)?

3. Acceptability is considered from the perspective of the commander by reviewing the strategic objectives.

4. Are COAs reconciled with external constraints, particularly ROE? This requires visualization of execution of the COA against each enemy capability. Although this process occurs during COA analysis and the test at this time is preliminary, it may be possible to declare a COA unacceptable if it violates the commander's definition of acceptable risk.

(d) **Distinguishable**—Must be sufficiently different from other COAs in the following:

1. The focus or direction of main effort.

2. The scheme of maneuver (land, air, maritime, and special operation).

3. Sequential versus simultaneous maneuvers.

4. The primary mechanism for mission accomplishment.

5. Task organization.

6. The use of reserves.

(e) **Complete**—Does it answer the questions who, what, where, when, how, and why? Must incorporate:

1. Objectives (including desired effects) and tasks to be performed.

2. Major forces required.

3. Concepts for deployment, employment, and sustainment.

4. Time estimates for achieving objectives.

5. Military end state and mission success criteria.

(16) **Conduct COA development brief to commander.** Figure IV-9 provides suggested sequence and content.

(17) **JFC provides guidance on COAs.**

(a) Review and approve COA(s) for further analysis.

(b) Direct revisions to COA(s), combinations of COAs, or development of additional COA(s).

Example Course of Action Development Briefing

- Operations Directorate of a Joint Staff (J-3)/Plans Directorate of a Joint Staff (J-5)

  - Context/background (i.e., road to war)
  - Initiation—review guidance for initiation
  - Strategic guidance—planning tasks assigned to supported commander, forces/resources apportioned, planning guidance, updates, defense agreements, theater campaign plan(s), Guidance for Employment of the Force/Joint Strategic Capabilities Plan
  - Forces apportioned/assigned

- Intelligence Directorate of a Joint Staff (J-2)

  - Joint Intelligence Preparation of the Operational Environment
  - Enemy courses of action (COAs)—most dangerous, most likely; strengths and weaknesses

- J-3/J-5

  - Update facts and assumptions
  - Mission statement
  - Commander's intent (purpose, method, end state)
  - End state: political/military
    - termination criteria
  - Center of gravity analysis results: critical factors; strategic/operational
  - Joint operations area/theater of operations/communications zone sketch
  - Phase 0 shaping activities recommended (for current theater campaign plan)
  - Flexible deterrent options with desired effect
  - For each COA, sketch and statement by phase
    - task organization
    - component tasking
    - timeline
    - recommended command and control by phase
    - lines of operation/lines of effort
    - logistics estimates and feasibility
    - COA risks
  - COA summarized distinctions
  - COA priority for analysis

- Commander's Guidance

Figure IV-9. Example Course of Action Development Briefing

(c) Direct priority for which enemy COA(s) will be used during wargaming of friendly COA(s).

(18) **Continue the staff estimate process.** The staff must continue to conduct their staff estimates of supportability for each COA.

(19) **Conduct vertical and horizontal parallel planning**

(a) Discuss the planning status of staff counterparts with both commander's and JFC components' staffs.

(b) Coordinate planning with staff counterparts from other functional areas.

(c) Permit adjustments in planning as additional details are learned from higher and adjacent echelons, and permit lower echelons to begin planning efforts and generate questions (e.g., requests for information).

d. **The Planning Directive**

(1) The ***planning directive*** identifies planning responsibilities for developing joint force plans. It provides guidance and requirements to the staff and subordinate commands concerning coordinated planning actions for plan development. The JFC normally communicates initial planning guidance to the staff, subordinate commanders, and supporting commanders by publishing a planning directive to ensure that everyone understands the commander's intent and to achieve unity of effort.

(2) Generally, the J-5 coordinates staff action for deliberate planning, and the J-3 coordinates staff action for CAP. The J-5 staff receives the JFC's initial guidance and combines it with the information gained from the initial staff assessments. The JFC, through the J-5, may convene a preliminary planning conference for members of the JPEC who will be involved with the plan. This is the opportunity for representatives to meet face-to-face. At the conference, the JFC and selected members of the staff brief the attendees on important aspects of the plan and may solicit their initial reactions. Many potential conflicts can be avoided by this early exchange of information.

6. **Course of Action Analysis**

a. **Introduction**

(1) COA analysis is the process of closely examining potential COAs to reveal details that will allow the commander and staff to tentatively identify COAs that are valid, and then compare these COAs. COA analysis identifies advantages and disadvantages of each proposed friendly COA. The commander and staff analyze each tentative COA separately according to the commander's guidance. While time-consuming, COA analysis should answer two primary questions: ***Is the COA feasible, and is it acceptable?***

(2) ***Wargaming*** is a primary means to conduct this analysis. Wargaming is a conscious attempt to visualize the flow of the operation, given joint force strengths and dispositions, adversary capabilities and possible COAs, the OA, and other aspects of the operational environment. Each critical event within a proposed COA should be wargamed based upon time available using the action, reaction, and counteraction method of friendly and/or opposing force interaction. The basic wargaming method (modified to fit the specific mission and operational environment) can apply to noncombat as well as combat operations.

(3) COA wargaming allows the commander, staff, and subordinate commanders and their staffs to gain a common understanding of friendly and enemy COAs. This common understanding allows them to determine the advantages and disadvantages of each COA and forms the basis for the commander's comparison and approval. COA wargaming involves a detailed assessment of each COA as it pertains to the enemy and the operational

environment. Each friendly COA is wargamed against selected enemy COAs. The commander will select the COAs he wants wargamed and provide wargaming guidance along with *evaluation criteria.*

(4) Wargaming stimulates thought about the operation so the staff can obtain ideas and insights that otherwise might not have occurred. This process highlights tasks that appear to be particularly important to the operation and provides a degree of familiarity with operational-level possibilities that might otherwise be difficult to achieve. An objective, comprehensive analysis of tentative COAs is difficult even without time constraints. Based upon time available, the commander should wargame each tentative COA against the most probable and the most dangerous adversary COAs (or most difficult objectives in noncombat operations) identified through the JIPOE process. Figure IV-10 shows the key inputs and outputs associated with COA analysis.

b. **Analysis and Wargaming Process**

(1) The analysis and wargaming process can be as simple as a detailed narrative effort that describes the action, probable reaction, counteraction, assets, and time used. A more comprehensive version is the "sketch-note" technique, which adds operational sketches and notes to the narrative process in order to gain a clearer picture. The most sophisticated form of wargaming is computer-aided modeling and simulation.

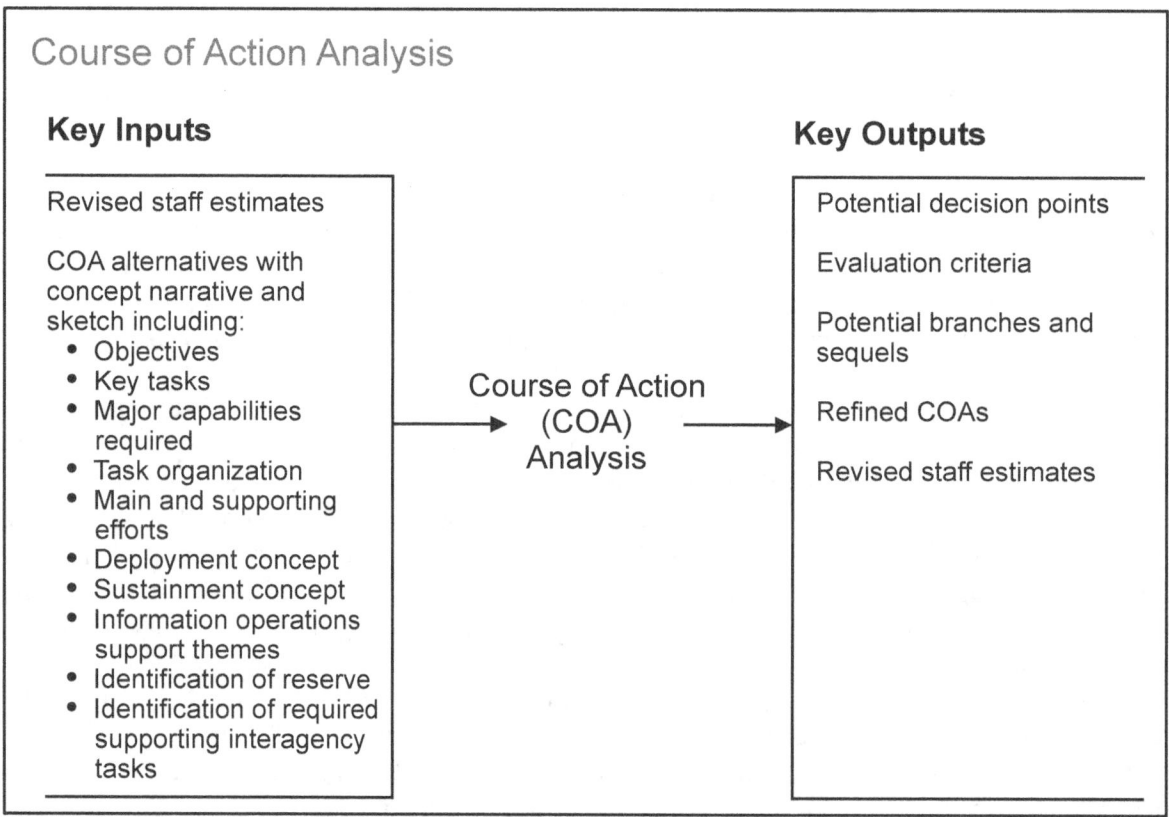

Figure IV-10. Course of Action Analysis

(2) The heart of the commander's estimate process is analysis of multiple COAs. During COA development, the staff considers opposing COAs based on adversary capabilities, objectives, an estimate of the adversary's intent, and integrated actions by other actors (neutral, other adversaries, and even friendly actions that would not be favorable) that would challenge achievement of the end state. The staff then develop friendly COAs based on the joint force mission and capabilities. In the analysis and wargaming step, the staff analyzes the probable effect *each opposing COA has on the chances of success of each friendly COA.* The aim is to develop a sound basis for determining the *feasibility* and *acceptability* of the COAs. Analysis also provides the planning staff with a greatly improved understanding of their COAs and the relationship between them. COA analysis identifies which COA best accomplishes the mission while best positioning the force for future operations. It also helps the commander and staff to:

(a) Determine how to maximize combat power against the enemy while protecting the friendly forces and minimizing collateral damage.

(b) Have as near an identical visualization of the operation as possible.

(c) Anticipate events in the operational environment and potential reaction options.

(d) Determine conditions and resources required for success while also identifying gaps and seams.

(e) Determine when and where to apply the force's capabilities.

(f) Focus intelligence collection requirements.

(g) Determine the most flexible COA.

(h) Identify potential decision points.

(i) Determine task organization options.

(j) Develop data for use in a synchronization matrix or related tool.

(k) Identify potential plan branches and sequels.

(l) Identify high-value targets.

(m) Assess risk.

(n) Determine COA advantages and disadvantages.

(o) Recommend CCIRs.

(3) Wargaming is a disciplined process, with rules and steps that attempt to visualize the flow of the operation. The process considers friendly dispositions, strengths, and weaknesses; enemy assets and probable COAs; and characteristics of the physical

environment. It relies heavily on joint doctrinal foundation, tactical judgment, and operational experience. It focuses the staff's attention on each phase of the operation in a logical sequence. It is an iterative process of action, reaction, and counteraction. Wargaming stimulates ideas and provides insights that might not otherwise be discovered. It highlights critical tasks and provides familiarity with operational possibilities otherwise difficult to achieve. Wargaming is a critical portion of the planning process and should be allocated more time than any other step. **Each retained COA should, at a minimum, be wargamed against both the most likely and most dangerous enemy COAs.**

(4) During the war game, the staff takes a COA statement and begins to add more detail to the concept, while determining the strengths or weaknesses of each COA. Wargaming tests a COA and can provide insights that can be used to improve upon a developed COA. The commander and staff (and subordinate commanders and staffs if the war game is conducted collaboratively) may change an existing COA or develop a new COA after identifying unforeseen critical events, tasks, requirements, or problems.

(5) For the war game to be effective, the commander should indicate what aspects of the COA should be examined and tested. Wargaming guidance may include a list of friendly COAs to be wargamed against specific threat COAs (e.g., COA 1 against the enemy's most likely, most dangerous), the timeline for the phase or stage of the operations, a list of critical events, and level of detail (i.e., two levels down).

(6) **COA Analysis Considerations.** *Evaluation criteria* and known *critical events* are two of the many important considerations as COA analysis begins.

(a) The commander and staff use evaluation criteria during follow-on COA comparison (JOPP step 5) for the purpose of selecting the best COA. The commander and staff consider various potential evaluation criteria during wargaming, and select those that the staff will use during COA comparison to assess the effectiveness and efficiency of one COA relative to others following the war game. These evaluation criteria help focus the wargaming effort and provide the framework for data collection by the staff. These criteria are those aspects of the situation (or externally imposed factors) that the commander deems *critical* to mission accomplishment. Figure IV-11 shows examples of potential evaluation criteria.

(b) Evaluation criteria change from mission to mission. Though these criteria will be applied in the next step, COA comparison (JOPP step 6), it will be helpful during this wargaming step for all participants to be familiar with the criteria so that any insights into a given COA that influence a criterion are recorded for later comparison. The criteria may include anything the commander desires. If they are not received directly, the staff can derive them from the commander's intent statement. Evaluation criteria do not stand alone. Each must have a clearly defined definition. Defining the criteria in precise terms reduces subjectivity and ensures that the interpretation of each remains constant. The following sources provide a good starting point for developing a list of potential evaluation criteria.

1. Commander's guidance and commander's intent.

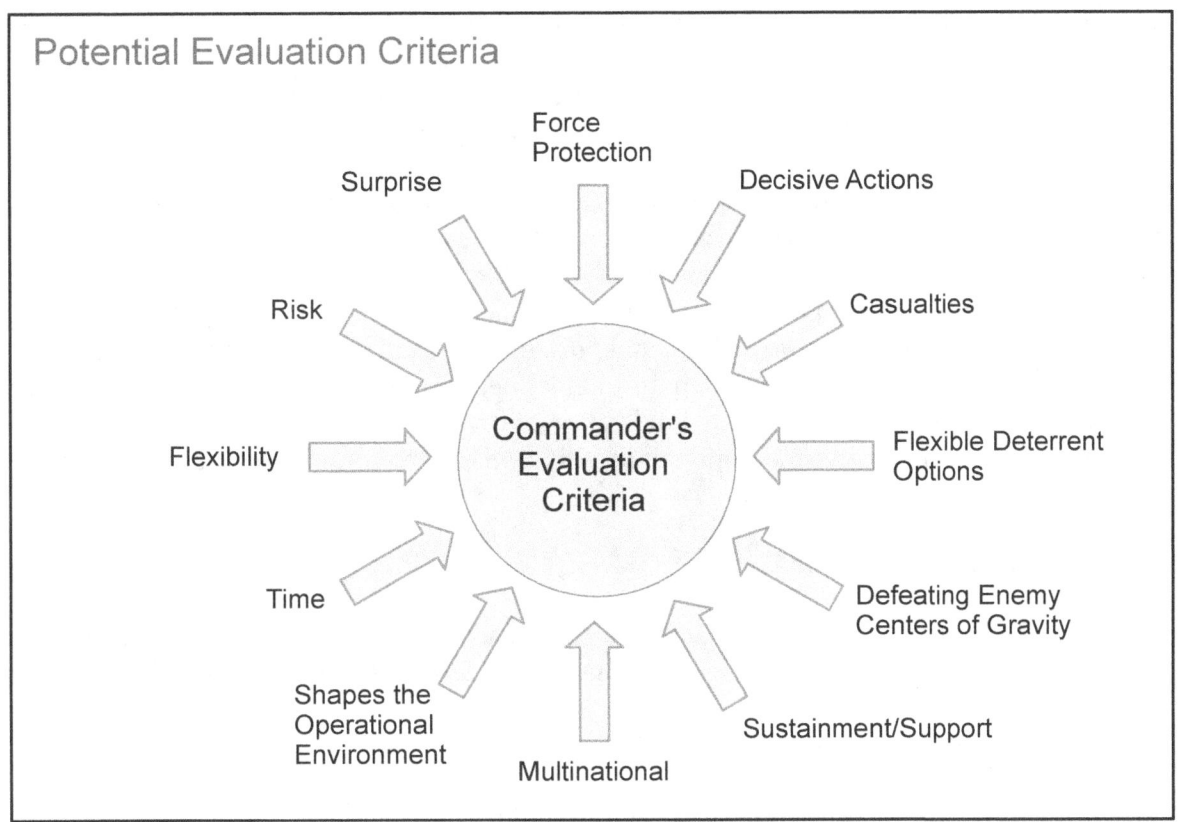

Figure IV-11. Potential Evaluation Criteria

2. Mission accomplishment at an acceptable cost.

3. The principles of joint operations.

4. Doctrinal fundamentals for the type of operation being conducted.

5. The level of residual risk in the COA.

6. Implicit significant factors relating to the operation (e.g., need for speed, security).

7. Factors relating to specific staff functions.

8. Elements of operational design.

9. Other factors to consider: political constraints, risk, financial costs, flexibility, simplicity, surprise, speed, mass, sustainability, C2, infrastructure survivability, etc.

(c) **List Known Critical Events.** These are essential tasks, or a series of critical tasks, conducted over a period of time that require detailed analysis (such as the series of component tasks to be performed on D-day). This may be expanded to review component tasks over a phase(s) of an operation (e.g., lodgment phase) or over a period of time (C-day through D-day). The planning staff may wish at this point to also identify decision points (those decisions in time and space that the commander must make to ensure timely execution and synchronization of resources). These decision points are most likely linked to a critical event (e.g., commitment of the JTF reserve force).

(7) **There are two key decisions to make before COA analysis begins.** The *first* decision is to decide **what type of war game will be used.** This decision should be based on commander's guidance, time and resources available, staff expertise, and availability of simulation models. At this point in the planning process, there may be no phases developed for the COA; *pre-hostilities*, *hostilities*, and *post-hostilities* may be the only considerations at this point. Phasing comes later when the planner begins to flesh out the selected COA into a strategic concept. The *second* decision is to **prioritize the enemy COAs** the war game is to be analyzed against. In time-constrained situations, it may not be possible to wargame against all COAs.

c. **Conducting the War Game**

(1) The primary steps are *prepare for the war game, conduct the war game and assess the results,* and *prepare products.* Figure IV-12 shows sample wargaming steps.

(2) **Prepare for the War Game**

(a) The two forms of war games are *computer-assisted* and *manual.* There are many forms of computer-assisted war games; most require a significant spin-up time to load scenarios and then to train users. However, the potential to utilize the computer model for multiple scenarios or blended scenarios makes it valuable. For both types, consider how to organize the players in a logical manner.

(b) For manual wargaming, three distinct methods are available to run the event:

1. **Deliberate Timeline Analysis.** Consider actions day-by-day or in other discrete blocks of time. This is the most thorough method for detailed analysis when time permits.

2. **Operational Phasing.** Used as a framework for COA analysis. Identify significant actions and requirements by functional area and/or JTF component.

3. **Critical Events/Sequence of Essential Tasks.** The sequence of essential tasks, also known as the critical events method, highlights the initial shaping actions necessary to establish a sustainment capability and to engage enemy units in the deep battle area. At the same time, it enables the planners to adapt if the enemy executes a reaction that necessitates the reordering of the essential tasks. This technique also allows war gamers to analyze concurrently the essential tasks required to execute the CONOPS. Focus on specific critical events that encompass the essence of the COA. If necessary, different MOEs should be developed for assessing different types of critical events (e.g., destruction, blockade, air control, neutralization, ensure defense). As with the focus on

---

Sample Wargaming Steps

1 **Prepare for the War Game**
- Gather tools
- List and review friendly forces and capabilities
- List and review opposing forces and capabilities
- List known critical events
- Determine participants
- Determine opposing course of action (COA) to war game
- Select wargaming method
  - manual or computer-assisted
- Select a method to record and display wargaming results
  - narrative
  - sketch and note
  - war game worksheets
  - synchronization matrix

2 **Conduct War Game and Assess Results**
- Purpose of war game (identify gaps, visualization, etc.)
- Basic methodology (e.g., action, reaction, counteraction)
- Record results

3 **Prepare Products**
- Results of the war game brief
  - potential decision points
  - evaluation criteria
  - potential branches and sequels
- Revised staff estimates
- Refined COAs
- Time-phased force and deployment data refinement and transportation feasibility
- Feedback through the COA decision brief

Figure IV-12. Sample Wargaming Steps

operational phasing, the critical events discussion identifies significant actions and requirements by functional area and/or by JTF component.

(c) Red Cell. The J-2 staff will provide a red cell to role play and model the adversaries during planning and specifically during wargaming.

1. A robust, well-trained, imaginative, and skilled red cell that aggressively pursues the adversary's point of view during wargaming is essential. By accurately portraying the full range of realistic capabilities and options available to the enemy, they help the staff address friendly responses for each adversary COA.

2. The red cell is normally composed of personnel from the joint force J-2 staff and when available they may be augmented by other subject experts.

3. The red cell develops critical decision points, projects adversary reactions to friendly actions, and estimates impacts and implications on the adversary forces

and objectives. By trying to win the war game, the red cell helps the staff identify weaknesses and vulnerabilities before a real enemy does.

　　　　4. Given time constraints, as a minimum, the most dangerous and most likely adversary COAs should be wargamed and role played by the red cell during the war game.

　　　　(d) **White Team.** A small team of arbitrators normally composed of senior individuals familiar with the plan is a smart investment to ensure the war game does not get bogged down in unnecessary disagreement or arguing. The white team will provide overall oversight to the war game and any adjudication required between participants. The white team may also include the facilitator and/or highly qualified experts as required.

　　　　(3) **Conduct the War Game and Assess the Results**

　　　　(a) The facilitator and the red team commander get together to agree on the rules of the war game. The war game begins with an event designated by the facilitator. It could be an enemy offensive/defensive action or it could be a friendly offensive or defensive action. They decide where (in the OA) and when (H-hour or L-hour) it will begin. They review the initial array of forces. Of note, they must come to an agreement on the effectiveness of ISR capabilities and shaping actions by both sides prior to the war game. The facilitator must ensure that all members of the war game know what critical events will be wargamed and what techniques will be used. This coordination within the friendly team and between the friendly and the red team must be done well in advance.

　　　　(b) Within each wargaming method, the war game normally has three total moves. If necessary, that portion of the war game may be extended beyond the three moves. The facilitator decides how many moves are made in the war game.

　　　　(c) During the war game, the players must continually assess the COA's feasibility. Can it be supported? Can this be done? Are more combat power, more ISR capabilities, or more time needed? Are necessary logistics and communications available? Is the OA large enough? Has the threat successfully countered a certain phase or stage of a friendly COA? Based on the answers to the above questions, revisions to the friendly COA may be required. We don't make major revisions to a COA in the midst of a war game. Instead, we stop the war game, make the revisions, and start over at the beginning.

　　　　(d) The war game is for comparing and contrasting friendly COAs with the adversary COAs. Planners compare and contrast friendly COAs with each other in the fifth step of JOPP, COA comparison. They avoid becoming emotionally attached to a friendly COA as it leads to overlooking the COA shortcomings and weaknesses. Planners avoid comparing one friendly COA with another friendly COA during the war game and remain unbiased. The facilitator ensures adherence to the timeline. A war game for one COA at the JTF level may take six to eight hours. The facilitator must allocate enough time to ensure the war game will thoroughly test a COA.

　　　　(e) A **synchronization matrix** is a decision-making tool and a method of recording the results of wargaming. Key results that should be recorded include decision points, potential evaluation criteria, CCIRs, COA adjustments, branches, and sequels. Using a synchronization matrix helps the staff visually synchronize the COA across time and space in relation to the adversary's possible COAs. The war game and synchronization matrix efforts will be particularly useful in identifying cross-component support resource requirements.

(f) The war game considers friendly dispositions, strengths, and weaknesses; adversary assets and probable COAs; and characteristics of the OA. Through a logical sequence, it focuses the players on essential tasks to be accomplished.

(g) When the war game is complete and the worksheet and synchronization matrix are filled out, there should be enough detail to flesh out the bones of the COA and begin orders development (once the COA has been selected by the commander in a later JOPP step).

(h) Additionally, the war game will produce a refined event template and the initial decision support template (DST), or decision support tools. These are similar to a football coach's game plan. The tools can help predict what the threat will do. The tools also provide the commander options for employing forces to counter an adversary action. The tools will prepare the commander (coach) and the staff (team) for a wide range of possibilities and a choice of immediate solutions.

(i) The war game relies heavily on doctrinal foundation, tactical judgment, and experience. It generates new ideas and provides insights that might have been overlooked. The dynamics of the war game require the red team commander and the red team members to be aggressive, but realistic, in the execution of threat activities. The war game:

1. Records advantages and disadvantages of each COA as they become evident.

2. Creates decision support tools (a game plan).

3. Focuses the planning team on the threat *and* commander's evaluation criteria.

(4) **Prepare Products.** Certain products should result from the war game in addition to wargamed COAs. Planners enter the war game with a rough event template and must complete the war game with a refined, more accurate event template. The event template with its named areas of interest (NAIs) and time-phase lines will help the J-2 focus the ISR effort. An event matrix can be used as a "script" for the intelligence report during the war game. It can also tell planners if they are relying too much on one or two collection platforms and if assets have been overextended.

(a) A first draft of a DST and DSM should also come out of the COA war game. As more information about friendly forces and threat forces becomes available, the DST and DSM may change.

(b) The critical events are associated with the essential tasks identified in mission analysis. The decision points are tied to points in time and space when and where the commander must make a critical decision. Decision points will be tied to the CCIRs. Remember, CCIRs generate two types of information requirements: PIRs and FFIRs. The commander approves CCIRs. From a threat perspective, PIRs tied to a decision point will require an intelligence collection plan prioritizing and tasking collection assets to gather information about the threat. JIPOE ties PIRs to NAIs, which are linked to adversary COAs. The synchronization matrix is a tool that will help determine if adequate resources are available. Primary outputs are:

1. Wargamed COAs with graphic and narrative. Branches and sequels identified.

2. Information on commander's evaluation criteria.

3. Initial task organization.

4. Critical events and decision points.

5. Newly identified resource shortfalls to include force augmentation.

6. Refined/new CCIRs and event template/matrix.

7. Initial DST/DSM.

8. Fleshed out synchronization matrix.

9. Refined staff estimates.

(c) The outputs of the COA war game will be used in the comparison/decision step, orders development, and transition. The outputs on the slide are products. The results of the war game are the strengths and weaknesses of each friendly COA, the core of the back brief to the commander.

(d) The commander and staff normally will compare advantages and disadvantages of each COA during *course of action comparison*. However, if the *suitability*, *feasibility*, or *acceptability* of any COA becomes questionable during the *analysis* step, the commander should *modify or discard* it and concentrate on other COAs. The need to create additional combinations of COAs may also be required.

7. **Course of Action Comparison**

a. **Introduction**

(1) COA comparison is a subjective process whereby COAs are considered independently and evaluated/compared against a set of criteria that are established by the staff and commander. The goal is to identify and recommend the COA that has the highest probability of success against the enemy COA that is of the most concern to the commander.

(2) Figure IV-13 depicts inputs and outputs for COA comparison. Other products not graphically shown in the chart include updated JIPOE products, updated CCIRs, staff estimates, commander's identification of branches for further planning, and a WARNORD as appropriate.

(3) COA comparison facilitates the commander's decision-making process by balancing the **ends, means, ways, and risk** of each COA. The end product of this task is a briefing to the commander on a COA recommendation and a decision by the commander. COA comparison helps the commander answer the following questions:

(a) What are the differences between each COA?

(b) What are the advantages and disadvantages?

(c) What are the risks?

b. **COA Comparison Process**

(1) In COA comparison, the staff evaluates all COAs against established evaluation criteria and selects the COA that best accomplishes the mission. The commander reviews the criteria list and adds or deletes as he sees fit. The number of evaluation criteria will vary, but there should be enough to differentiate COAs. Consequently, COAs are not compared with each other, but rather they are individually evaluated against the criteria that are established by the staff and commander.

(2) Staff officers may each use their own matrix, such as the example in Figure IV-14, to compare COAs with respect to their functional areas. Matrices use the evaluation criteria developed before the war game. Decision matrices alone cannot provide decision solutions. Their greatest value is providing a method to compare COAs against criteria that, when met, produce mission success. They are analytical tools that staff officers use to

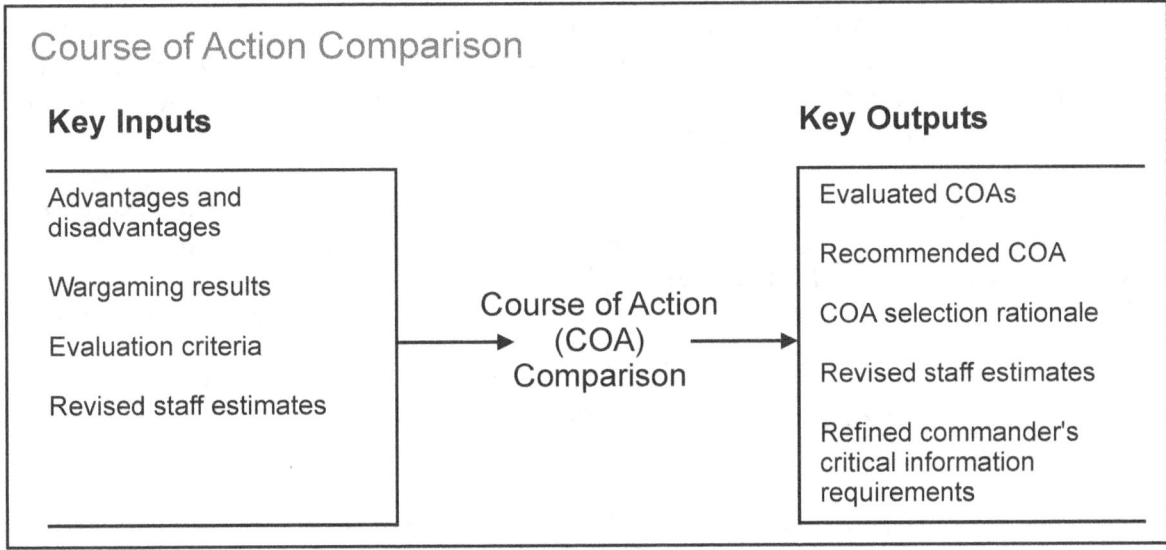

Figure IV-13. Course of Action Comparison

Staff Estimate Matrix (Intelligence Estimate)

Evaluation Criteria	Frontal Course of Action 1	Envelopment Course of Action 2
Effects of Terrain		✓
Effects of Weather	✓	
Utilizes Surprise		✓
Attacks Critical Vulnerabilities		✓
Collection Support		✓
Counterintelligence	✓	
Totals	2	4

Figure IV-14. Staff Estimate Matrix (Intelligence Estimate)

prepare recommendations. Commanders provide the solution by applying their judgment to staff recommendations and making a decision.

(3) The staff helps the commander identify and select the COA that best accomplishes the mission. The staff supports the commander's decision-making process by clearly portraying the commander's options and recording the results of the process. The staff compares feasible COAs to identify the one with the highest probability of success against the most likely enemy COA and the most dangerous enemy COA.

(4) **Prepare for COA comparison.** The commander and staff develop and evaluate a list of important criteria. Using the evaluation criteria discussed during COA analysis and wargaming, the staff outlines each COA, highlighting advantages and disadvantages. Comparing the strengths and weaknesses of the COAs identifies their advantages and disadvantages relative to each other.

(a) Determine/define comparison/evaluation criteria. As discussed earlier, criteria are based on the particular circumstances and should be relative to the situation. There is no standard list of criteria, although the commander may prescribe several core criteria that all staff directors will use. Individual staff sections, based on their estimate process, select the remainder of the criteria.

1. Criteria are based on the particular circumstances and should be relative to the situation.

2. Review commander's guidance for relevant criteria.

<u>3.</u> Identify implicit significant factors relating to the operation.

<u>4.</u> Each staff identifies criteria relating to that staff function.

<u>5.</u> Other criteria might include:

<u>a.</u> Political, social, and safety constraints; requirements for coordination with embassy/interagency personnel.

<u>b.</u> Fundamentals of joint warfare, including stability operations.

<u>c.</u> Elements of operational art.

<u>d.</u> Mission accomplishment.

<u>e.</u> Risks.

<u>f.</u> Costs.

(b) Define and determine the standard for each criterion.

<u>1.</u> Establish standard definitions for each evaluation criterion. Define the criteria in precise terms to reduce subjectivity and ensure the interpretation of each evaluation criterion remains constant between the various COAs.

<u>2.</u> Establish definitions prior to commencing COA comparison to avoid compromising the outcome.

<u>3.</u> Apply standards for each criterion to each COA.

(c) The staff evaluates feasible COAs using those evaluation criteria most important to the commander to identify the one COA with the highest probability of success. The selected COA should also:

<u>1.</u> Mitigate risk to the force and mission to an acceptable level.

<u>2.</u> Place the force in the best posture for future operations.

<u>3.</u> Provide maximum latitude for initiative by subordinates.

<u>4.</u> Provide the most flexibility to meet unexpected threats and opportunities.

c. **Determine the comparison method and record.** Actual comparison of COAs is critical. The staff may use any technique that facilitates reaching the best recommendation and the commander making the best decision. There are a number of techniques for comparing COAs. Examples of several decision matrices can be found in Appendix G, "Course of Action Comparison."

d. **COA comparison remains a subjective process and should not be turned into a mathematical equation.** The key element in this process is the ability to articulate to the commander why one COA is preferred over another.

8. **Course of Action Approval**

    a. **Introduction**

      (1) In this JOPP step, the staff briefs the commander on the COA comparison and the analysis and wargaming results, including a review of important supporting information. The staff determines the best COA to recommend to the commander. Figure IV-15 depicts the COA approval inputs and outputs.

      (2) The nature of a potential contingency could make it difficult to determine a specific end state until the crisis actually occurs. In these cases, the JFC may choose to present two or more valid COAs for approval by higher authority. A single COA can then be approved when the crisis occurs and specific circumstances become clear. However, in CAP, the desired end state should be represented by the set of objectives the President approves before committing forces to combat.

    b. **Prepare and present the COA decision briefing.** The staff briefs the commander on the COA comparison and the analysis and wargaming results. The briefing should include a review of important supporting information such as the current status of the joint force; the current JIPOE; and assumptions used in COA development. All principal staff directors and the component commanders should attend this briefing (physically or electronically). Figure IV-16 shows a sample COA briefing guide.

    c. **Commander selects/modifies the COA.** COA approval/selection is the end result of the COA comparison process. Throughout the COA development process, the commander conducts an independent analysis of the mission, possible COAs, and relative merits and risks associated with each COA. The commander, upon receiving the staff's

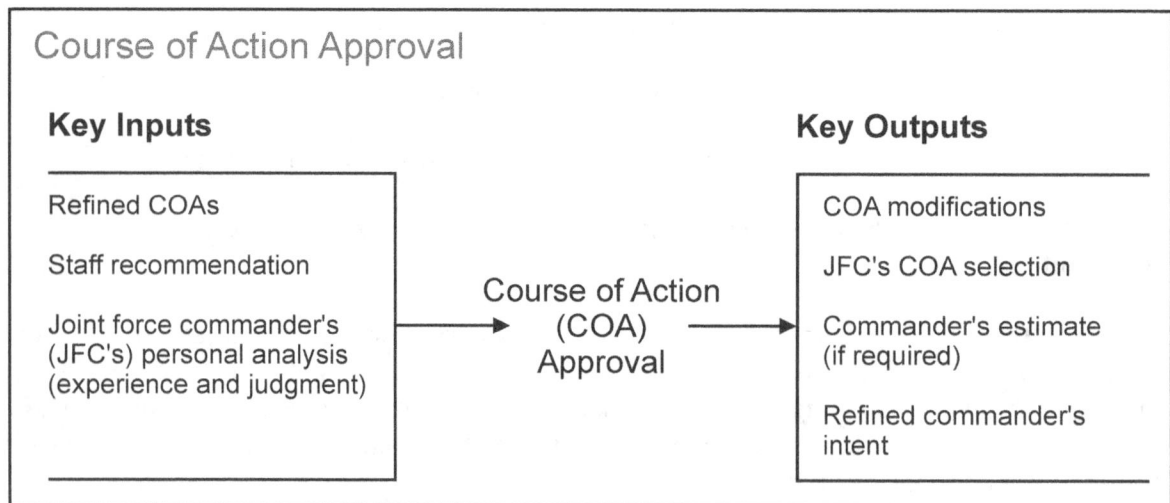

Figure IV-15. Course of Action Approval

Sample Course of Action Briefing Guide

- Purpose of the briefing
- Opposing situation
  - **Strength.** A review of opposing forces, both committed and available for reinforcement
  - **Composition.** Order of battle, major weapons systems, and operational characteristics
  - **Location and disposition.** Ground combat and fire support forces; air, naval, and missile forces; logistics forces and nodes; command and control facilities; and other combat power
  - **Reinforcements.** Land; air; naval; missile; chemical, biological, radiological, and nuclear; other advanced weapons systems; capacity for movement of these forces
  - **Logistics** Summary of opposing forces ability to support combat operations
  - **Time and space factors.** The capacity to move and reinforce positions
  - **Combat efficiency.** The state of training, readiness, battle experience, physical condition, morale, leadership, motivation, tactical doctrine, discipline, and significant strengths and weaknesses
- Friendly situation (similar elements as opposing situation)
- Mission statements
- Commander's intent statement
- Operational concepts and courses of action (COAs)
  - Any changes from the mission analysis briefing in the following areas:
    - assumptions
    - limitations
    - adversary and friendly centers of gravity (COGs)
    - phasing of the operation (if phased)
    - lines of operation/lines of effort
  - Present courses of action. As a minimum, discuss:
    - COA# _____ (short name, e.g., "Simultaneous Assault")
    - COA statement (brief concept of operations)
    - COA sketch
    - COA architecture
      - task organization
      - command relationships
      - organization of the operational area
    - major differences between each COA
    - summaries of COAs
  - COA analysis
    - review of the joint planning group's wargaming efforts
    - add considerations from own experiences
  - COA comparisons
    - description of comparison criteria (e.g., evaluation criteria) and comparison methodology
    - weigh strengths and weaknesses with respect to comparison criteria
  - COA recommendations
    - staff
    - components

Figure IV-16. Sample Course of Action Briefing Guide

recommendation, combines his analysis with the staff recommendation, resulting in a selected COA. It gives the staff a concise statement of how the commander intends to accomplish the mission, and provides the necessary focus for execution planning and contingency plan development. During this step, the commander should:

(1) Review staff recommendations.

(2) Apply results of own COA analysis and comparison.

(3) Consider any separate recommendations from supporting and subordinate commanders.

(4) Review guidance from the higher headquarters/strategic guidance.

(5) The commander may:

(a) Concur with staff/component recommendations, as presented.

(b) Concur with recommended COAs, but with modifications.

(c) Select a different COA from the staff/component recommendation.

(d) Direct the use of a COA not formerly considered.

(e) Defer the decision and consult with selected staff/commanders prior to making a final decision.

d. **Refine Selected COA.** Once the commander selects a COA, the staff will begin the refinement process of that COA into a clear decision statement to be used in the commander's estimate. At the same time, the staff will apply a final "acceptability" check.

(1) Staff refines commander's COA selection into clear decision statement.

(a) Develop a brief statement that **clearly and concisely** sets forth the COA selected and provides only whatever information is necessary to develop a plan for the operation (no defined format).

(b) Describe what the force is to do as a whole, and as much of the elements of when, where, and how as may be appropriate.

(c) Express decision in terms of what is to be accomplished, if possible.

(d) Use simple language so the meaning is unmistakable.

(e) Include statement of what is acceptable risk.

(2) Apply final "acceptability" check.

(a) Apply experience and an understanding of situation.

(b) Consider factors of acceptable risk versus desired outcome consistent with higher commander's intent and concept. Determine if gains are worth expenditures.

e. **Prepare the Commander's Estimate**

(1) Once the commander has made a decision on a selected COA, provided guidance, and updated intent, the staff completes the commander's estimate. The commander's estimate provides a **concise narrative statement** of how the commander intends to accomplish the mission and provides the necessary focus for campaign planning and contingency plan development. Further, it responds to the establishing authority's requirement to develop a plan for execution. The commander's estimate provides a continuously updated source of information from the perspective of the commander. Commanders at various levels use estimates during JOPP to support all aspects of COA determination and plan or order development.

(2) Outside of formal APEX requirements, a commander may or may not use a commander's estimate as the situation dictates. The commander's initial intent statement and planning guidance to the staff can provide sufficient information to guide the planning process. Although the commander will tailor the content of the commander's estimate based on the situation, a typical format for an estimate that a commander submits is shown at Figure IV-17.

(a) Precise contents may vary widely, depending on the nature of the crisis, time available to respond, and the applicability of prior planning. In a rapidly developing situation, the formal commander's estimate may be initially impractical, and the entire estimate process may be reduced to a commanders' conference.

(b) In practice, with appropriate horizontal and vertical coordination, the commander's COA selection could already have been briefed to and approved by SecDef. In the current global environment, where major military operations are both politically and strategically significant, even a commander's selected COA is normally briefed to and approved by the President or SecDef. The commander's estimate then becomes a matter of formal record keeping and guidance for component and supporting forces.

(3) The supported commander may use simulation and analysis tools in the collaborative environment to assess a variety of options, and may also choose to convene a concept development conference involving representatives of subordinate and supporting commands, the Services, JS, and other interested parties. Review of the resulting commander's estimate (also referred to as the strategic concept) requires maximum collaboration and coordination among all planning participants. The supported commander may highlight issues for future interagency consultation, review, or resolution to be presented to SecDef during the IPR.

(4) **CJCS Estimate Review.** The estimate review determines whether the scope and concept of planned operations satisfy the tasking and will accomplish the mission; determines whether the assigned tasks can be accomplished using available resources in the timeframes contemplated by the plan; and ensures the plan is proportional and worth the

---

Commander's Estimate

Operational Description

- Purpose of the operation

- References

- Description of military operations

Narrative—Five Paragraphs

- Mission

- Situation and courses of action

- Analysis of opposing courses of action (adversary capabilities and intentions)

- Comparison of friendly courses of action

- Recommendation or decision

Remarks

- Remarks—Cite plan identification number of the file where detailed requirements have been loaded into the Joint Operation Planning and Execution System.

Figure IV-17. Commander's Estimate

expected costs. Once approved for further planning by SecDef during the concept development IPR (IPR C), the commander's estimate becomes the CONOPS for the plan.

9. Plan or Order Development

a. **Concept of Operations**

(1) **Deliberate planning will result in plan development, while CAP typically will lead directly to OPORD development.** During plan or order development, the commander and staff, in collaboration with subordinate and supporting components and organizations, expand the approved COA into a detailed joint contingency plan or OPORD by first developing an executable **CONOPS—the eventual centerpiece of the contingency plan or OPORD.**

(2) The CONOPS clearly and concisely expresses what the JFC intends to accomplish and how it will be done using available resources. It describes how the actions of the joint force components and supporting organizations will be integrated, synchronized, and phased to accomplish the mission, including potential branches and sequels. The CONOPS:

(a) States the commander's intent.

(b) Describes the central approach the JFC intends to take to accomplish the mission.

(c) Provides for the application, sequencing, synchronization, and integration of forces and capabilities in time, space, and purpose (including those of multinational and interagency organizations as appropriate).

(d) Describes when, where, and under what conditions the supported commander intends to give or refuse battle, if required.

(e) Focuses on friendly and adversary COGs and their associated critical vulnerabilities.

(f) Avoids discernible patterns and makes full use of ambiguity and deception.

(g) Provides for controlling the tempo of the operation.

(h) Visualizes the campaign in terms of the forces and functions involved.

(i) Relates the joint force's objectives and desired effects to those of the next higher command and other organizations as necessary. This enables assignment of tasks to subordinate and supporting commanders.

(3) The staff writes (or graphically portrays) the CONOPS in sufficient detail so that subordinate and supporting commanders understand their mission, tasks, and other requirements and can develop their supporting plans accordingly. During CONOPS development, the commander determines the best arrangement of simultaneous and sequential actions and activities to accomplish the assigned mission consistent with the approved COA. This arrangement of actions dictates the sequencing of forces into the OA, providing the link between the CONOPS and force planning. The link between the CONOPS and force planning is preserved and perpetuated through the TPFDD structure. The structure must ensure unit integrity, force mobility, and force visibility as well as the ability to transition to branches or sequels rapidly as operational conditions dictate. Planners ensure that the CONOPS, force plan, deployment plans, and supporting plans provide the flexibility to adapt to changing conditions, and are consistent with the JFC's intent.

(4) If the scope, complexity, and duration of the military action contemplated to accomplish the assigned mission warrant a campaign, then the staff outlines the series of military operations and associated objectives in a strategic concept. They develop the CONOPS for the preliminary part of the campaign in sufficient detail to impart a clear understanding of the commander's concept of how the assigned mission will be accomplished.

(5) During CONOPS development, the JFC must assimilate many variables under conditions of uncertainty to determine the essential military conditions, sequence of actions, and application of capabilities and associated forces to create effects and achieve objectives.

JFCs and their staffs must be continually aware of the higher-level objectives and associated desired and undesired effects that influence planning at every juncture. If operational objectives are not linked to strategic objectives, the inherent linkage or "nesting" is broken and eventually tactical considerations can begin to drive the overall strategy at cross-purposes.

The CJCSM 3122.01 series volumes provide detailed guidance on CONOPS content and format.

b. **Format of Military Plans and Orders.** Plans and orders can come in many varieties from very detailed campaign plans and contingency plans to simple verbal orders. They also include OPORDs, WARNORDs, PLANORDs, ALERTORDs, EXORDs, and FRAGORDs, as well as PTDOs, DEPORDs, and GFMAP Annex Schedule modifications. The more complex directives will contain much of the amplifying information in appropriate annexes and appendices. However, the directive should always contain the essential information in the main body. The form may depend on the time available, the complexity of the operation, and the levels of command involved. However, in most cases, the directive will be standardized in the five-paragraph format that is described in Appendix A, "Joint Operation Plan Format." Following is a brief description of each of these paragraphs.

(1) **Paragraph 1—Situation.** The commander's summary of the general situation that ensures subordinates understand the background of the planned operations. Paragraph 1 will often contain subparagraphs describing the higher commander's intent, friendly forces, and enemy forces.

(2) **Paragraph 2—Mission.** The commander inserts his mission statement.

(3) **Paragraph 3—Execution.** This paragraph contains commander's intent, which will enable commanders two levels down to exercise initiative while keeping their actions aligned with the overall purpose of the mission. It also specifies objectives, tasks, and assignments for subordinates (by phase, as applicable—with clear criteria denoting phase completion).

(4) **Paragraph 4—Administration and Logistics.** This paragraph describes the concept of support for logistics, personnel, and medical services.

(5) **Paragraph 5—Command and Control.** This paragraph specifies the command relationships, succession of command, and overall plan for communications.

c. **Plan or Order Development**

(1) For plans and orders developed per JSCP direction or as a result of a Presidential or SecDef tasking (normally transmitted through the CJCS), the CJCS, in coordination with the supported and supporting commanders and other members of the JCS, monitors planning activities, resolves shortfalls when required, and reviews the supported commander's contingency plan for adequacy, feasibility, acceptability, completeness, and compliance with joint doctrine. The supported commander will conduct one or more plan approval IPRs with SecDef (or designated approval authority) to confirm the plan's strategic

guidance and receive approval of assumptions, the mission statement, the concept, the plan, and any further guidance required for plan refinement. During IPR F, the CJCS and USD(P) will include issues arising from, or resolved during, plan review (e.g., key risks, decision points). The intended result of IPR F is SecDef approval of the basic plan and required annexes, the resolution of any remaining key issues, and approval to proceed with plan assessment (as applicable) with any amplifying guidance or direction. If the President or SecDef decides to execute the plan, all three APEX operational activities—situational awareness, planning, and execution—continue in a complementary and iterative process.

(2) The JFC guides plan development by issuing a PLANORD or similar planning directive to coordinate the activities of the commands and agencies involved. A number of activities are associated with plan development, as Figure IV-18 shows. These planning activities typically will be accomplished in a parallel, collaborative, and iterative fashion rather than sequentially, depending largely on the planning time available. The same flexibility displayed in COA development is seen here again, as planners discover and eliminate shortfalls.

(3) The CJCSM 3122 series provides specific guidance on these activities for organizations required to prepare a plan per APEX procedures. However, these are typical types of activities that other organizations also will accomplish as they plan for joint operations. For example, a CCMD that is preparing a crisis-related OPORD at the President's direction will follow specific procedures and milestones in force planning, TPFDD development, and shortfall identification. If required, a JTF subordinate to the CCMD will support this effort even as the JTF commander and staff are planning for their specific mission and tasks.

(a) **Application of Forces and Capabilities**

1. When planning the application of forces and capabilities, the **JFC should not be completely constrained by force apportionment if additional resources are justifiable and no other COA within the apportioned forces reasonably exists.** The additional capability requirements will be coordinated with JS through the allocation process.

Plan Development Activities

- Force planning

- Support planning

- Nuclear strike planning

- Deployment and redeployment planning

- Shortfall identification

- Feasibility analysis

- Refinement

- Documentation

- Plan review and approval

- Supporting plan development

Figure IV-18. Plan Development Activities

Risk assessments will include results using both apportioned capabilities and augmentation capabilities. Operation planning is inherently an iterative process, with forces being requested and approved for certain early phases, while other forces may be needed or withdrawn for the later phases. This process is particularly complex when planning a campaign because of the potential magnitude of committed forces and length of the commitment. Finally, when making this determination, the **JFC should also consider withholding some capability as an operational reserve.**

2. When developing contingency plan, the supported JFC should designate the **main effort** and **supporting efforts** as soon as possible. This action is necessary for economy of effort and for allocating disparate forces, to include MNFs. The main effort is based on the supported JFC's prioritized objectives. It identifies where the supported JFC will concentrate capabilities to achieve specific objectives. Designation of the main effort can be addressed in geographical (area) or functional terms. **Area tasks and responsibilities** focus on a specific area to control or conduct operations. An example is the assignment of areas of operations for Army forces and Marine Corps forces operating in the same JOA. **Functional tasks and responsibilities** focus on the performance of continuing efforts that involve the forces of two or more Military Departments operating in the same domain—air, land, maritime, or space—or where there is a need to accomplish a distinct aspect of the assigned mission. An example is the designation of the maritime component commander as the joint force air component commander when the Navy component commander has the preponderance of the air assets and the ability to effectively plan, task, and control joint air operations. In either case, designating the main effort will establish where or how a major portion of available friendly forces and assets are employed, often to attain the primary objective of a major operation or campaign.

3. Designating a main effort facilitates the synchronized and integrated employment of the joint force while preserving the initiative of subordinate commanders. After the main effort is identified, joint force and component planners determine those tasks essential to accomplishing objectives. The supported JFC assigns these tasks to subordinate commanders along with the capabilities and support necessary to accomplish them. As such, the CONOPS must clearly specify the nature of the main effort.

4. The main effort can change during the course of the operation based on numerous factors, including changes in the operational environment and how the adversary reacts to friendly operations. When the main effort changes, support priorities must change to ensure success. Both horizontal and vertical coordination within the joint force and with multinational and interagency partners is essential when shifting the main effort. Secondary efforts are important, but are ancillary to the main effort. They normally are designed to complement or enhance the success of the main effort (for example, by diverting enemy resources). Only necessary secondary efforts, whose potential value offsets or exceeds the resources required, should be undertaken, because these efforts may divert resources from the main effort. Secondary efforts normally lack the operational depth of the main effort and have fewer forces and capabilities, smaller reserves, and more limited objectives.

(b) **Force Planning**

1. The primary purposes of force planning are to identify all forces needed to accomplish the supported component commanders' CONOPS with some rigor and effectively phase the forces into the OA. Force planning consists of determining the force requirements by operation phase, mission, mission priority, mission sequence, and operating area. It includes force allocation review, major force phasing, integration planning, force list structure development, and force list development. Force planning is the responsibility of the CCDR, supported by component commanders in coordination with JS and JFPs. Force planning begins early during CONOPS development and focuses on applying the right force to the mission while ensuring force visibility, force mobility, and adaptability. The commander determines force requirements; develops a TPFDD letter of instruction (LOI) specific to the OA; and designs force modules to align and time-phase the forces in accordance with the CONOPS. Proper force planning allows major forces and elements to be selected from those apportioned or allocated for planning and included in the supported commander's CONOPS by operation phase, mission, and mission priority. Service components then collaboratively make tentative assessments of the specific sustainment capabilities required in accordance with the CONOPS. Upon direction to execute, the CCDR then submits the refined force requests to JS. JS assigns a JFP to each force request and directs the JFP to forward a recommended sourcing solution (execution sourcing). The JFP provides the recommended sourcing solution with the operational and force provider risk for SecDef decision. The allocation decision is published in a modification to the CJCS GFMAP annex that directs the JFP to direct the force provider to deploy forces or provide capabilities. The JFP then publishes a modification to the GFMAP Annex Schedule to order the force provider to deploy forces. After the actual units or capabilities are identified (sourced), the CCDR refines the force plan by identifying and inserting contracted support requirements to ensure it supports the CONOPS, provides force visibility, and enables flexibility. The commander identifies and resolves or reports shortfalls with a risk assessment.

2. In CAP, force planning focuses on the actual units designated to participate in the planned operation and their readiness for deployment. The supported commander identifies force requirements as operational capabilities in the form of force packages to facilitate sourcing the GFM process. A force package is a list (group of force capabilities) of the various forces (force requirements) that the supported commander requires to conduct the operation described in the CONOPS. The supported commander typically describes required force requirements in the form of broad capability descriptions or unit type codes, depending on the circumstances. The supported commander submits the required force packages through JS to the force providers for sourcing. Force providers review the readiness and deployability posture of their available units before deciding which units to allocate to the supported commander's force requirements. Services and their component commands also determine mobilization requirements and plan for the provision of non-unit sustainment. The supported commander will review the sourcing recommendations through the GFM process to ensure compatibility with capability requirements and CONOPS.

(c) **Support Planning.** The purpose of support planning is to determine the TPFDD sequencing of the personnel, logistic, and other support necessary to provide mission support, distribution, maintenance, civil engineering, medical support, personnel service support, and sustainment for the joint force in accordance with the CONOPS. Support planning is conducted in parallel with other planning and encompasses such essential factors as IO, SC, lead component identification, assignment of responsibility for base operating support, communications and network support, airfield operations, management of non-unit replacements, health service support, personnel service support, personnel management, personnel visibility, financial management, handling of prisoners of war and detainees, theater civil engineering policy, logistic-related environmental considerations, IFO, support of noncombatant evacuation operations and other retrograde operations, and nation assistance. The GCC and subordinate commanders must review inter-Service support agreements. The GCC may designate a Service component commander as the single-Service manager for theater postal operations and morale, welfare, and recreation. The GCC must decide whether to delegate directive authority for logistics to a subordinate JFC and what will be the specific authority by function and scope. The GCC must also decide whether to assign specific common user logistic functions to a lead Service and what size, roles, and functions a joint deployment and distribution operations center will have if a common user logistic lead is assigned. The GCC planning guidance must clearly articulate the degree of reliance on HNS, acquisition and cross-servicing agreement, or contract support within each phase of operations. Finally, the GCC must decide whether or not to establish a joint command for logistics or to delegate the authority to a subordinate Service component. Support planning is primarily the responsibility of the Service component commanders and begins during CONOPS development. Service component commanders identify and update support requirements in coordination with the Services, Defense Logistics Agency, and USTRANSCOM. Service component commanders initiate the procurement of critical and low-density inventory items, determine HNS availability, determine contract support requirements and plans, develop plans for asset visibility, and establish phased delivery plans for sustainment in line with the phases and priorities of the CONOPS. They develop and train for battle damage repair, develop reparable retrograde plans, develop container management plans, develop force and LOC protection plans, develop supporting phased transportation and support plans aligned to the CONOPS, and report movement support requirements. Service component commanders continue to refine their mission support, sustainment, and distribution requirements as the force providers identify and source force requirements. During distribution planning, the supported CCDR and USTRANSCOM resolve gross distribution feasibility questions impacting intertheater and intratheater movement and sustainment delivery. If these feasibility questions are identified shortfalls due to inadequate resources, then planners must address these shortfalls as discussed in paragraph 9c(3)(f), "Shortfall Identification." USTRANSCOM and other transportation providers identify air, land, and sea transportation resources to support the approved CONOPS. These resources may include apportioned intertheater transportation, GCC-controlled theater transportation, and transportation organic to the subordinate commands. USTRANSCOM and other transportation providers develop transportation schedules for movement requirements identified by the supported commander. A transportation schedule does not necessarily mean that the supported commander's CONOPS is transportation feasible; rather, the schedules provide the most effective and realistic use of available transportation resources in relation to the phased CONOPS.

For additional information on the joint deployment and distribution operation center and the GCC's options for assigning logistics responsibilities, see JP 4-0, Joint Logistics.

<u>1</u>. **Logistics supportability analysis** is conducted to confirm the sourcing of logistic requirements in accordance with strategic guidance and to assess the adequacy of resources provided through support planning. This analysis ensures support is phased in accordance with the CONOPS; refines support C2 planning; and integrates support plans across the supporting commands, Service components, and agencies. It ensures an effective but minimum logistics footprint for each phase of the CONOPS.

<u>2</u>. **Transportation refinement** simulates the planned movement of resources that require lift support to ensure that the plan is transportation feasible. The supported commander evaluates and adjusts the CONOPS to achieve end-to-end transportation feasibility if possible, or requests additional resources if the level of risk is unacceptable. Transportation plans must be consistent and reconciled with plans and timelines required by providers of Service-unique combat and support aircraft to the supported CCDR. Planning also must consider requirements of international law; commonly understood customs and practices; and agreements or arrangements with foreign nations with which the US requires permission for overflight, access, and diplomatic clearance. If significant changes are made to the CONOPS, it should be assessed for transportation feasibility and refined to ensure it is acceptable.

(d) **Nuclear Strike Planning.** Commanders must assess the military as well as political impact a nuclear strike would have on their operations. Nuclear planning guidance issued at the CCDR level is based on national-level political considerations and is influenced by the military mission. Although United States Strategic Command (USSTRATCOM) conducts nuclear planning in coordination with the supported GCC and certain allied commanders, the supported commander does not effectively control the decision to use nuclear weapons.

(e) **Deployment and Redeployment Planning.** Deployment and redeployment planning is conducted on a continuous basis for all approved contingency plans and as required for specific crisis action plans. Planning for redeployment should be considered throughout the operation and is best accomplished in the same time-phased process in which deployment was accomplished. In all cases, mission requirements of a specific operation define the scope, duration, and scale of both deployment and redeployment operation planning. Unity of effort is paramount, since both deployment and redeployment operations involve numerous commands, agencies, and functional processes. Procedures and standards to attain and maintain visibility of personnel must be formulated. Because the ability to adapt to unforeseen conditions is essential, supported CCDRs must ensure that their deployment plans for each contingency or crisis action plan support global force visibility requirements. When operations that may be lengthy are planned, consideration must be given to force rotations. Units must rotate without interrupting operations. Planning should consider joint reception, staging, onward movement, and integration (JRSOI), turnover time, relief-in-place, transfer of authority, and time it takes for the outbound unit to redeploy. This information is vital for the JFPs to develop force rotations in the GFMAP Annex Schedule if the operation is executed.

<u>1</u>. **Operational Environment.** For a given plan, deployment planning decisions are based on the anticipated operational environment, which may be permissive,

uncertain, or hostile. The anticipated operational environment dictates the type of entry operations, deployment concept, mobility options, predeployment training, and force integration requirements. Normally, supported CCDRs, their subordinate commanders, and their Service components are responsible for providing detailed situation information, mission statements by operation phase, theater support parameters, strategic and operational lift allocations by phase (for both force movements and sustainment), HNS information and environmental standards, and pre-positioned equipment planning guidance.

2. **Deployment and Redeployment Concept.** Supported CCDRs must develop a deployment concept and identify specific predeployment standards necessary to meet mission requirements. Supporting CCDRs provide trained and mission-ready forces to the supported CCMD deployment concept and predeployment standard. Services recruit, organize, train, and equip interoperable forces. The Services' predeployment planning and coordination with the supporting CCMD must ensure that predeployment standards specified by the supported CCDR are achieved, supporting personnel and forces arrive in the supported theater fully prepared to perform their mission, and deployment delays caused by duplication of predeployment efforts are eliminated. The Services and supporting CCDRs must ensure unit contingency plans are prepared, forces are tailored and echeloned, personnel and equipment movement plans are complete and accurate, command relationship and integration requirements are identified, mission-essential tasks are rehearsed, mission-specific training is conducted, force protection is planned and resourced, and both logistics and personnel service support sustainment requirements are identified. Careful and detailed planning ensures that only required personnel, equipment, and materiel deploy; unit training is exacting; missions are fully understood; deployment changes are minimized during execution; and the flow of personnel, equipment, and movement of materiel into theater aligns with the CONOPS. Supported CCDRs must also develop a redeployment CONOPS to identify how forces and materiel will either redeploy to home station or to support another JFC's operation. This redeployment CONOPS is especially relevant and useful if force rotations are envisioned to provide the requisite forces for a long-term operation. CCDRs may not have all planning factors to fully develop this CONOPS, but by using the best available information for redeployment requirements, timelines, and priorities, the efficiency and effectiveness of redeployment operations may be greatly improved. Topics addressed in this early stage of a redeployment CONOPS may include a proposed sequence for redeployment of units, individuals, and materiel. Responsibilities and priorities for recovery, reconstitution, and return to home station may also be addressed along with transition requirements during mission handover. As a campaign or operation moves through the different operational plan phases, the CCDR will be able to develop and issue a redeployment order based on a refined redeployment CONOPS. Effective redeployment operations are essential to ensure supporting Services and rotational forces have sufficient time to fully source and prepare for the next rotation.

For additional information on deployment and redeployment planning, see JP 3-35, Deployment and Redeployment Operations.

3. **Movement Planning.** Movement planning integrates the activities and requirements of units with partial or complete self-deployment capability, activities of units that require lift support, and the transportation of sustainment and retrogrades. Movement

planning is highly collaborative and is enhanced by coordinated use of simulation and analysis tools.

a. If a plan is executed, the supported command forwards force requests in an RFF to JS. These force requests are allocated in a modification to the appropriate GFMAP annex. The JFP then publishes the GFMAP Annex Schedule specifying the latest arrival date (LAD) and end date of each unit's deployment. These allocated forces begin the process of building the TPFDD. The individual force requirements and the deployment information (available-to-load date, earliest arrival date, personnel increment number, ready-to-load date, etc.) are loaded into the execution plan identification number and further refined.

b. The supported command is responsible for movement control, including sequence of arrival, and exercises this authority through the TPFDD and the APEX validation process. During execution, the supported command may sequence movement within the limits specified in the GFMAP by SecDef. The supported commander will use the organic lift and nonorganic, common-user, strategic lift resources made available for planning by the CJCS. Competing requirements for limited strategic lift resources, support facilities, and intratheater transportation assets will be assessed in terms of impact on mission accomplishment. If additional resources are required, the supported command will identify the requirements and provide rationale for those requirements in an RFF. The supported commander's operational priorities and any movement constraints (e.g., assumptions concerning the potential use of WMD) are used to prepare a movement plan. The plan will consider en route staging locations and the ability of these locations to support the scheduled activity. This information, together with an estimate of required site augmentation, will be communicated to appropriate supporting commanders. The global force manager and USTRANSCOM use the Joint Flow Analysis and Sustainment for Transportation model to assess transportation feasibility and develop recommendations on final port of embarkation selections for those units without organic lift capability. Movement feasibility requires current analysis and assessment of movement C2 structures and systems; available organic, strategic, and theater lift assets; transportation infrastructure; and competing demands and restrictions.

c. After coordinated review of the movement analysis by USTRANSCOM, the supported command, and the JFPs, the supported command may adjust the CONOPS to improve movement feasibility where operational requirements remain satisfied. Commander, USTRANSCOM, should adjust or reprioritize transportation assets to meet the supported commander's operational requirements. If this is not an option due to requirements from other commanders, then the supported commander adjusts TPFDD requirements or is provided additional strategic and theater lift capabilities using (but not limited to) Civil Reserve Air Fleet and/or Voluntary Intermodal Sealift Agreement capabilities as necessary to achieve end-to-end transportation feasibility.

d. Operational requirements may cause the supported commander and/or subordinate commanders to alter their plans, potentially impacting the deployment priorities or force/capability requirements. Planners must understand and anticipate the impact of change. There is a high potential for a sequential pattern of disruption when changes are made to the TPFDD either in altering the flow of previously planned movements, or adding movements to deploy or redeploy additional forces or capabilities. A unit displaced by a change might not simply move on the next available lift, but may require reprogramming for movement at a later time. This may not only disrupt the flow, but may also interrupt the operation. Time is also a factor in TPFDD changes. Airlift can respond to short-notice changes, but at a cost in efficiency. Sealift, on the other hand, requires longer lead times, and cannot respond to change in a short period. These plan changes and the resulting modifications to the TPFDDs must be handled during the planning cycles.

4. **JSROI.** JRSOI planning is conducted to ensure deploying forces arrive and become operational in the OA as scheduled. Establishing personnel visibility for force protection purposes is necessary for joint forces immediately upon their arrival in the OA, and plans to accomplish this task are issued by the manpower and personnel directorate of a joint staff (J-1) at the CCMD level. JRSOI planning is also conducted to ensure forces can be scheduled in the GFMAP Annex Schedule to rotate without impacting operations. Effective integration of the force into the joint operation is the primary objective of the deployment process.

5. **CJCS and Supported GCC TPFDD LOIs.** The supported commander publishes supplemental instructions for TPFDD development in the TPFDD LOI. The LOI provides operation-specific guidance for utilizing the APEX processes and systems to provide force visibility and tracking, force mobility, and operational agility through the TPFDD and the validation process. It provides procedures for the deployment, redeployment, and rotations of the operation's forces. The LOI provides instructions on force planning sourcing, reporting, and validation. It defines planning and execution milestones and details movement control procedures and lift allocations to the commander's components, supporting commanders, and other members of the JPEC. A TPFDD must ensure force visibility, be tailored to the phases of the concept of operation, and be transportation feasible.

6. **Deployment and JRSOI Refinement.** Deployment, JRSOI, and logistics TPFDD refinement is conducted by the supported command in coordination with JS, JFPs, USTRANSCOM, the Services, and supporting commands. During execution, the flexibility of refinement of LADs and end dates is specified in the GFMAP. The purpose of the deployment and JRSOI refinement is to ensure the force deployment plan maintains force mobility throughout any movements, provides for force visibility and tracking at all times, provides for effective force preparation, and fully integrates forces into a joint operation while enabling unity of effort. This refinement conference examines planned missions, the priority of the missions within the operation phases, and the forces assigned to those missions. By mission, the refinement conference examines force capabilities, force size, support requirements, mission preparation, force positioning/basing, weapon systems, major equipment, force protection, and sustainment requirements. The refinement conference should assess the feasibility of force closure by the commander's required delivery date and the feasibility of successful mission execution within the timeframe established by the commander under the deployment concept. This refinement conference should assess potential success of all force integration requirements. Transition criteria for all phases should be evaluated for force redeployment, including rotation requirements.

For more information on JRSOI, see JP 3-35, Deployment and Redeployment Operations.

7. For lesser-priority plans that may be executed simultaneously with higher-priority plans or ongoing operations, CCMD and USTRANSCOM planners may develop several different deployment scenarios to provide the CCDR a range of possible transportation conditions under which the plan may have to be executed based on risk to this plan and the other ongoing operations. This will help both the supported and supporting CCDRs identify risk associated with having to execute multiple operations in a transportation-constrained environment.

(f) **Shortfall Identification.** Along with hazard and threat analysis, shortfall identification is conducted throughout the plan development process. The supported commander continuously identifies limiting factors and capabilities shortfalls and associated risks as plan development progresses. Where possible, the supported commander resolves the shortfalls and required controls and countermeasures through planning adjustments and coordination with supporting and subordinate commanders. If the shortfalls and necessary controls and countermeasures cannot be reconciled or the resources provided are inadequate to perform the assigned task, the supported commander reports these limiting factors and assessment of the associated risk to the CJCS. The CJCS and the Service Chiefs consider shortfalls and limiting factors reported by the supported commander and coordinate resolution. However, the completion of assigned plans is not delayed pending the resolution of shortfalls. If shortfalls cannot be resolved within the JSCP timeframe, the completed plan will include a consolidated summary and impact assessment of unresolved shortfalls and associated risks.

(g) **Feasibility Analysis.** This step in plan or order development is similar to determining the feasibility of a COA, except that it typically does not involve simulation-based wargaming. The focus in this step is on ensuring the assigned mission can be accomplished using available resources within the time contemplated by the plan. The results of force planning, support planning, deployment and redeployment planning, and shortfall identification will affect contingency plan or OPORD feasibility. The primary factors considered are whether the apportioned or allocated resources can be deployed to the JOA when required, sustained throughout the operation, and employed effectively, or whether the scope of the plan exceeds the apportioned resources and supporting capabilities. Measures to enhance feasibility include adjusting the CONOPS, ensuring sufficiency of resources and capabilities, and maintaining options and reserves.

(h) **Documentation.** When the TPFDD is complete and end-to-end transportation feasibility has been achieved and is acceptable to the supported CCDR, the supported CCDR completes the documentation of the final contingency plan or OPORD and coordinates access to the transportation-feasible TPFDD as appropriate.

(i) **Plan Review and Approval.** When the final contingency plan or OPORD is complete, the supported commander then submits it with the associated TPFDD file to the CJCS for JPEC review. The JPEC reviews the supported commander's contingency plan or OPORD and provides the results of the review to the CJCS. The CJCS reviews and recommends approval or disapproval of the contingency plan or OPORD to SecDef. The

JCS provides a copy of the plan to OSD to facilitate their parallel review of the plan and to inform USD(P)'s recommendation of approval/disapproval to SecDef. After the CJCS's and USD(P)'s review, SecDef or the President will review, approve, or modify the plan. The President or SecDef is the final approval authority for OPORDs, depending upon the subject matter.

(j) Supporting Plan Development

1. Supporting commanders prepare plans that encompass their role in the joint operation. Employment planning is normally accomplished by the JFC (CCDR or subordinate JFC) who will direct the forces if the plan is executed. Detailed employment planning may be delayed when the politico–military situation cannot be clearly forecast, or it may be excluded from supporting plans if employment is to be planned and executed within a multinational framework.

2. The supported commander normally reviews and approves supporting plans. However, the CJCS may be asked to resolve critical issues that arise during the review of supporting plans, and JS may coordinate the review of any supporting plans should circumstances so warrant. Deliberate planning does not conclude when the supported commander approves the supporting plans. Planning refinement and maintenance continues until the operation terminates or the planning requirement is cancelled or superseded.

(4) **Transition.** Transition is critical to the overall planning process. It is an orderly turnover of a plan or order as it is passed to those tasked with execution of the operation. It provides information, direction, and guidance relative to the plan or order that will help to facilitate situational awareness. Additionally, it provides an understanding of the rationale for key decisions necessary to ensure there is a coherent shift from planning to execution. These factors coupled together are intended to maintain the intent of the CONOPS, promote unity of effort, and generate tempo. Successful transition ensures that those charged with executing an order have a full understanding of the plan. Regardless of the level of command, such a transition ensures that those who execute the order understand the commander's intent and CONOPS. Transition may be internal or external in the form of briefs or drills. Internally, transition occurs between future plans and future/current operations. Externally, transition occurs between the commander and subordinate commands.

(a) **Transition Brief.** At higher levels of command, transition may include a formal transition brief to subordinate or adjacent commanders and to the staff supervising execution of the order. At lower levels, it might be less formal. The transition brief provides an overview of the mission, commander's intent, task organization, and enemy and friendly situation. It is given to ensure all actions necessary to implement the order are known and understood by those executing the order. The brief may include items from the order or plan such as:

1. Higher headquarters' mission and commander's intent.

2. Mission.

<u>3.</u> Commander's intent.

<u>4.</u> CCIRs.

<u>5.</u> Task organization.

<u>6.</u> Situation (friendly and enemy).

<u>7.</u> CONOPS.

<u>8.</u> Execution (including branches and potential sequels).

<u>9.</u> Planning support tools (such as a synchronization matrix).

(b) **Confirmation Brief.** A confirmation brief is given by a subordinate commander after receiving the order or plan. Subordinate commanders brief the higher commander on their understanding of commander's intent, their specific tasks and purpose, and the relationship between their unit's missions and the other units in the operation. The confirmation brief allows the higher commander to identify potential gaps in the plan, as well as discrepancies with subordinate plans. It also gives the commander insights into how subordinate commanders intend to accomplish their missions.

(c) **Transition Drills.** Transition drills increase the situational awareness of subordinate commanders and the staff and instill confidence and familiarity with the plan. Sand tables, map exercises, and rehearsals are examples of transition drills.

Intentionally Blank

APPENDIX A
JOINT OPERATION PLAN FORMAT

SECTION A. INTRODUCTION

1. Below is a sample format that a joint force staff can use as a guide when developing a joint OPLAN. The exact format and level of detail may vary somewhat among joint commands, based on theater-specific requirements and other factors. However, joint OPLANs/CONPLANs will always contain the basic five paragraphs (such as paragraph 3, "Execution") and their primary subparagraphs (such as paragraph 3a, "Concept of Operations"). **The JPEC typically refers to a joint contingency plans that encompasses more than one major operation as a campaign plan, but JFCs prepare a plan for a campaign in joint contingency plan format.**

2. The CJCSM 3122.01 series volumes describe joint operation planning interaction between the President, SecDef, CJCS, the supported joint commander, and other JPEC members, and provides models of planning messages and estimates. The CJCSM 3122.01 series volumes provide the formats for joint OPLANs/CONPLANs when commanders must submit contingency plans in accordance with APEX policy requirements.

SECTION B. NOTIONAL OPERATION PLAN FORMAT

    a. Copy Number

    b. Issuing Headquarters

    c. Place of Issue

    d. Effective Date-Time Group

    e. OPERATION PLAN: (Number or Code Name)

    f. USXXXXCOM OPERATIONS TO . . .

    g. References: *(List any maps, charts, and other relevant documents deemed essential to comprehension of the plan.)*

1. **Situation**

(This section briefly describes the composite conditions, circumstances, and influences of the theater strategic situation that the plan addresses [see national intelligence estimate, any multinational sources, and strategic and commanders' estimates].)

    a. **General.** *(This section describes the general politico–military environment that would establish the probable preconditions for execution of the contingency plans. It should summarize the competing political goals that could lead to conflict. Identify primary* *antagonists. State US policy goals and the estimated goals of other parties. Outline political decisions needed from other countries to achieve US policy goals and conduct effective US military operations to achieve US military objectives. Specific items can be listed separately for clarity as depicted below.)*

(1) **Environment of Conflict.** *(Provide a summary of the national and/or multinational strategic context [JSCP, UCP].)*

(2) **Policy Goals.** *(This section relates the strategic guidance, end state, and termination objectives to the theater situation and requirements in its global, regional, and space dimensions, interests, intentions/criteria for termination.)*

(a) US/Multinational Policy Goals. *(Identify the national security, multinational or military objectives and strategic tasks assigned to or coordinated by the CCMD.)*

(b) End State. *(Describe the national strategic end state and relate the military end state to the national strategic end state.)*

(3) **Non-US National Political Decisions**

(4) **Operational Limitations.** *(List actions that are prohibited or required by higher or multinational authority [ROE, law of armed conflict, termination criteria, etc.].)*

b. **Area of Concern**

(1) **Operational Area.** *(Describe the JFC's OA. A map may be used as an attachment to graphically depict the area.)*

(2) **Area of Interest.** *(Describe the area of concern to the commander, including the area of influence, areas adjacent thereto, and extending into enemy territory to the objectives of current or planned operations. This area also includes areas occupied by enemy forces who could jeopardize the accomplishment of the mission.)*

c. **Deterrent Options.** *(Delineate FDOs desired to include those categories specified in the current JSCP. Specific units and resources must be prioritized in terms of LAD relative to C-day. Include possible diplomatic, informational, or economic deterrent options accomplished by non-DOD agencies that would support US mission accomplishment. See Appendix E, "Flexible Deterrent Options," for examples of FDOs.)*

d. **Risk.** *(Risk is the probability and severity of loss linked to hazards. List the specific hazards that the joint force may encounter during the mission. List risk mitigation measures.)*

e. **Adversary Forces.** *(Identify the opposing forces expected upon execution and appraise their general capabilities. Refer readers to annex B [Intelligence] for details. However, this section should provide the information essential to a clear understanding of* *the magnitude of the hostile threat. Identify the adversary's strategic and operational COGs and critical vulnerabilities as depicted below.)*

    (1) **Adversary Centers of Gravity**

        (a) Strategic.

        (b) Operational.

    (2) **Adversary Critical Factors**

        (a) Strategic.

        (b) Operational.

    (3) **Adversary Courses of Action** *(most likely and most dangerous to friendly mission accomplishment).*

        (a) General.

        (b) Adversary's End State.

        (c) Adversary's Strategic Objectives.

        (d) Adversary's Operational Objectives.

        (e) Adversary CONOPS.

    (4) **Adversary Logistics and Sustainment**

    (5) **Other Adversary Forces/Capabilities**

    (6) **Adversary Reserve Mobilization**

  f. **Friendly Forces**

    (1) **Friendly Centers of Gravity.** *(This section should identify friendly COGs, both strategic and operational; this provides focus to force protection efforts.)*

        (a) Strategic.

        (b) Operational.

    (2) **Friendly Critical Factors**

        (a) Strategic.

        (b) Operational.

(3) **Multinational Forces**

(4) **Supporting Commands and Agencies.** *(Describe the operations of unassigned forces, other than those tasked to support this contingency plan, that could have a direct and significant influence on the operations in the plan. Also list the specific tasks of friendly forces, commands, or government departments and agencies that would directly support execution of the contingency plan, for example, USTRANSCOM, USSTRATCOM, Defense Intelligence Agency, and so forth.)*

g. **Assumptions.** *(List all reasonable assumptions for all participants contained in the JSCP or other tasking on which the contingency plan is based. State expected conditions over which the JFC has no control. Include assumptions that are directly relevant to the development of the plan and supporting plans and assumptions to the plan as a whole. Include both specified and implied assumptions that, if they do not occur as expected, would invalidate the plan or its CONOPS. Specify the mobility [air and sea lift], the degree of mobilization assumed, i.e., total, full, partial, selective, or none.)*

(1) **Threat Warning/Timeline.**

(2) **Pre-Positioning and Regional Access** *(including international support and assistance).*

(3) **In-Place Forces.**

(4) **Strategic Assumptions** *(including those pertaining to nuclear weapons employment).*

(5) **Legal Considerations.** *(List those significant legal considerations on which the plan is based.)*

(a) ROE.

(b) International law, including the law of armed conflict.

(c) US law.

(d) Host-nation and partner nation policies.

(e) Status-of-forces agreements.

(f) Other bilateral treaties and agreements including Article 98 agreements.

2. Mission

(State concisely the essential task[s] the JFC has to accomplish. This statement should address who, what, when, where, and why.)

3. Execution

a. **Concept of Operations.** (For a CCDR's contingency plan, the appropriate strategic concept(s) can be taken from the campaign plan and developed into a strategic concept of operation for a theater campaign or OPLAN. Otherwise, the CONOPS will be developed as a result of the COA selected by the JFC during COA development. The concept should be stated in terms of who, what, where, when, why, and how. It also contains the JFC's strategic vision, intent, and design in the strategic concept of operation for force projection operations, including mobilization, deployment, employment, sustainment, and redeployment of all participating forces, activities, and agencies.) **(Refer to annex C.)**

(1) **Commander's Intent.** *(This should describe the JFC's intent (purpose and end state), overall and by phase. This statement deals primarily with the military conditions that lead to mission accomplishment, so the commander may highlight selected objectives and their supporting effects. It may also include how the posture of forces at the end state facilitates transition to future operations. It may also include the JFC's assessment of the adversary commander's intent and an assessment of where and how much risk is acceptable during the operation. The commander's intent, though, is not a summary of the CONOPS.)*

(a) Purpose and End State. *(See Chapter II, "Strategic Direction and Joint Operation Planning," for details on determining the end state.)*

(b) Objectives.

(c) Effects, if discussed.

(2) **General.** *(Base the CONOPS on the JFC's selected COA. The CONOPS states how the commander plans to accomplish the mission, including the forces involved, the phasing of operations; the general nature and purpose of operations to be conducted, and the interrelated or cross-Service support. For a CCDR's contingency plan, the CONOPS should include a statement concerning the perceived need for Reserve Component mobilization based on plan force deployment timing and Reserve Component force size requirements. The CONOPS should be sufficiently developed to include an estimate of the level and duration of conflict to provide supporting and subordinate commanders a basis for preparing adequate supporting plans. To the extent possible, the CONOPS should incorporate the following:)*

(a) JFC's military objectives, supporting desired effects, and operational focus.

(b) Orientation on the adversary's strategic and operational COGs.

(c) Protection of friendly strategic and operational COGs.

(d) Phasing of operations, to include the commander's intent for each phase.

<u>1</u>. Phase I:

<u>a</u>. JFC's intent.

b. Timing.

c. Objectives and desired effects.

d. Risk.

e. Execution.

f. Employment.

(1) Land Forces.

(2) Air Forces.

(3) Maritime Forces.

(4) Space Forces.

(5) SOF.

g. Operational Fires. List those significant fires considerations on which the plan is based. The fires discussion should reflect the JFC's concept for application of available fires assets. Guidance for joint fires may address the following:

(1) Joint force policies, procedures, and planning cycles.

(2) Joint fire support assets for planning purposes.

(3) Priorities for employing target acquisition assets.

(4) Areas that require joint fires to support operational maneuver.

(5) Anticipated joint fire support requirements.

(6) Fire support coordinating measures (if required).

See JP 3-09, Joint Fire Support, *for a detailed discussion.*

2. Phases II through XX. *(Cite information as stated in subparagraph 3a(2)(d)1 above for each subsequent phase based on expected sequencing, changes, or new opportunities.)*

b. **Tasks.** *(List the tasks assigned to each element of the supported and supporting commands in separate subparagraphs. Each task should be a concise statement of a mission to be performed either in future planning for the operation or on execution of the OPORD. The task assignment should encompass all key actions that subordinate and supporting elements must perform to fulfill the CONOPS, including operational and tactical deception. If the actions cannot stand alone without exposing the deception, they must be published separately to receive special handling.)*

c. **Coordinating Instructions.** *(Provide instructions necessary for coordination and synchronization of the joint operation that apply to two or more elements of the command. Explain terms pertaining to the timing of execution and deployments.)*

4. **Administration and Logistics**

a. **Concept of Sustainment.** *(This should provide broad guidance for the theater strategic sustainment concept for the campaign or operation, with information and instructions broken down by phases. It should cover functional areas of logistics, transportation, personnel policies, and administration.)*

b. **Logistics.** *(This paragraph should address sustainment priorities and resources; base development and other civil engineering requirements, HNS, contracted support, environmental considerations, mortuary affairs, and Service responsibilities. Identify the priority and movement of major logistic items for each option and phase of the concept. Note: Logistic phases must complement the operation's phases. Identify strategic and theater ports of embarkation and debarkation for resupply. Outline transportation policies, guidance, and procedures for all options and phases.)*

c. **Personnel.** *(Identify detailed planning requirements and subordinate taskings. Assign tasks for establishing and operating joint personnel facilities, managing accurate and timely personnel accountability and strength reporting, and making provisions for staffing them. Discuss the administrative management of participating personnel, the reconstitution of forces, command replacement and rotation policies, and required joint individual augmentation to command headquarters and other operational requirements.)* Refer to annex E (if published).

d. **Public Affairs.** Refer to annex F.

e. **Civil–Military Operations.** Refer to annex G.

f. **Meteorological and Oceanographic Services.** Refer to annex H.

g. **Environmental Considerations.** Refer to annex L. See JP 3-34, *Joint Engineer Operations.*

h. **Geospatial Information and Services.** Refer to annex M.

i. **Health Service Support.** Refer to annex Q. *(Identify planning requirements and subordinate taskings for health service support functional areas. Address critical medical supplies and resources. Assign tasks for establishing joint medical assumptions and include them in a subparagraph.)*

5. **Command and Control**

a. **Command**

      (1) **Command Relationships.** *(State the organizational structure expected to exist during plan implementation. Indicate any changes to major C2 organizations and the time of expected shift. Identify all command arrangement agreements and memorandums of understanding used and those that require development.)*

      (2) **Command Posts.** *(List the designations and locations of each major headquarters involved in execution. When headquarters are to be deployed or the plan provides for the relocation of headquarters to an alternate command post, indicate the location and time of opening and closing each headquarters.)*

      (3) **Succession to Command.** *(Designate in order of succession the commanders responsible for assuming command of the operation in specific circumstances.)*

   b. **Joint Communications System Support.** *(Provide a general statement concerning the scope of communications systems and procedures required to support the operation. Highlight any communications systems or procedures requiring special emphasis.)* Refer to annex K.

[Signature]
[Name]
[Rank/Service]
Commander

Annexes:

    A—Task Organization

    B—Intelligence

    C—Operations

    D—Logistics

    E—Personnel

    F—Public Affairs

    G—Civil–Military Operations

    H—Meteorological and Oceanographic Operations

    J—Command Relationships

    K—Communications Systems

    L—Environmental Considerations

    M—Geospatial Information and Services

N—Space Operations

P—Host-Nation Support

Q—Medical Services

R—Reports

S—Special Technical Operations

T—Consequence Management

U—Notional Counterproliferation Decision Guide

V—Interagency Coordination

W—Contingency Contracting

X—Execution Checklist

Y—Strategic Communication

Z—Distribution

Note: Annexes A–D, K, and Y are required annexes for a CAP OPORD per APEX. All others may either be required by the JSCP or deemed necessary by the supported commander.

Intentionally Blank

APPENDIX B
STRATEGIC ESTIMATE

SECTION A. INTRODUCTION

1. The strategic estimate is an analytical tool available to CCDRs prior to the development of theater strategies or the design of global campaign plans or TCPs and subordinate campaign plans or OPLANs. CCDRs use continuous strategic estimates to facilitate the employment of military forces across the range of military operations. The strategic estimate is more comprehensive in scope than the estimates of subordinate commanders as it encompasses all aspects of the CCDR's operational environment, and it is the basis for the development of the GCC's theater strategy.

2. The CCDR, the CCMD staff, supporting commands, and agencies assess the broad strategic factors that influence the strategic environment, thus informing the ends, ways, means, and risks involved in accomplishing the theater strategic end state outlined in the GEF and JSCP.

3. Both supported and supporting CCDRs prepare strategic estimates based on assigned tasks. CCDRs who support multiple commands may prepare strategic estimates for each supporting operation.

4. Section B presents a notional format that a CCMD staff can use as a guide when developing a strategic estimate. The J-5 may provide the lead staff organization for the conduct of the strategic estimate with significant participation from the other staff directorates. The exact format and level of detail may vary somewhat among commands, based on theater-specific requirements and other factors.

5. The result of the strategic estimate is a better understanding and visualization of the complete security environment to include potential adversaries, friends, and neutrals. The strategic estimate process is dynamic and continuous, and provides input for designing and developing theater strategies and campaign plans. This strategic estimate is also the starting point for conducting the commander's estimate of the situation for a specific plan or order focusing on specific problems to be solved using deliberate planning or CAP.

SECTION B. NOTIONAL STRATEGIC ESTIMATE FORMAT

1. **Strategic Direction**

(This section analyzes broad policy, strategic guidance, and authoritative direction to the theater situation and identifies theater strategic requirements in global and regional dimensions.)

    a. **US Policy Goals.** *(Identify the US national security or military objectives and strategic tasks assigned to or coordinated by the CCMD.)*

b. **Non-US/Multinational Policy Goals.** *(Identify the multinational (alliance or coalition) security or military objectives and strategic tasks that may also be assigned to, or coordinated by the CCMD.)*

c. **End State(s).** *(Describe the strategic end state[s] and related military end state[s] to be maintained or accomplished.)*

2. **Strategic Environment**

(Analyze the information on the characteristics of the strategic environment.)

a. **Area of Responsibility.** *(Provide a visualization of the relevant geographic, political, economic, social, demographic, historic, and cultural factors in the AOR assigned to the CCDR.)*

b. **Area of Interest.** *(Describe the area of interest to the commander, including the area of influence and adjacent areas and extending into adversary or potential enemy territory. This area also includes areas occupied by enemy forces that could jeopardize the accomplishment of the mission.)*

c. **Adversary Forces.** *(Identify all states, groups, or organizations expected to be hostile to, or that may threaten, US and partner nation interests, and appraise their general objectives, motivations, and capabilities. Provide the information essential for a clear understanding of the magnitude of the potential threat.)*

d. **Friendly Forces.** *(Identify all relevant friendly states, forces, and organizations. These include assigned US forces, regional allies, and anticipated multinational partners. Describe the capabilities of the other instruments of power (diplomatic, economic, and informational), US military supporting commands, and other agencies that could have a direct and significant influence on the operations in this AOR.)*

e. **Neutral Forces.** *(Identify all other relevant states, groups, or organizations in the AOR and determine their general objectives, motivations, and capabilities. Provide the information essential for a clear understanding of their motivations and how they may impact US and friendly multinational operations.)*

3. **Assessment of the Major Strategic and Operational Challenges**

a. This is a continuous appreciation of the major challenges in the AOR that the CCDR may be tasked to deal with.

b. These may include a wide range of challenges, from direct military confrontation, peacekeeping, security cooperation, and building partner capacity, to providing response to atrocities, humanitarian assistance, disaster relief, and stability operations.

4. Potential Opportunities

a. This is an analysis of known or anticipated circumstances as well as emerging situations that the CCMD may use as positive leverage to improve the theater strategic situation and further US or partner nation interests.

b. Each potential opportunity must be carefully appraised with respect to existing strategic guidance and operational limitations.

5. Assessment of Risks

Risk is the probability and severity of loss linked to hazards.

a. This assessment matches a list of the potential challenges with anticipated capabilities in the operational environment.

b. Risks associated with each major challenge should be analyzed separately and categorized according to significance or likelihood (most dangerous or most likely).

c. The CCMD staff should develop a list of possible mitigation measures to these risks.

Intentionally Blank

APPENDIX C
STAFF ESTIMATES

1. Role of Estimates

a. Commander and staff estimates are central to formulating and updating military action to meet the requirements of any situation. Estimates should be comprehensive and continuous and must visualize the future, but at the same time they must optimize the limited time available and not become overly time-consuming. *Comprehensive* estimates consider both the quantifiable and the intangible aspects of military operations. They translate friendly and enemy strengths, weapons systems, training, morale, and leadership into combat capabilities. The estimate process requires the ability to visualize the battle or crisis situations requiring military forces.

b. Estimates must be as thorough as time and circumstances permit. The JFC and staff must constantly collect, process, and evaluate information. They update their estimates:

    (1) When the commander and staff recognize new facts.

    (2) When they replace assumptions with facts or find their assumptions invalid.

    (3) When they receive changes to the mission or when changes are indicated.

c. Estimates for the current operation can often provide a basis for estimates for future missions as well as changes to current operations. Technological advances and near-real-time information estimates ensure that estimates can be continuously updated. Estimates must *visualize the future* and support the commander's visualization. They are the link between current operations and future plans. The commander's vision directs the end state. Each subordinate unit commander must also possess the ability to envision the organization's end state. Estimates contribute to this vision. Failure to make staff estimates can lead to errors and omissions when developing, analyzing, and comparing COAs.

d. Not every situation will allow or require an extensive and lengthy planning effort. It is conceivable that a commander could review the assigned task, receive oral briefings, make a quick decision, and direct writing of the plan to commence. This would complete the process and might be suitable if the task were simple and straightforward.

e. Most commanders, however, are more likely to demand a thorough, well-coordinated plan that requires a complex staff estimate process. Written staff estimates are carefully prepared, coordinated, and fully documented.

f. Because of the unique talents of each JS division, involvement of all is vital. Each staff estimate takes on a different focus that identifies certain assumptions, detailed aspects of the COAs, and potential deficiencies that are simply not known at any other level, but nevertheless must be considered (see Figure C-1). Such a detailed study of the COAs involves the corresponding staffs of subordinate and supporting commands.

Functional Staff Estimates

Mobilization

Identify and address actions that must occur to integrate and synchronize the use of Reserve Component forces in the tentative courses of action (COAs).

Personnel

Identify and address known or anticipated personnel factors that may influence the tentative COAs, including the anticipated need for individual and small-unit replacements; the anticipated use of civilian, contract support, or indigenous personnel; and the anticipated individual and unit rotation policy.

Intelligence

Identify relevant information about the operational environment. Provide information about the adversary's military system, including the anticipated military situation at the beginning of the operation, enemy centers of gravity, limitations, intentions, most likely and most dangerous COAs, and priority intelligence requirements. Provide information on other systems in the operational environment, including the populace, infrastructure, social issues, political factors and relationships, and information architecture. Identify and address known or anticipated foundational intelligence data requirements of the weapon systems employed in each COA to ensure such data are current, accurate, and available to those units.

Logistics

Identify and address known or anticipated factors that may influence the feasibility of providing required logistic support to sustain the timing, intensity, and duration of the tentative COAs, including the required time-phasing to position support personnel and contractors to receive and integrate required combat forces and to move sustainment stocks.

Legal Support

Identify legal issues that may affect tentative COAs, including those related to the rules of engagement, laws of armed conflict, US laws, host-nation laws, and status-of-forces agreements.

Engineering

Identify and address known or anticipated engineering factors that may influence preparatory tasks, force deployment, force protection, and the reception, staging, onward movement, and integration of forces. Identify construction requirements that may need emergency or contingency construction authority.

Force Protection

Identify and examine known or anticipated force protection factors that may influence the tentative COAs.

Interagency Coordination

Identify opportunities for interagency cooperation to facilitate unity of effort. Identify requirements for interagency support of joint operations.

Figure C-1. Functional Staff Estimates

Functional Staff Estimates (continued)

Health Service Support

Identify and address known or anticipated health threat factors that may affect health service support. These factors include theater patient movement policy; required medical treatment, evacuation, and hospitalization capabilities; preventive medicine, veterinary, and dental support required; medical logistics; and the medical aspects of chemical, biological, radiological, and nuclear defensive operations.

Transportation and Movement

Identify available transportation capabilities and coordination requirements to support the time-phased deployment, employment, and sustainment of tentative COAs. Include requirements for intertheater and intratheater transportation assets and requirements to protect critical transportation nodes and lines of communications. Include procedures for integrating transportation of contractors and contractor support equipment into the force flow.

Joint Reception, Staging, Onward Movement, and Integration

Identify available capabilities and coordination requirements for joint reception, staging, onward movement, and integration of forces, including potential external sources of support (host-nation support and operational contract support).

Communications Systems Support

Identify and examine the feasibility of providing adequate communications systems support for tentative COAs. Address the adequacy and security of networks used to manage, store, manipulate, and transmit operational or logistical data.

Special Technical Operations

Identify and examine factors that may influence special technical operations that support and are integrated with tentative COAs.

Incident Response

Identify and examine factors that may influence incident response operations that support and are integrated with tentative COAs. Incident responses are actions taken to maintain or restore essential services and manage and mitigate problems resulting from disasters and catastrophes, including natural, man-made, or terrorist incidents.

Multinational Capabilities and Support

Identify, consolidate, and integrate opportunities to leverage multinational capabilities to include host-nation support required for the tentative COAs. Include the anticipated transportation and other support that the supported commander must provide to multinational partners to achieve unity of effort.

Operational Contract Support

Identify and address anticipated operational or environmental factors that affect the use of contract support for operational or sustainment requirements.

Integrated Financial Operations

Identify ways to integrate, synchronize, prioritize, and target fiscal resources and capabilities across US Government departments and agencies, multinational partners, and nongovernmental organizations against adversaries and in support of the population. Minimize the possibility that such resources and capabilities will be diverted or inadvertently misused to support an enemy's financial networks.

Figure C-1. Functional Staff Estimates (continued)

g. Each staff directorate:

(1) Reviews the mission and situation from its own staff functional perspective;

(2) Examines the factors and assumptions for which it is the responsible staff;

(3) Analyzes each COA from its staff functional perspective; and

(4) Concludes whether the mission can be supported.

h. **The products of this process are revised, documented staff estimates.** These are extremely useful to the J-5, which extracts information from them for the commander's estimate. The estimates are also valuable to planners in subordinate and supporting commands as they prepare supporting plans. Although documenting the staff estimates can be delayed until after the preparation of the commander's estimate, they should be sent to subordinate and supporting commanders in time to help them prepare annexes for their supporting plans.

i. The principal elements of the staff estimates normally include **mission, situation and considerations, analysis of opposing COAs, comparison of friendly COAs, and conclusions.** The coordinating staff and each staff principal develop facts, assessments, and information that relate to their functional field. Types of estimates generally include, but are not limited to, operations, personnel, intelligence, logistics, communications, civil–military operations, and special staff. The details in each basic category vary with the staff performing the analysis. The principal staff directorates have a similar perspective—they focus on friendly COAs and their supportability. However, the J-2 estimates on intelligence (provided at the beginning of the process) concentrate on the enemy: enemy situation, including strengths and weaknesses; enemy capabilities and an analysis of those capabilities; and conclusions drawn from that analysis. The analysis of adversary capabilities includes an analysis of the various COAs available to the adversary according to its capabilities, which include attacking, withdrawing, defending, and delaying. The J-2's conclusion will indicate the adversary's most likely COA and identify adversary COGs.

j. In many cases, the steps in the COA development phase are not separate and distinct, as the evolution of the refined COA illustrates. During planning guidance and early in the staff estimates, the initial COAs may have been developed from initial impressions and based on limited staff support. But as concept development progresses, COAs are refined and evolve to include many of the following considerations:

(1) What military operations are considered?

(2) Where they will be performed?

(3) Who will conduct the operation?

(4) When is the operation planned to occur?

(5) How will the operation be conducted?

k. **An iterative process of modifying, adding to, and deleting from the original tentative list is used to develop these refined COAs.** The staff continually evaluates the situation as the planning process continues. Early staff estimates are frequently given as oral briefings to the rest of the staff. In the beginning, they tend to emphasize information collection more than analysis. It is only in the later stages of the process that the staff estimates are expected to indicate which COAs can be best supported.

l. **Sample Estimate Format.** The following is a sample format that a JFC and joint force staff can use as a guide when developing an estimate. The exact format and level of detail may vary somewhat among joint commands and primary staff sections (J-1, J-2, etc.) based on theater-specific requirements and other factors. Refer to the CJCSM 3122.01 series volumes for the specific format when there is a requirement for the supported JFC to submit a commander's estimate.

SAMPLE ESTIMATE FORMAT

1. Mission

   a. Mission Analysis

      (1) Determine the higher command's purpose. Analyze national security and national military strategic direction as well as appropriate guidance in partner nations' directions, including long- and short-term objectives for conflict termination. Determine a clearly defined military end state and related termination criteria.

      (2) Determine specified, implied, and essential tasks and their priorities.

      (3) Determine objectives and consider desired and undesired effects.

   b. Mission Statement

      (1) Express in terms of who, what, when, where, and why (purpose).

      (2) Frame as a clear, concise statement of the essential tasks to be accomplished and the purpose to be achieved.

2. Situation and Courses of Action

   a. Situation Analysis

      (1) Geostrategic Context

(a) Domestic and international context: political and/or diplomatic long- and short-term causes of conflict; domestic influences, including public will, competing demands for resources, and political, economic, legal, and moral constraints; and international interests (reinforcing or conflicting with US interests, including positions of parties neutral to the conflict), international law, positions of intergovernmental organizations, and other competing or distracting international situations. Similar factors must be considered for noncombat operations.

(b) A systems perspective of the operational environment: all relevant political, military (see next paragraph), economic, social, information, infrastructure and other aspects. See Chapter III, "Operational Art and Operational Design," for a discussion of developing a systems perspective.

(2) Analysis of the Adversary. Scrutiny of the opponent situation, including capabilities and vulnerabilities (at the theater level, commanders normally will have available a formal intelligence estimate), should include the following:

(a) Broad military courses of action (COAs) being taken and available in the future.

(b) Political and military intentions and objectives (to extent known).

(c) Military strategic and operational advantages and limitations.

(d) Possible external military support.

(e) Centers of gravity (strategic and operational) and decisive points.

(f) Specific operational characteristics such as strength, composition, location, and disposition; reinforcements; logistics; time and space factors (including basing utilized and available); and combat/noncombat efficiency and proficiency in joint operations.

(3) Friendly Situation. Should follow the same pattern used for the analysis of the adversary. At the theater level, combatant commanders (CCDRs) normally will have available specific supporting estimates, including personnel, logistics, and communications estimates; multinational operations require specific analysis of partner nations' objectives, capabilities, and vulnerabilities. Interagency coordination required for the achievement of objectives must also be considered.

(4) Operational Limitations. Actions either required or prohibited by higher authority, such as constraints or restraints, and other restrictions that limit the commander's freedom of action, such as diplomatic agreements,

political or economic conditions in affected countries, and host-nation issues.

(5) **Assumptions.** Assumptions are intrinsically important factors upon which the conduct of the operation is based and must be noted as such.

(6) **Deductions.** Deductions from the above analysis should yield estimates of relative combat power, including enemy capabilities that can affect mission accomplishment.

b. **Course of Action Development and Analysis.** COAs are based on the above analysis and a creative determination of how the mission will be accomplished. Each COA must be adequate, feasible, and acceptable. State all practical COAs open to the commander that, if successful, will accomplish the mission. For a CCDR's strategic estimate, each COA typically will constitute an alternative theater strategic or operational concept and should outline the following:

(1) Major strategic and operational tasks to be accomplished in the order in which they are to be accomplished.

(2) Major forces or capabilities required (to include joint, interagency, and multinational).

(3) Command and control concept.

(4) Sustainment concept.

(5) Deployment concept.

(6) Estimate of time required to achieve the termination criteria.

(7) Concept for establishing and maintaining a theater reserve.

3. **Analysis of Adversary Capabilities and Intentions**

a. Determine the probable effect of possible adversary capabilities and intentions on the success of each friendly COA.

b. Conduct this analysis in an orderly manner by time phasing, geographic location, and functional event. Consider:

(1) The potential actions of subordinates two echelons down.

(2) Conflict termination issues; think through own action, opponent reaction, and counteraction.

(3) The potential impact on friendly desired effects and the likelihood that the adversary's actions will cause specific undesired effects.

c. Conclude with revalidation of friendly COAs. Determine additional requirements, make required modifications, and list advantages and disadvantages of each adversary capability.

4. Comparison of Own Courses of Action

a. Evaluate the advantages and disadvantages of each COA.

b. Compare with respect to evaluation criteria.

(1) Fixed values for joint operations (the principles of joint operations, the fundamentals of joint warfare, and the elements of operational design).

(2) Other factors (for example, political constraints).

(3) Mission accomplishment.

c. If appropriate, merge elements of different COAs into one.

5. Recommendation

Provide an assessment of which COAs are supportable, an analysis of the risk for each, and a concise statement of the recommended COA with its requirements.

APPENDIX D
ASSESSMENT

1. Introduction

a. Assessment is a process that measures progress of the joint force toward mission accomplishment. The focus is on measuring progress toward the end state and delivering relevant reliable feedback into the planning process to adjust operations during execution. Assessment involves deliberately comparing forecasted outcomes with actual events to determine the overall effectiveness of force employment. More specifically, assessment helps the commander determine progress toward attaining the desired end state, achieving objectives, or performing tasks. Commanders continuously assess the operational environment and the progress of operations and compare them to their initial vision and intent. Based on their assessment, commanders adjust operations to ensure objectives are met and the military end state is achieved.

b. **The assessment process is continuous and directly tied to the commander's decisions** throughout planning, preparation, and execution of operations. Staffs help the commander by monitoring the numerous aspects that can influence the outcome of operations and providing the commander timely information needed for decisions. **The CCIR process is linked to the assessment process** by the commander's need for timely information and recommendations to make decisions. The assessment process helps staffs by identifying key aspects of the operation that the commander is interested in closely monitoring and where the commander wants to make decisions. Examples of commander's critical decisions include when to transition to another phase of a campaign, what the priority of effort should be, or how to adjust command relationships between component commanders.

c. The assessment process begins during mission analysis when the commander and staff consider what to measure and how to measure it **to determine progress toward accomplishing a task, creating an effect, or achieving an objective.** During planning and preparation for an operation, for example, the staff assesses the joint force's ability to execute the plan based on available resources and changing conditions in the operational environment. However, **the discussion in this section focuses on assessment for the purpose of determining the progress of the joint force toward mission accomplishment.**

d. **Commanders and their staffs determine relevant assessment actions and measures during planning.** They consider assessment measures as early as mission analysis and include assessment measures and related guidance in commander and staff estimates. **They use assessment considerations to help guide operational design because these considerations can affect the sequence and type of actions along LOOs/lines of effort.** During execution, they continually monitor progress toward accomplishing tasks, creating effects, and achieving objectives. Assessment actions and measures help commanders adjust operations and resources as required, determine when to execute branches and sequels, and make other critical decisions to ensure current and future operations remain aligned with the mission and end state.

(1) Normally, the joint force J-3 or J-5, assisted by the J-2, is responsible for coordinating assessment activities. For subordinate commanders' staffs, this may be accomplished by equivalent elements within joint functional and/or Service components. The chief of staff facilitates the assessment process and determination of CCIRs by incorporating them into the headquarters' battle rhythm. Various elements of the JFC's staff use assessment results to adjust both current operations and future planning.

(2) Friendly, adversary, and neutral diplomatic, informational, and economic actions applied in the operational environment can impact military actions and objectives. When relevant to the mission, the commander also must anticipate using assessment to evaluate the results of these actions. This typically requires collaboration with other agencies and multinational partners—preferably within a common, accepted process—in the interest of unified action. For example, failure to coordinate overflight and access agreements with foreign governments in advance or to adhere to international law regarding sovereignty of foreign airspace could result in mission delay, failure to meet US objectives, and/or an international incident. Many of these organizations may be outside the JFC's authority. Accordingly, the JFC should grant some joint force organizations authority for direct coordination with key outside organizations—such as interagency elements from DOS or the Department of Homeland Security, national intelligence agencies, intelligence sources in other nations, and other CCMDs—to the extent necessary to ensure timely and accurate assessments.

2. Assessment Process

a. Assessment is continuous; it precedes and guides every operations process activity and concludes each operation or phase of an operation. Broadly, assessment consists of the following activities:

(1) Monitoring the current situation to collect relevant information.

(2) Evaluating progress toward attaining end state conditions, achieving objectives, and performing tasks.

(3) Recommending or directing action for improvement.

b. **Monitoring**

(1) *Monitoring* **is continuous observation of those conditions relevant to the current operation.** Monitoring within the assessment process allows staffs to collect relevant information, specifically that information about the current situation that can be compared with the forecasted situation described in the commander's intent and CONOPS. Progress cannot be judged, nor execution or adjustment decisions made, without an accurate understanding of the current situation.

(2) During planning, commanders monitor the situation to develop facts and assumptions that underlie the plan. During preparation and execution, commanders and staffs monitor the situation to determine if the facts are still relevant, if their assumptions remain valid, and if new conditions emerged that affect their operations.

(3) CCIRs and decision points focus the staff's monitoring activities and prioritize the unit's collection efforts. Information requirements concerning the enemy, terrain and weather, and civil considerations are identified, assigned priorities, and synchronized by the J-2. The operations officers use friendly reports to coordinate other assessment-related information requirements. To prevent duplicated collection efforts, information requirements associated with assessing the operation are integrated into both the ISR plan and FFIRs by the J-3 in coordination with the JFC's staff.

(4) Staffs monitor and collect information from the common operational picture and friendly reports. This information includes operational and intelligence summaries from subordinate, higher, and adjacent headquarters and communications and reports from liaison teams. The staff also identifies information sources outside military channels and monitors their reports. These other channels might include products from civilian, host-nation, and other agencies. Staffs apply information management principles to facilitate getting this information to the right people at the right time.

(5) Staff sections record relevant information in running estimates. Each staff section maintains a continuous assessment of current operations as a basis to determine if they are proceeding according to the commander's intent. In their running estimates, staff sections use this new information, updated facts, and assumptions as the basis for evaluation.

c. **Evaluating**

(1) The staff analyzes relevant information collected through monitoring to evaluate the operation's progress. ***Evaluating* is using criteria to judge progress toward desired conditions and determining why the current degree of progress exists.** Evaluation is the heart of the assessment process where most of the analysis occurs. Evaluation helps commanders determine what is working, determine what is not working, and gain insights into how to better accomplish the mission.

(2) Criteria in the forms of MOEs and MOPs aid in determining progress toward performing tasks, achieving objectives, and attaining end state conditions. MOEs help determine if a task is achieving its intended results. MOPs help determine if a task is completed properly. MOEs and MOPs are simply criteria—they do not represent the assessment itself. MOEs and MOPs require relevant information in the form of indicators for evaluation.

(3) MOEs are criteria used to assess changes in system behavior, capability, or operational environment that is tied to measuring the attainment of an end state, achievement of an objective, or creation of an effect. MOEs help measure changes in conditions, both positive and negative. MOEs help to answer the question, *Are we doing the right things?* MOEs are used at the strategic, operational, and tactical levels to assess the impact of military operations and measure changes in the operational environment, changes in system behavior, or changes to adversary capabilities. MOEs are based on observable or collectable indicators. Several indicators may make up an MOE, just like several MOEs may assist in assessing progress toward the achievement of an objective or moving toward a potential crisis or branch plan execution. Indicators provide evidence that a certain condition exists or

certain results have or have not been attained, and enable decision makers to direct changes to ongoing operations to ensure the mission remains focused on the end state. MOE assessment is implicit in the continuous nature of the JIPOE process. Upon the collection of indicators, JIPOE analysts can compare the baseline intelligence estimate used to inform the plan against the current situation to measure changes. MOEs are commonly found and tracked in formal assessment plans. Examples of MOEs for the objective *provide a safe and secure environment* may include:

    (a) Increase/decrease in insurgent activity.

    (b) Increase/decrease in reporting of insurgent activity to host-nation security forces.

    (c) Increase/decrease in civilian injuries involving mines and unexploded ordnance.

    (d) Attitude/opinion/behavioral changes in selected populations.

    (e) Changes in media portrayal of events.

    (4) MOPs are criteria used to assess friendly actions that are tied to measuring task accomplishment. MOPs help to answer questions such as *Was the action taken?* or *Were the tasks completed to standard?* A MOP confirms or denies that a task has been properly performed. MOPs are commonly found and tracked at all levels in execution matrixes. MOPs are also heavily used to evaluate training. MOPs help to answer the question, *Are we doing things right?*

    (5) In general, operations consist of a series of collective tasks sequenced in time, space, and purpose to accomplish missions. The current operations cells use MOPs in execution matrixes and running estimates to track completed tasks. Evaluating task accomplishment using MOPs is relatively straightforward and often results in a *yes* or *no* answer. Examples of MOPs include:

    (a) Route X cleared.

    (b) Generators delivered, are operational, and secured at Villages A, B, and C.

    (c) $15,000 spent for schoolhouse completion.

    (d) Aerial dissemination of 60,000 military information support leaflets over Village D.

    (e) Completed 15 media engagements.

    (f) Sent 35 press releases.

    (6) In the context of assessments, an indicator is an item of information that provides insight into MOEs or MOPs. Indicators used to perform MOE analysis inform

changes to the operational environment, system behavior, or adversary capabilities. Indicators used to inform MOP assessments should consider the friendly force capabilities required to perform assigned tasks. This consideration enhances the nexus between MOP and FFIR to enable decision makers to direct changes in resources. The J-2 uses indicators to shape the collection effort as part of ISR synchronization. Indicators take the form of reports from subordinates, surveys and polls, and information requirements. Indicators help to answer the question, *What is the current status of this MOE or MOP?* A single indicator can inform multiple MOPs and MOEs. Examples of indicators for the MOE *decrease in insurgent activity* are:

        (a) Number of hostile actions per area each week.

        (b) Number of munitions caches found per area each week.

        (7) Evaluation includes analysis of why progress is, or is not, being made according to the plan. Commanders and staffs propose and consider possible causes. In particular, the question of whether changes in the situation can be attributed to friendly actions is addressed. Subject matter experts, both internal and external to the staff, are consulted on whether the correct underlying causes for specific changes in the situation have been identified. Assumptions identified in the planning process are challenged to determine if they are still valid.

        (8) **A key aspect of evaluation is determining variances**—the difference between the actual situation and what the plan forecasted the situation would be at the time or event. Based on the significance of the variances, the staff makes recommendations to the commander on how to adjust operations to accomplish the mission more effectively.

        (9) Evaluating includes considering whether the desired conditions have changed, are no longer achievable, or are not achievable through the current operational approach. This is done by continually challenging the key assumptions made when framing the problem. When an assumption is invalidated, then reframing may be in order.

d. **Recommending or Directing Action**

        (1) Monitoring and evaluating are critical activities; however, assessment is incomplete without recommending or directing action. Assessment may diagnose problems, but unless it results in recommended adjustments, its use to the commander is limited.

        (2) Based on the evaluation of progress, the staff brainstorms possible improvements to the plan and makes preliminary judgments about the relative merit of those changes. Staff members identify those changes possessing sufficient merit and provide them as recommendations to the commander or make adjustments within their delegated authority. Recommendations to the commander range from continuing the operation as planned, executing a branch, or making adjustments not anticipated. Making adjustments includes assigning new tasks to subordinates, reprioritizing support, adjusting the ISR plan, and significantly modifying the COA. Commanders integrate recommendations from the staff, subordinate commanders, and other partners with their personal assessment. From those

recommendations, they decide if and how to modify the operation to better accomplish the mission.

(3) Assessment diagnoses threats, suggests improvements to effectiveness, and reveals opportunities. The staff presents the results and conclusions of its assessments and recommendations to the commander as an operation develops. Just as the staff devotes time to analysis and evaluation, so too must it make timely, complete, and actionable recommendations. The chief of staff or executive officer ensures the staff completes its analyses and recommendations in time to affect the operation and for information to reach the commander when it is needed.

(4) When developing recommendations, the staff draws from many sources and considers its recommendations within the larger context of the operations. While several ways to improve a particular aspect of the operation might exist, some recommendations could impact other aspects of the operation. As with all recommendations, the staff should address any future implications.

3. Levels of War and Assessment

a. Assessment occurs at all levels and across the entire range of military operations. Even in operations that do not include combat, assessment of progress is just as important and can be more complex than traditional combat assessment. **As a general rule, the level at which a specific operation, task, or action is directed should be the level at which such activity is assessed.** To do this, JFCs and their staffs consider assessment ways, means, and measures during planning, preparation, and execution. This properly focuses assessment and collection at each level, reduces redundancy, and enhances the efficiency of the overall assessment process. See Figure D-1.

b. Assessment at the operational and strategic levels typically is broader than at the tactical level (e.g., combat assessment) and uses MOEs that support strategic and operational mission accomplishment. Strategic- and operational-level assessment efforts concentrate on broader tasks, effects, objectives, and progress toward the end state. Continuous assessment helps the JFC and joint force component commanders determine if the joint force is doing the right things to achieve objectives, not just doing things right. The JFC also can use MOEs to determine progress toward success in those operations for which tactical-level combat assessment ways, means, and measures do not apply.

c. Tactical-level assessment typically uses MOPs to evaluate **task accomplishment.** The results of tactical tasks are often physical in nature, but also can reflect the impact on specific functions and systems. Tactical-level assessment may include assessing progress by phase lines; neutralization of enemy forces; control of key terrain or resources; and security, relief, or reconstruction tasks. Assessment of results at the tactical level helps commanders determine operational and strategic progress, so JFCs must have a comprehensive, integrated assessment plan that links assessment activities and measures at all levels.

d. **Combat assessment** is an example of a tactical-level assessment and is a term that can encompass many tactical-level assessment actions. Combat assessment typically focuses

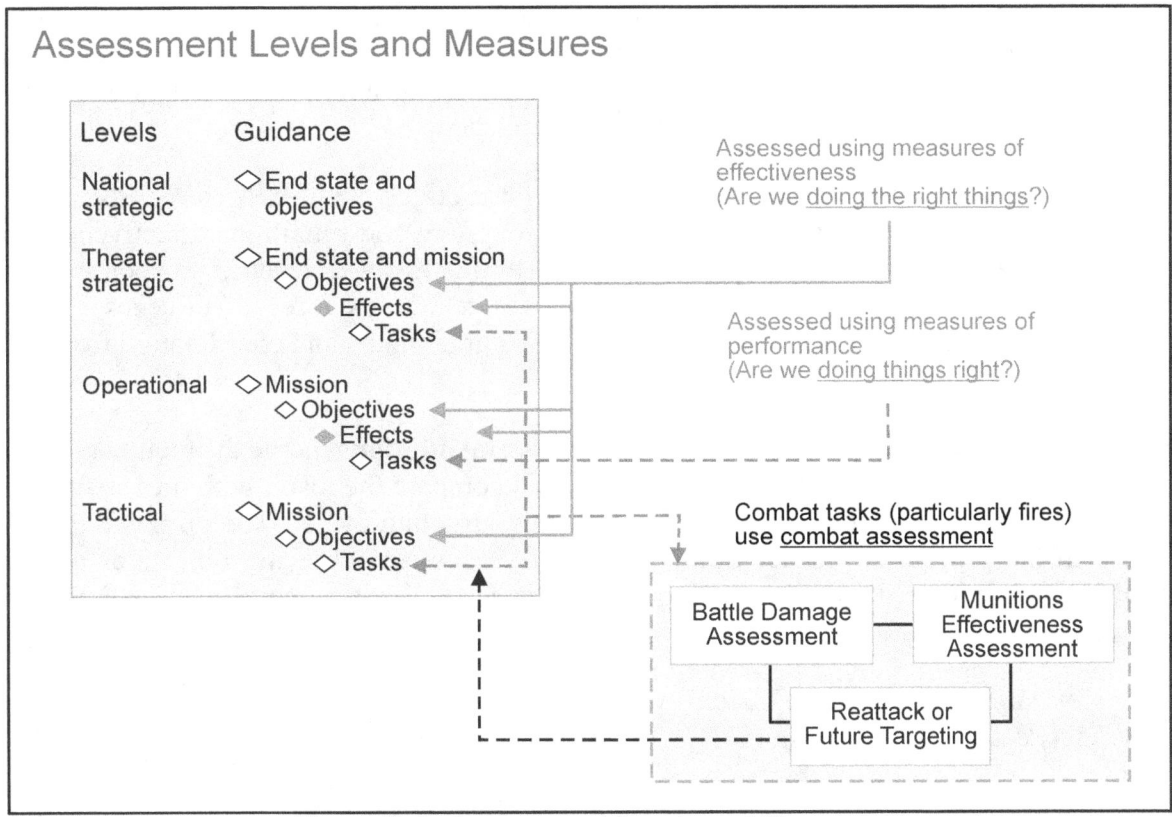

Figure D-1. Assessment Levels and Measures

on determining the results of weapons engagement (with both lethal and nonlethal capabilities), and thus is an important component of joint fires and the joint targeting process (see JP 3-60, *Joint Targeting*). **Combat assessment is composed of three related elements: battle damage assessment (BDA), munitions effectiveness assessment (MEA), and future targeting or reattack recommendations.** However, combat assessment methodology also can be applied by joint force functional and Service components to other tactical tasks not associated with joint fires (e.g., disaster relief delivery assessment, relief effectiveness assessment, and future relief recommendations).

(1) **BDA** is an estimate resulting from the application of lethal or nonlethal capabilities. BDA is composed of physical damage assessment, functional damage assessment, and target system assessment.

(a) **Physical damage assessment** is the estimate of the quantitative extent of physical damage (through munitions blast, fragmentation, and/or fire damage effects) to a target resulting from the application of force. This assessment is based upon observed or interpreted damage.

(b) **Functional damage assessment** is the estimate of the effects of force to degrade or destroy the functional or operational capability of the target to perform its intended mission and on the level of success in achieving operational objectives established against the target. This assessment is based upon all-source information, and includes an estimation of the time required for recuperation or replacement of the target function.

(c) **Target system assessment** is the broad assessment of the overall impact and effectiveness of the full spectrum of military force applied against the operation of an enemy target system or total combat effectiveness (including significant subdivisions of the system) relative to the operational objectives established.

(2) **MEA** is conducted concurrently and interactively with BDA, the assessment of the military force applied in terms of the weapon system and munitions effectiveness to determine and recommend any required changes to the methodology, tactics, weapon system, munitions, fusing, and/or weapon delivery parameters to increase force effectiveness. MEA is primarily the responsibility of operations with required inputs and coordination from the intelligence community.

(3) **Future targeting and reattack recommendations** merge the picture of what was done (BDA) with how it was done (MEA) and compare the result with predetermined MOEs that were developed at the start of the joint targeting cycle. The purposes of this phase in the process are to determine degree of success in achieving objectives and to formulate any required follow-up action, or to indicate readiness to move on to new tasks in the path to achieving the overall JFC objectives.

For more information on BDA and MEA, see JP 3-60, Joint Targeting, and Defense Intelligence Agency publication DI-2820-4-03, Battle Damage Assessment (BDA) Quick Guide.

4. Assessment Process and Measures

a. **The assessment process uses MOPs to evaluate task performance at all levels of war and MOEs to determine progress of operations toward achieving objectives.** MOEs help answer questions such as *Are we doing the right things, are our actions producing the desired effects, or are alternative actions required?* MOPs are closely associated with task accomplishment. MOPs help answer questions such as *Was the action taken, were the tasks completed to standard, or how much effort was involved?* Well-devised measures can help the commanders and staffs understand the causal relationship between specific tasks and desired effects.

(1) **MOEs assess changes in system behavior, capability, or operational environment.** They measure the attainment of an end state, achievement of an objective, or creation of an effect; they do not measure task performance. These measures typically are more subjective than MOPs and can be crafted as either qualitative or quantitative. MOEs can be based on quantitative measures to reflect a trend and show progress toward a measurable threshold. The Measuring Progress in Conflict Environments Framework provides good examples of MOEs that have been vetted by the interagency, cover all five sectors of stability operations, and address both drivers of conflict and institutional performance in dealing with them. Some examples include:

(a) Perception among identity group members that loss of power (e.g., to other identity groups) will eliminate the prospect of regaining power in the future.

(b) Dispute resolution mechanisms exist and are being used to clarify or resolve remaining vital issues among parties to the conflict.

(c) Percent of military-aged population that expresses an inclination to support or join a violent faction (by identity group).

(d) Degree to which members of formerly warring factions and competing identity groups can travel freely in areas controlled by their rivals.

(e) Detainees/prisoners are subjected to torture, cruel, or inhuman treatment, beatings or psychological pressures (by identity group).

(f) Safe and sustainable return of displaced persons and refugees to former neighborhoods.

(g) Estimated percentage of gross domestic product accounted for by illicit economic transactions.

(h) Level of public satisfaction with electrical power delivery (by identity group and region).

(i) Perception that ethnic identity polarizes society (by identity group).

(j) Perception of heads of households that, under normal conditions, they are able to meet their food needs either by growing foodstuffs/raising livestock or purchasing food on the market.

(2) **MOPs measure task performance.** They are generally quantitative, but also can apply qualitative attributes to task accomplishment. MOPs are used in most aspects of combat assessment, since it typically seeks specific, quantitative data or a direct observation of an event to determine accomplishment of tactical tasks. But MOPs have relevance for noncombat operations as well (e.g., tons of relief supplies delivered or noncombatants evacuated). MOPs also can be used to measure operational and strategic tasks, but the type of measurement may not be as precise or as easy to observe.

b. The assessment process and related measures should be **relevant, measurable, responsive,** and **resourced** so there is no false impression of accomplishment. Quantitative measures can be helpful in this regard.

(1) **Relevant.** MOPs and MOEs should be relevant to the task, effect, operation, operational environment, end state, and commander's decisions. This criterion helps avoid collecting and analyzing information that is of no value to a specific operation. It also helps ensure efficiency by eliminating redundant efforts.

(2) **Measurable.** Assessment measures should have qualitative or quantitative standards they can be measured against. To effectively measure change, a baseline measurement should be established prior to execution to facilitate accurate assessment throughout the operation. Both MOPs and MOEs can be quantitative or qualitative in nature,

but meaningful quantitative measures are preferred because they are less susceptible to subjective interpretation.

(3) **Responsive.** Assessment processes should detect situation changes quickly enough to enable effective response by the staff and timely decisions by the commander. The JFC and staff should consider the time required for an action or actions to produce desired results within the operational environment and develop indicators that can respond accordingly. Many actions directed by the JFC require time to implement and may take even longer to produce a measurable result.

(4) **Resourced.** To be effective, assessment must be adequately resourced. Staffs should ensure that resource requirements for data collection efforts and analysis are built into plans and monitored. Effective assessment can help avoid both duplication of tasks and unnecessary actions, which in turn can help preserve combat power.

c. Commanders and staffs derive relevant assessment measures during the planning process and reevaluate them continuously throughout preparation and execution. They consider assessment measures during mission analysis, refine these measures in the JFC's planning guidance and in commander's and staff's estimates, wargame the measures during COA development, and include MOEs and MOPs in the approved plan or order. An integrated data collection management plan is critical to the success of the assessment process and should encompass all available tactical, theater, and national intelligence sources.

d. Just as tactical tasks relate to operational- and strategic-level tasks, effects, and objectives, there is a relationship between assessment measures. By monitoring available information and using MOEs and MOPs as assessment tools during planning, preparation, and execution, commanders and staffs determine progress toward creating desired effects, achieving objectives, and attaining the military end state, and modify the plan as required. Well-devised MOPs and MOEs, supported by effective information management, help the commanders and staffs understand the linkage between specific tasks, the desired effects, and the JFC's objectives and end state.

APPENDIX E
FLEXIBLE DETERRENT OPTIONS

1. General

FDOs are preplanned, deterrence-oriented actions carefully tailored to send the right signal and influence an adversary's actions. They can be established to dissuade actions before a crisis arises or to deter further aggression during a crisis. FDOs are developed **for each instrument of national power—diplomatic, informational, military, and economic—but they are most effective when used to combine the influence across instruments of national power.** FDOs facilitate early strategic decision making, rapid de-escalation, and crisis resolution by laying out a wide range of interrelated response paths. ***Examples of FDOs*** for each instrument of national power are listed in Figures E-1 through E-4. **Key goals of FDOs are:**

a. Deter aggression through communicating the strength of US commitments to treaty obligations and regional peace and stability.

b. Confront the adversary with unacceptable costs for their possible aggression.

c. Isolate the adversary from regional neighbors and attempt to split the adversary coalition.

d. Rapidly improve the military balance of power in the AOR without precipitating armed response from the adversary.

Examples of Requested Diplomatic Flexible Deterrent Options

- Alert and introduce special teams (e.g., public diplomacy).
- Reduce international diplomatic ties.
- Increase cultural group pressure.
- Promote democratic elections.
- Initiate noncombatant evacuation procedures.
- Identify the steps to peaceful resolution.
- Restrict activities of diplomatic missions.
- Prepare to withdraw or withdraw US embassy personnel.
- Take actions to gain support of allies and friends.
- Restrict travel of US citizens.
- Gain support through the United Nations.
- Demonstrate international resolve.

Figure E-1. Examples of Requested Diplomatic Flexible Deterrent Options

```
Examples of Requested Informational
Flexible Deterrent Options

  • Impose sanctions on communications systems and intelligence, surveillance, and
    reconnaissance (ISR) technology transfer.

  • Protect friendly communications systems and ISR assets (computer network
    defense, operations security, information assurance).

  • Increase public awareness of the problem and potential for conflict.

  • Make public declarations of nonproliferation policy.

  • Increase communication systems and ISR processing and transmission
    capability.

  • Interrupt satellite downlink transmissions.

  • Publicize violations of international law.

  • Publicize increased force presence, joint exercises, military capability.

  • Increase informational efforts:

       ○ Influence adversary decision makers (political, military, and social).
       ○ Promote mission awareness.
       ○ Increase measures directed at the opponent's military forces.

  • Implement meaconing, interference, jamming, and intrusion of enemy
    informational assets.

  • Maintain an open dialogue with the news media.

  • Take steps to increase US public support.

  • Ensure consistency of strategic communication messages.
```

Figure E-2. Examples of Requested Informational Flexible Deterrent Options

2. **Description of Deterrent Actions**

   a. **Deterrence is the prevention of an adversary's undesired action.** Deterrence is a state of mind brought about by the adversary's perception of three factors: being denied the expected benefits of his action; having excessive costs imposed for taking the action; and that restraint is an acceptable alternative. These effects are the results of a synchronized and coordinated use of all instruments of national power. **FDOs are deterrent-oriented response options** that are requested and may be initiated based on evaluation of indicators of heightened regional tensions.

   b. **FDOs serve two basic purposes. First,** they assist in bringing an issue to early resolution before armed conflict by sending an appropriate message to belligerent parties. **Second,** they position US forces in a manner that facilitates implementation of OPLANs/CONPLANs or OPORDs if hostilities are unavoidable. They also facilitate an early decision by laying out a wide range of interrelated response paths that are carefully tailored to avoid the classic response of "too much, too soon, or too little, too late." They are

Examples of Requested Military
Flexible Deterrent Options

- Increase readiness posture of in-place forces.
- Upgrade alert status.
- Increase intelligence, surveillance, and reconnaissance.
- Initiate or increase show-of-force actions.
- Increase training and exercise activities.
- Increase defense support to public diplomacy.
- Increase information operations.
- Deploy forces into or near the potential operational area.
- Increase active and passive protection measures.

Figure E-3. Examples of Requested Military Flexible Deterrent Options

initiated before and after unambiguous warning. **Although they are not intended to place US forces in jeopardy if deterrence fails, risk analysis should be an inherent step in determining which FDO to use and how and when that FDO should be used.** FDOs have the advantage of rapid de-escalation if the situation precipitating the FDO changes.

3. Flexible Deterrent Option Implementation

The President or SecDef directs FDO implementation, and the specific FDO or combination selected will vary with each situation. Their use will be consistent with the US

Examples of Requested Economic
Flexible Deterrent Options

- Freeze or seize real property in the US where possible.
- Freeze monetary assets in the US where possible.
- Freeze international assets where possible.
- Encourage US and international financial institutions to restrict or terminate financial transactions.
- Encourage US and international corporations to restrict transactions.
- Embargo goods and services.
- Enact trade sanctions.
- Enact restrictions on technology transfer.
- Cancel or restrict US-funded programs.
- Reduce security assistance programs.

Figure E-4. Examples of Requested Economic Flexible Deterrent Options

NSS. FDOs can be used individually, in packages, sequentially, or concurrently, but **are primarily designed to be used in groups that maximize integrated results from all the diplomatic, informational, military, and economic instruments of national power.** It is imperative that extensive, continuous coordination occurs with interagency and multinational partners to maximize the impact of FDOs.

APPENDIX F
FLEXIBLE RESPONSE OPTIONS

1. General

A flexible response option (FRO) is an operational to strategic-level concept of operation that is easily scalable, provides military options, and facilitates rapid decision making by national leaders in response to heightened terrorist threats or actual terrorist attacks against the US homeland or US interests.

2. Description of Flexible Response Options

a. The basic purpose of FROs is to preempt and/or respond to terrorist attacks against the US and/or US interests. FROs are intended to facilitate early decision making by developing a wide range of prospective actions carefully tailored to produce desired effects, congruent with national security policy objectives. A FRO is the venue in which various military capabilities are made available to the President and SecDef, with actions appropriate and adaptable to existing circumstances, in reaction to any terrorist threat or attack.

b. FROs are used to address both specific, transregional threats and nonspecific, heightened threats. FROs are operations that are first and foremost designed to preempt enemy attacks, but also provide DOD the necessary planning framework to fast-track requisite authorities and approvals necessary to address dynamic and evolving terrorist threats.

c. FROs are developed as directed by the CJCS and maintained by the CCMDs to address the entire range of possible terrorist threats. FROs should support both long-term regional and national security policy objectives. Initially, FROs are developed pre-crisis by CCMDs, based on intelligence collection and analysis and critical factors analysis, and then modified and/or refined or developed real-time. FRO content guidelines are listed in Figure F-1.

d. FROs should not be limited to current authorities or approvals; rather, planning should be based on DOD's capabilities (overt, clandestine, low visibility, and covert) to achieve objectives, independent of risk. While entirely unconstrained planning is not realistic or prudent, the intent of FROs is to provide national leaders a full range of military options to include those prohibited in the current operational environment.

e. FROs are divided into three broad categories. These planning categories determine the scope of FRO planning efforts:

(1) Interdict terrorist organization to deny a subgroup, affiliate, and ally or network the capability to function with global reach, access, and effectiveness.

(2) Interdict safe haven to deny the enemy and associated networks specific geographic safe haven and/or support bases.

Flexible Response Option Content Guidelines

- Identify critical enemy vulnerabilities and specific targets for each major vulnerability
- Operations objectives
- Desired effects
- Essential tasks
- Major forces and capabilities required
- Concept of deployment
- Concept of employment to include phasing, timing, major decision points, and essential interagency supporting actions
- Concept for sustainment
- Estimated time to accomplish objectives
- Military end state(s)
- Additional resources or shifts essential for execution
- Additional recommended changes in authority and approval required
- Additional risks associated with execution and mitigation approaches

Figure F-1. Flexible Response Option Content Guidelines

(3) Interdict enemy critical network capabilities to deny the enemy specific functional capabilities.

f. **Flexible Response Option Characteristics**

(1) Follows a standardized framework to provide military options to national leadership.

(2) Military CONOPS at the operational or strategic-level.

(3) Preplanned or developed real-time.

(4) Provides a *start point* for iterative planning.

(5) Scalable based on situation and SecDef guidance.

(6) Focused on enemy critical vulnerabilities.

(7) Nested with national and regional strategy.

(8) Deliberate and synchronized expansion of the campaign against transnational terrorist organizations rather than disparate actions.

(9) A combination of direct and indirect actions.

(10) Decisive action or set conditions for follow-on operations.

---

3. Flexible Response Option Implementation

a. The planning engine for FROs is the deliberate planning process. In the event that SecDef directs the execution of a FRO, the supported CCMD, would initiate planning to determine existing options or develop new ones for SecDef and to enable acquisition of authorities and approvals necessary to conduct appropriate military operations to disrupt terrorist threats and/or respond to attacks on the US or US interests.

b. **Applications of Flexible Response Options**

(1) **Disrupt** is used to address both specific, transregional threats and nonspecific, heightened threats. Disrupt options are lethal and nonlethal operations that are first and foremost designed to preempt enemy attacks, but also provide DOD the necessary planning framework to fast track requisite authorities and approvals necessary to address dynamic and evolving threats.

(a) **Specific Threats.** Disrupt contingencies are triggered by specific indications and warnings or identified attack plans spanning more than one AOR or otherwise requiring global synchronization, as determined by JS.

(b) **Nonspecific Threats.** Disrupt is also triggered by general indications of increased terrorist threats, in the absence of actionable intelligence against a specific threat. Periodically, intelligence assessments indicate that enemy strength has increased despite current operations or terrorist attack preparations have progressed to the point that national leadership is willing to consider additional operations, actions, and activities.

(2) **Response.** Respond contingencies are triggered as a result of a successful or unsuccessful attack against the US, or its interests. If efforts fail to preempt, disrupt, or defeat a major attack, respond options rapidly provide flexible and scalable options to respond with global operations against the entire scope of the enemy (see Figure F-2). The following are examples of FRO scalability. Operations in each category can be executed individually, concurrently, or sequentially.

(a) **Rapid Response.** Priority of effort is to demonstrate US resolve through speed of action. Rapid responses would most likely be unilateral strikes, raids, computer network operations, and IO against known targets with low collateral damage.

(b) **Limited Response.** Priority of effort is to attack terrorist organizations directly attributed to the attack. The goal of this category is to maximize perceived legitimacy of US response. Limited response demonstrates restraint and is more likely to garner international cooperation. Disadvantages may include uncertain timeline due to requirement for attribution and continued vulnerability to networks not directly associated with the current attack.

Flexible Response Option Scalability

Rapid Response Demonstrate Resolve	**Limited Response** Target Those Directly Responsible	**Decisive Response** Defeat Violent Extremist Organization
Priority of Effort: • Speed	**Priority of Effort:** • Legitimacy via attribution	**Priority of Effort:** • Direct attack on enemy center of gravity
Advantages: • Demonstrate resolve • Least impact of current operations	**Advantages:** • Response aimed directly at those responsible • Demonstrates restraint • International cooperation more likely	**Advantages:** • Proactive vice reactive • Targets critical enemy vulnerabilities • Greater impact on enemy
Disadvantages: • Limited strategic effect • More likely lethal in nature • Probable negative international reaction • More likely unilateral action	**Disadvantages:** • Uncertain timeline • Persistent operation may require reallocation of resources • US remains vulnerable to other extremist organization elements	**Disadvantages:** • Potential to destabilize region of focus • Perception of US overreaction • Higher risk • Unintended consequences

Figure F-2. Flexible Response Option Scalability

(c) **Decisive Response.** Priority of effort is to attack the enemy operational COG to achieve a long-term disruption of its operational capability. This category is proactive vice reactive and seeks greater long-term impact on the enemy network. Disadvantages may include perception of US overreaction and inadvertent spread of violent extremist ideology.

APPENDIX G
COURSE OF ACTION COMPARISON

The most common technique for COA comparison is the decision matrix, which uses evaluation criteria to determine the COA that has the highest probability of success based upon the evaluation criteria. COAs are not compared to each other directly. Each COA is considered independently and is compared with evaluation criteria. The CCDR may direct some of these criteria, but most criteria are developed by the JPG. These evaluation criteria will vary based on a number of factors, including the nature and scope of the campaign or contingency plan, being derived from elements of the CCDR's intent, or areas of expertise resident in the JPG. Below are examples of common methods.

1. Weighted Numerical Comparison Technique

a. The example below provides a numerical aid for differentiating COAs. Values reflect the relative advantages or disadvantages of each COA for each criterion selected. Certain criteria have been weighted to reflect greater value (Figures G-1 and G-2).

b. Determine the weight of each criterion based on its relative importance and the commander's guidance. The commander may give guidance that results in weighting certain criteria. The staff member responsible for a functional area scores each COA using those criteria. Multiplying the score by the weight yields the criterion's value. The staff member then totals all values. However, the staff member must be careful not to portray subjective conclusions as the results of quantifiable analysis. Comparing COAs by category is more accurate than comparing total scores.

(1) Criteria are those selected through the process described earlier.

(2) The criteria can be rated (or weighted). The most important criteria are rated with the highest numbers. Lesser criteria are weighted with progressively lower numbers.

(3) The highest number is best. The best criterion and the most advantageous COA ratings are those with the highest number. Values reflect the relative strengths and weaknesses of each COA.

(4) Each staff section does this separately, perhaps using different criteria on which to base the COA comparison. The staff then assembles and arrives at a consensus for the criterion and weights. The chief of staff or JTF deputy commander should approve the staff's recommendations concerning the criteria and weights to ensure completeness and consistency throughout the staff sections.

2. Non-Weighted Numerical Comparison Technique

The same as the previous method except the criteria are not weighted. Again, the highest number is best for each of the criteria.

Example Numerical Comparison

Criteria	Weight	COA 1		COA 2		COA 3	
		Rating	Product	Rating	Product	Rating	Product
Exploits maneuver	2	3	6	2	4	1	2
Attacks COGs	3	2	6	3	9	1	3
Integrates maneuver and interdiction	2	2	4	3	6	1	2
Exploits deception	2	1	2	2	4	3	6
Provides flexibility	2	1	2	3	6	2	4
CSS (best use of transportation)	1	3	3	2	2	1	1
Total		12		15		9	
Weighted total			23		31		18

- The joint force commander's intent explained that the most important criterion was "attacking the enemy's COGs." Therefore, assign a value of 3 for that criterion and lower numbers for other criteria that the staff devises (**this is the weighing criterion**).

- For attacking the enemy COGs, COA 2 was rated the best (with a number of 3). Therefore, COA 2 = 9, COA 1 = 6, and COA 3 = 3.

- After the relative COA **rating** is multiplied by the **weight** given each criterion and the product columns are added, COA 2 (with a score of 31) is rated the most appropriate according to the criteria used to evaluate it.

Legend

COA   course of action   COG   center of gravity   CSS   combat service support

Figure G-1. Example Numerical Comparison

Example #2 Course of Action Comparison Matrix Format

Evaluation Criterion	Weight	COA 1		COA 2		COA 3	
		Score	Weighted	Score	Weighted	Score	Weighted
Surprise	2	3	6	1.5	3	1.5	3
Risk	2	3	6	1	2	2	4
Flexibility	1	3	3	1.5	1.5	1.5	1.5
Retaliation	1	1.5	1.5	3	3	1.5	1.5
Damage to alliance	1	3	3	1.5	1.5	1.5	1.5
Legal basis	1	2	2	3	3	1	1
External support	1	3	3	2	2	1	1
Force protection	1	2.5	2.5	2.5	2.5	1	1
OPSEC	1	3	3	1.5	1.5	1.5	1.5
Total			30		20		16

Legend

COA   course of action   OPSEC   operations security

Figure G-2. Example #2 Course of Action Comparison Matrix Format

3. Narrative or Bulletized Descriptive Comparison of Strengths and Weaknesses or Advantages and Disadvantages

Summarize comparison of all COAs by analyzing strengths and weaknesses or advantages and disadvantages for each criterion. See Figures G-3 and G-4 for examples.

4. Plus/Minus/Neutral Comparison

Base this comparison on the broad degree to which selected criteria support or are reflected in the COA. This is typically organized as a table showing (+) for a positive influence, (0) for a neutral influence, and (–) for a negative influence. Figure G-5 is an example.

5. Descriptive Comparison

This is simply a description of advantages and disadvantages of each COA. See Figure G-4.

Criteria for Strengths and Weaknesses Example

	Criteria 1		Criteria 2		Criteria 3	
	Strengths	Weaknesses	Strengths	Weaknesses	Strengths	Weaknesses
COA 1	• •	• •	• •	• •	• •	• •
COA 2	Strengths • •	Weaknesses • •	Strengths • •	Weaknesses • •	Strengths • •	Weaknesses • •
COA 3	Strengths • •	Weaknesses • •	Strengths • •	Weaknesses • •	Strengths • •	Weaknesses • •

Legend

COA   course of action

Figure G-3. Criteria for Strengths and Weaknesses Example

Descriptive Comparison Example

	Criteria 1		Criteria 2		Criteria 3	
	Advantages	Disadvantages	Advantages	Disadvantages	Advantages	Disadvantages
COA 1	• •	• •	• •	• •	• •	• •
COA 2	Advantages • •	Disadvantages • •	Advantages • •	Disadvantages • •	Advantages • •	Disadvantages • •
COA 3	Advantages • •	Disadvantages • •	Advantages • •	Disadvantages • •	Advantages • •	Disadvantages • •

Legend

COA   course of action

Figure G-4. Descriptive Comparison Example

Plus/Minus/Neutral Comparison Example

Criteria	COA 1	COA 2
Casualty estimate	+	−
Casualty evacuation routes	−	+
Suitable medical facilities	0	0
Flexibility	+	−

Legend

COA   course of action

Figure G-5. Plus/Minus/Neutral Comparison Example

Intentionally Blank

APPENDIX H
GLOBAL FORCE MANAGEMENT

1. Global Force Management Processes

GFM is a compilation of three related processes: assignment, allocation, and apportionment used to align US forces.

a. **Assignment.** Title 10, USC, Sections 161, 162, and 167 outline force assignment guidance and requirements. The President, through the UCP, instructs SecDef to document his direction for assigning forces in the Forces for Unified Commands Memorandum (Forces For). The Secretaries of the Military Departments shall assign forces under their jurisdiction to unified and specified CCMDs to perform missions assigned to those commands. Such assignment defines the combatant command (command authority) (COCOM) and shall be made as directed by SecDef, including the command to which forces are to be assigned. Assignment is further explained in the biennial GFMIG. Included within Section 2 of the GFMIG are the annually updated Forces For tables. During odd-numbered years, the Forces For is published separately and posted on the JS J-8 Web site. Forces not assigned to a CCDR are retained under the Secretary of the Military Department and are commonly referred to as "Service retained" or "unassigned."

b. **Allocation**

(1) Pursuant to Title 10, USC, Section 162, "[a] force assigned to a combatant command...may be transferred from the command to which it is assigned only by authority of SecDef; and under procedures prescribed by the Secretary and approved by the President." Under this authority, SecDef allocates forces between CCDRs. When transferring forces, the Secretary will specify the command relationship the gaining commander will exercise and the losing commander will relinquish.

(2) Decisions by SecDef to allocate forces are published within the four annexes of the CJCS GFMAP. The GFMAP directs the JFPs to publish a GFMAP Annex Schedule that serves as the DEPORD directing force providers to deploy forces at the specified dates. The GFMAP also allows force providers some leeway in determining which unit will deploy and on the ordered LADs that the force provider must deploy to account for realities, such as TPFDD refinement, based on transportation analysis or minor operational adjustments by the CCDR, based on operational necessities.

(a) Annex A is Conventional Forces with Services as the JFPs.

(b) Annex B is SOF with United States Special Operations Command as the JFP.

(c) Annex C is Mobility Forces with USTRANSCOM as the JFP.

(d) Annex D is Joint Individual Augmentation (JIA) with Services as the JFPs.

(3) Since most operational forces are assigned, each **allocation** is a decision to take a force from one CCDR and deploy it to another. Each allocation has risks that must be weighed to balance the operational necessity of deploying the force with the risk to the force provider. These risks also include the financial cost and the stress on the Service and Service men and women. The allocation decision process is necessarily centralized with SecDef making the final decisions. When unassigned forces are allocated to a CCDR, they are normally attached. When assigned forces are allocated from one CCDR to another, the gaining CCDR is usually tasked to exercise operational control (OPCON), for the time the unit will be in the gaining CCDR's control. The providing CCDR relinquishes OPCON or tactical control (TACON) of that unit during its deployment and resumes OPCON or TACON following the deployment. The providing CCDR retains COCOM of the unit. Specific command relationships are specified in the CJCS GFMAP and the Annex Schedule.

(4) Allocation is divided into emergent and rotational:

(a) **Emergent.** The emergent process begins with the CCDR identifying a force or individual requirement that cannot be met using available assigned forces or forces already allocated. The CCDR documents each force requirement, usually one unit per requirement. The force requirement contains information of what type of force is needed as well as the operational risk if the force is not provided. Each requirement is validated by the CCDR and assigned a force tracking number (FTN). Each FTN is forwarded electronically to JS for validation. The force request is also transmitted to JS with a RFF message that requests sourcing of one or more FTNs. JS validates each force request, provides priority based on the GEF and sourcing guidance, and assigns one of the three JFPs to provide a recommended sourcing solution. At the direction of JS, the JFPs staff the force requirement with the Services via their assigned Service components to determine the recommended sourcing options and force provider risk. The JFP generates a recommended sourcing solution, drafts a modification to their respective GFMAP annex, staffs the draft annex, and forwards the recommendations with the operational and force provider risks to JS. JS forwards the draft GFMAP annex modification to the CCMDs, Services, CSAs, other DOD agencies, and OSD and briefs the solutions through the CJCS to endorse, and to SecDef for a decision. For some contentious issues, the Global Force Management Board (GFMB) may meet to review and endorse sourcing recommendations prior to the CJCS. Once SecDef decides to allocate, JS publishes the modification to the GFMAP annex, and the JFP publishes the GFMAP Annex Schedule.

<u>1.</u> **Joint Individual Augmentation Sourcing.** The JIA execution sourcing allocation process mirrors the force sourcing process with the following exceptions: the format and information requirements of the JIA request are different and a distinct automated data processing tool, Electronic Joint Manpower and Personnel System, is used to track and account for the JIA Service member. When a CCDR is directed to create a JTF headquarters, the CCDR creates a joint manning document (JMD), sourced as much as possible from CCMD resources, that is forwarded to JS J-1 for JIA sourcing approval. A CCDR message requesting JIA modification to an existing JMD is called an out-of-cycle change request. JS coordinates directly with the Services vice their assigned Service components for identifying recommended sourcing solutions for JIA requirements. The

Service may delegate the responsibility for generating JIA sourcing recommendations to the appropriate assigned Service component.

2. **Allocation and the Interagency Process.** Although requests for interagency capabilities are not usually part of the allocation process, the interagency process is detailed in JP 3-08, *Interorganizational Coordination During Joint Operations.* There are cases in which a CCDR will request a capability via the allocation process and a non-DOD agency appears to offer the best solution. In these cases, JS serves as the JFP to coordinate between the agencies. The CJCS GFMAP annex and JFP GFMAP Annex Schedules are used to relay the sourcing solution back to the JPEC. However, SecDef does not have authority to direct people and capabilities of other USG departments and agencies.

(b) **Rotational.** The rotational process begins with a PLANORD from JS directing the CCDRs to submit force and JIA requirements for an entire fiscal year (FY); this process normally begins two years prior to the start of the FY required. The rotational process mirrors the emergent process with the rotational submission being the first RFF for the FY. As there are many force requirements, each with its own FTN in the rotational submissions, many of the steps of the emergent process are done via conferences. The number of requests being staffed simultaneously also necessitates some changes in the staffing process, but the force requests sourcing recommendations, to include risk, are identical. The GFMB meets to endorse the JFP rotational sourcing recommendations, and the first GFMAP annexes produced for the FY are called the base order.

(5) During the allocation process, the JFP collaboratively determines sourcing recommendations. Execution sourced forces are forces recommended and identified by JFPs, assisted by their Service components (who are responsible for coordinating with their Services). The recommended sourcing solution is reviewed through the GFM allocation process and becomes sourced when approved by SecDef for the execution of an approved operation or potential/imminent execution of an OPLAN. The GFMAP annex and GFMAP Annex Schedule specify the ordered force provider. The GFMAP allows the force provider and JFP some flexibility in identifying the appropriate unit for deployment. Execution sourcing solutions are grouped into five types.

(a) **Standard Force Solution.** A mission ready, joint capable force with associated table of organization and equipment executing its core mission.

(b) **Joint Force/Capability Solution.** Joint sourcing encompasses Services providing a force/capability in place of another Service's core mission. As in a standard force solution, the capability is performing its core mission.

(c) **In Lieu Of (ILO).** ILO sourcing is an overarching sourcing methodology that provides alternative force sourcing solutions when preferred force sourcing options are not available. An ILO force/capability is a standard force, including associated table of organization and equipment, that is deployed/employed to execute missions and tasks outside its core competencies.

(d) **Ad Hoc.** An ad hoc capability is consolidating individuals and equipment from various commands/Services and forming a deployable/employable entity, properly manned, trained, and equipped to meet the supported CCDR's requirements.

(e) **Joint Individual Augmentation.** An unfunded temporary manpower requirement (or a Service member filling an unfunded temporary manpower position) identified on a supported CCDR JMD to augment JTF staff operations during a contingency. JIA fill task force headquarters requirements. Tactical level deployments are not appropriate for JIA sourcing. Sourcing by JIA is meant to be the last method for obtaining joint manpower for positions.

More detailed description of force requirements can be found in the Annual CJCS Rotational Forces Request PLANORD. *The* CJCS Annual JFP PLANORD *contains details of the staffing process and requirements for force recommendations.*

Specifications for RFFs can be found in the CJCSM 3122.01 series volumes. The staffing process is detailed in the Joint Staff Force Sourcing Business Rules *and* Secretary of Defense Operations Book *process. The JIA sourcing process is explained in CJCSI 1301.01C,* Individual Augmentation Procedures, *and the* Joint Staff Individual Augmentation Business Rules.

c. **Apportionment.** Apportionment is the distribution of forces and capabilities as a starting point for planning. Pursuant to Title 10, USC, Section 153, "The CJCS shall be responsible for preparing strategic plans, including plans which conform with resource levels projected by SecDef to be available for the period of time for which the plans are to be effective." Pursuant to the JSCP, "apportioned forces are types of combat and related support forces provided to CCDRs as a starting point for planning purposes only." Forces apportioned for planning purposes may not be those allocated for execution. The CJCS approves force apportionment based on SecDef guidance in the GEF. The apportionment tables are contained in Chapter 4 of the GFMIG and are utilized to determine apportioned forces, starting with assigned forces and then subtracting the number of forces allocated to the high-priority operations (global demand). The result is the number of apportioned forces, which is published in the apportionment tables of the GFMIG. Apportioned forces are a quantity of a given type of force. During odd-numbered years, the apportionment tables are published separately and posted on the JS J-8 Web site.

d. The three processes of assignment, allocation, and apportionment are related. Figure H-1 shows the entire DOD force pool (every military unit, Soldier, Sailor, Airman, and Marine). This force pool is further divided by assigned (Forces For) to a CCMD and unassigned (dashed black line). Most allocated forces come from the assigned operational forces, but in some instances, the Service may be directed to provide (allocate) forces from unassigned forces. Unassigned and assigned forces may also be used by the Service to meet Service institutional requirements. This is the reason the projected employed forces crosses the dashed line and extends into the institutional Service forces box. The CCDR to which forces are assigned often employs and deploys assigned forces. Since the CCDR already has COCOM, and OPCON is inherent in COCOM, the forces do not need to be allocated. As

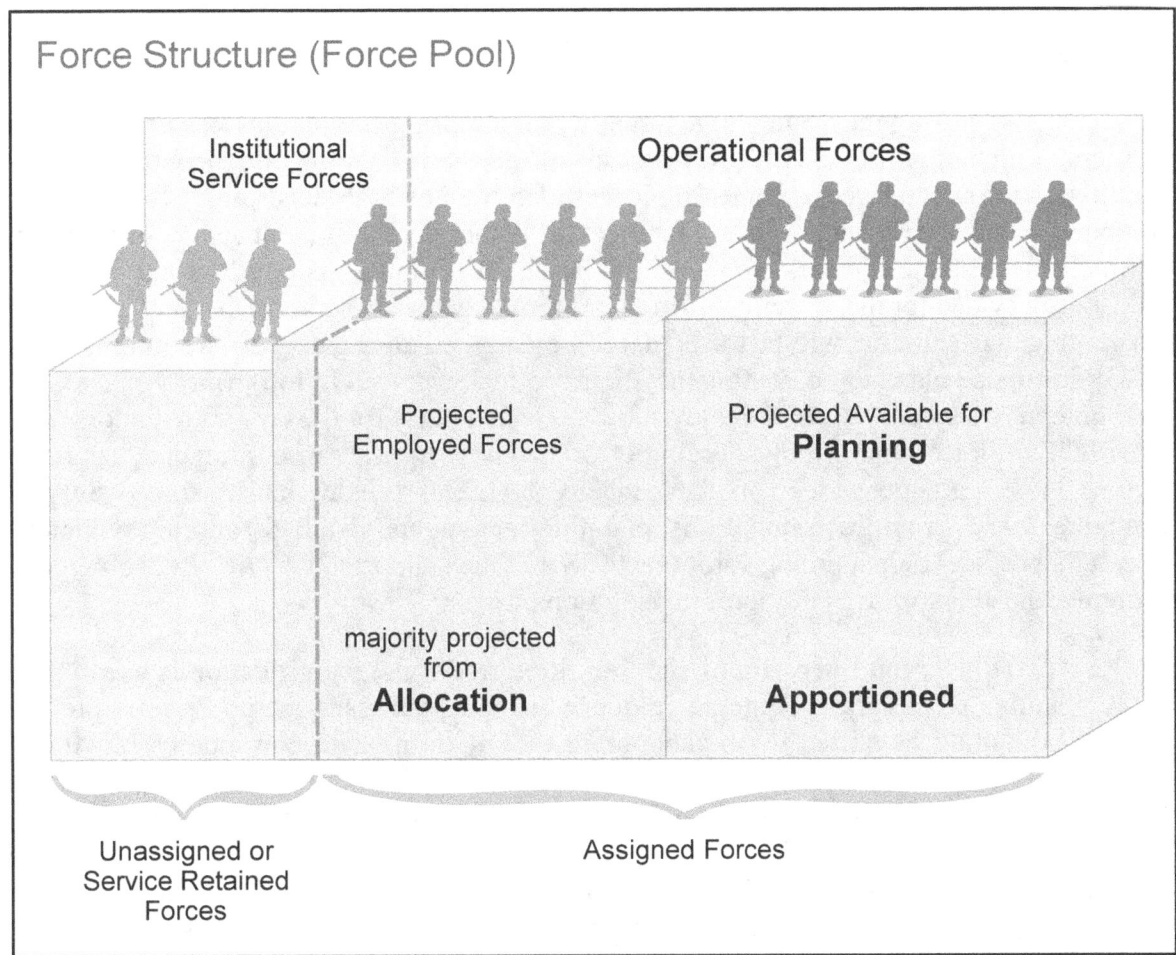

Figure H-1. Force Structure (Force Pool)

apportioned forces are calculated by subtracting global demand from the assigned forces, and the fact that some assigned forces are employed performing Service institutional missions or are performing missions for their assigned CCDR, the employed and apportioned forces in Figure H-1 overlap. CCDR force requests are constantly changing to respond to world events. To determine the projected employed forces, analysis of the current CCDR force requests must be conducted to project the number of employed forces in order to calculate the number of forces left that can reasonably be expected to be available or apportioned.

2. Force Sourcing and Global Force Management

a. **Force Sourcing.** Force sourcing is done by all commands and Services across the JPEC, and there are nuances at various stages. The definition of force sourcing covers a range of methodologies that identify units to meet a force requirement during planning, plan assessment, or execution. These methodologies include:

(1) **Execution Sourcing.** See allocation discussion on page H-1, paragraph 1b. It is the process of identifying forces recommended and identified by JFPs via their Service components and allocated by SecDef to meet CCDR force requirements. For execution sourcing during allocation, the JFP is the supported commander for the force planning steps

of identifying recommended sourcing solutions. All CCDRs, Services, CSAs, and other DOD agencies are in support.

(2) **Contingency Sourcing.** Usually begun during the plan assessment stage of deliberate planning, the CJCS may direct the JFPs to contingency source a plan. Contingency sourced forces are specific forces identified by JFPs, assisted by their Service components and the parent Services, that meet the planning requirement at a specified point in time. Because these forces are identified based on planning assumptions and planning guidance provided for the sourcing effort, there should be no expectation that forces sourced via contingency sourcing will be the actual forces sourced during execution sourcing. The CCDRs propose plans to be contingency sourced to JS (normally top-priority plans). JS recommends a schedule to contingency source selected plans for the GFMB to endorse and the CJCS to direct contingency sourcing efforts. The frequency of contingency sourcing actions is, in part, dependent on the capacity of the JFPs and their assigned Service components. JS provides assumptions, planning factors, and detailed sourcing guidance. The JFPs provide their sourcing solutions to JS and the supported CCDR. In contingency sourcing, the JFP approves the sourcing solutions.

(3) **Preferred Force Identification.** Preferred force identification is used in the entire planning process from strategic guidance through plan assessment. Preferred forces are forces that are identified by the supported CCDR in order to continue employment, sustainment, and transportation planning and to assess risk. These forces are planning assumptions only; they are not considered sourced units and do not indicate that these forces will be contingency or execution sourced. CCDR Service and functional components are encouraged to work with the JFPs and their Service components to make the best possible assumptions with respect to identifying preferred forces. The preferred forces identified for a plan by the CCDR should not be greater than the number of forces apportioned for planning unless the CJCS or his designee either grants permission or has provided amplifying planning guidance. The degree to which the CCDR is able to make good planning assumptions when identifying preferred forces determines the feasibility of a plan and may assist the JFP in identifying forces should the plan be designated for contingency sourcing or transitions to execution.

b. Throughout the planning process, planners consider the forces they have at their disposal to execute the plan and identify additional augmentation forces that are not apportioned or provided as a planning assumption by the CJCS (often referred to as allocated for planning).

3. **Force Planning and Global Force Management**

a. **Global Force Management During Deliberate Planning.** The apportionment tables provide the number of forces reasonably expected to be available for planning. These tables should be used as a beginning assumption in planning. As the plan is refined, there may be forces identified that are required above and beyond those apportioned. Those forces should be requested, as required, to be augmented, above the number apportioned for planning, or "augmentation forces." As the plan is briefed at the IPR level, leadership may approve planning to continue with the revised assumption of using the identified augmentation forces. These augmentation forces are then allocated for planning.

(1) Throughout COA and plan development, planners assess the plan as it is refined. To enable the assessments, the planners must assume that units are allocated to the identified plan force requirements and to enable plan assessments, planners identify preferred forces. As the plan is refined, the level of analysis used to identify preferred forces usually increases. Since contingency plans rely on a foundation of assumptions, if an event occurs that necessitates execution of a contingency plan, the planning assumptions have to be re-validated. The plan will usually enter a phase of CAP to adapt it to the realities surrounding the event rather than transitioning directly to execution.

(2) As a contingency plan is either approved or nearing approval, the CJCS may direct the JFPs to contingency source a plan to support the CJCS and/or SecDef strategic risk assessments. CCDRs may request contingency sourcing of specific plans. These requests are evaluated by the J-5, and a contingency sourcing schedule is presented to the GFMB. The GFMB endorses the schedule, and the CJCS orders the JFPs to contingency source specific plans per the schedule. (See paragraph 2a(2), "Contingency Sourcing.")

b. **Global Force Management During Crisis Action Planning.** The same planning steps that are used in deliberate planning are used in CAP, but the time to conduct the planning is constrained to the time available. Identification of preferred forces is done in CAP, just as in deliberate planning. Contingency sourcing is rarely used during CAP due to the time constraints involved; however, if time allows, the option exists for the CJCS to direct JFPs to contingency source a crisis action plan.

(1) In deliberate planning and CAP, the difference in force planning is the level of detail done with the force requirements for the plan. For deliberate planning, the number of planning assumptions prevents identifying the detailed force requirements needed by the JFPs to begin execution sourcing. During CAP, a known event has occurred and there are fewer assumptions. The focus of CAP is usually on transitioning to execution quickly. The detailed information requirements specified to support the execution sourcing process, either emergent or rotational, preclude completion until most assumptions are validated.

(2) CCDRs usually have a good understanding of the availability of their assigned forces. Availability entails the readiness of the unit, as well as the unit's time in the deployment cycle, and whether it meets SecDef dwell time requirements and whether the unit is already allocated to another mission. The supported CCDR generally reviews the force requirements for the contingency plan and conducts a review of assigned and previously allocated forces to determine if the mission can be done without requesting additional forces. If forces are already assigned and/or allocated that can perform the mission, the CCDR may direct those forces to perform the mission, within the constraints of the allocation authorities in the GFMAP. If additional forces are required, the CCDR will forward a RFF with all the details necessary for FTN(s), both electronically and by message RFF. The emergent force allocation process (discussed on page H-2) is the natural process for force requirements supporting CAP to follow.

(a) **Rotational Force Planning.** During execution, planning continues. The plan being executed is under constant review, and the next step or phase of the operation is under review. During Operation IRAQI FREEDOM and Operation ENDURING FREEDOM, SecDef directed that force requirements be reviewed and revalidated annually. This revalidation became the basis for rotational force planning. Today, all CCDRs review their ongoing operations and submit force requirements for the upcoming FY in their annual submission. The annual submission is, essentially, a consolidated RFF for the entire FY. CCDRs must review every operation in progress and determine what forces are needed for each operation. The CCDR must also project the force requirements for engagement and shaping operations to the maximum extent possible. To determine the operational requirements from ongoing operations, a way to organize this task is to review the forces currently conducting the operation and validate the continuing need for each force in the coming FY for the phase of the operation that the plan will be in. The electronic force requirement for the current unit is refined, validated, and submitted to JS to enter the rotational allocation process. It is important to link current forces and their force requirements because the JFPs must schedule units into the GFMAP Annex Schedule without interrupting the missions. Specifying the evolving missions and tasks for specific units is imperative so the Services can train, organize, and equip forces to be prepared to conduct those evolving missions. Once the annual force requirements have been submitted, newly identified, or refined, force requirements enter the emergent allocation process via a RFF.

(b) **Global Force Management in Exercise Planning and Sourcing and Executing.** RFFs to participate in exercises do not follow the same sourcing process as operational requests. Per CJCSI 3500.01, *Joint Training Policy and Guidance for the Armed Forces of the United States*, JFPs receive exercise force requests directly from the supported CCDRs. Supportability by JFPs and their Service components is determined, and the resulting sourcing solution is provided back directly to the supported CCDR. SecDef is not required to allocate forces for exercises, to include with other countries. Subsequent deployment of these exercise sourcing solutions is effected and tracked by the JFPs in concert with the supported CCDR. Under most circumstances, the GFMIG authorizes JFPs to transfer forces to support CCDR exercises (under TACON) and does not require a GFMAP modification to be approved by SecDef.

For detailed information and guidance on GFM and associated terminology, see SecDef's Global Force Management Implementation Guidance FY 2010–2011.

APPENDIX J
REFERENCES

The development of JP 5-0 is based on the following primary references:

1. General

    a. Title 10, USC, as amended.

    b. Title 22, USC, as amended.

    c. Unified Command Plan.

    d. National Security Strategy.

    e. Presidential Policy Directive–1, *Organization of the National Security Council System.*

2. Department of Defense

    a. National Defense Strategy.

    b. Secretary of Defense Memorandum, *Implementation of the Adaptive Planning Roadmap II*, March 2008.

    c. *Strategic Planning Guidance.*

    d. *Global Force Management Implementation Guidance FY 2004–2011.*

    e. *Guidance for Development of the Force.*

    f. *Guidance for Employment of the Force.*

    g. DOD Directive (DODD) 3000.06, *Combat Support Agencies.*

    h. DODD 3000.07, *Irregular Warfare.*

    i. DODD 5100.01, *Functions of the Department of Defense and Its Major Components.*

    j. DODD 5100.3, *Support of the Headquarters of Combatant and Subordinate Joint Commands.*

    k. DOD Instruction (DODI) 1100.22, *Policy and Procedures for Determining Workforce Mix.*

    l. DODI 3000.05, *Stability Operations.*

m. DODI 3020.41, *Contractor Personnel Authorized to Accompany the US Armed Forces.*

n. DODI 5000.68, *Security Force Assistance.*

4. Department of State

Briefing, Office of the Coordinator for Reconstruction and Stabilization, United States Department of State, *Post Conflict Reconstruction: Essential Tasks.*

5. Chairman of the Joint Chiefs of Staff

a. CJCSI 1301.01C, *Individual Augmentation Procedures.*

b. CJCSI 3100.01B, *Joint Strategic Planning System.*

c. CJCSI 3110.01G, *Joint Strategic Capabilities Plan.*

d. CJCSI 3141.01D, *Management and Review of Campaign and Contingency Plans.*

e. CJCSI 3401.01E, *Joint Combat Capability Assessment.*

f. CJCSI 3500.01, *Joint Training Policy and Guidance for the Armed Forces of the United States.*

g. CJCSI 5714.01C, *Policy for the Release of Joint Information.*

h. CJCSI 5715.01B, *Joint Staff Participation in Interagency Affairs.*

i. CJCSI 8501.01A, *Chairman of the Joint Chiefs of Staff, Combatant Commanders, and Joint Staff Participation in the Planning, Programming, Budgeting, and Execution System.*

j. CJCSM 3122.01A, *Joint Operation Planning and Execution System (JOPES), Volume I, Planning Policies and Procedures.*

k. CJCSM 3122.02C, *Joint Operation Planning and Execution System (JOPES), Volume III, Crisis Action Time-Phased Force and Deployment Data Development and Deployment Execution.*

l. CJCSM 3122.03C, *Joint Operation Planning and Execution System (JOPES), Volume II, Planning Formats.*

m. CJCSM 3150.01B, *Joint Reporting Structure General Instructions.*

n. *FY 10 Global Force Management Allocation Plan (GFMAP).*

o. National Military Strategy.

6. Joint Publications

    a. JP 1, *Doctrine for the Armed Forces of the United States.*

    b. JP 1-0, *Personnel Support to Joint Operations.*

    c. JP 1-02, *Department of Defense Dictionary of Military and Associated Terms.*

    d. JP 2-0, *Joint Intelligence.*

    e. JP 2-01.3, *Joint Intelligence Preparation of the Operational Environment.*

    f. JP 3-0, *Joint Operations.*

    g. JP 3-05, *Special Operations.*

    h. JP 3-08, *Interorganizational Coordination During Joint Operations.*

    i. JP 3-09, *Joint Fire Support.*

    j. JP 3-11, *Operations in Chemical, Biological, Radiological, and Nuclear (CBRN) Environments.*

    k. JP 3-13, *Information Operations.*

    l. JP 3-14, *Space Operations.*

    m. JP 3-16, *Multinational Operations.*

    n. JP 3-22, *Foreign Internal Defense.*

    o. JP 3-24, *Counterinsurgency Operations.*

    p. JP 3-30, *Command and Control for Joint Air Operations.*

    q. JP 3-33, *Joint Task Force Headquarters.*

    r. JP 3-34, *Joint Engineer Operations.*

    s. JP 3-35, *Deployment and Redeployment Operations.*

    t. JP 3-40, *Combating Weapons of Mass Destruction.*

    u. JP 3-60, *Joint Targeting.*

    v. JP 3-61, *Public Affairs.*

    w. JP 4-0, *Joint Logistics.*

    x. JP 4-01, *The Defense Transportation System.*

y. JP 4-02, *Health Service Support.*

z. JP 4-05, *Joint Mobilization Planning.*

aa. JP 4-06, *Mortuary Affairs.*

bb. JP 4-10, *Operational Contract Support.*

cc. JP 6-0, *Joint Communications System.*

7. **Service Publications**

a. Air Force Doctrine Document (AFDD) 2, *Operations and Organization.*

b. AFDD 3-1, *Air Warfare.*

c. AFDD 3-05, *Special Operations.*

d. AFDD 3-13, *Information Operations.*

e. AFDD 3-14, *Space Operations.*

f. AFDD 3-14.1, *Counterspace Operations.*

g. AFDD 3-17, *Air Mobility Operations.*

h. AFDD 3-70, *Strategic Attack.*

i. AFDD 6-0, *Command and Control.*

j. Marine Corps Doctrinal Publication (MCDP) 1-2, *Campaigning.*

k. MCDP 5, *Planning.*

l. Field Manual (FM) 3-0, *Operations.*

m. FM 3-07, *Stability Operations.*

n. FM 3-14, *Space in Support of Army Operations.*

o. FM 3-24, *Counterinsurgency.*

p. FM 5-0, *The Operations Process.*

q. FM 6-0, *Mission Command: Command and Control of Army Forces.*

r. Naval Doctrine Publication 1, *Naval Warfare.*

s. Navy Warfare Publication 3-62M, *Seabasing.*

t. *Army Mobilization and Operations Planning and Execution System.*

u. *Navy Capabilities and Mobilization Plan.*

v. *Marine Corps Capabilities Plan and Marine Corps Mobilization, Activation, Integration, Deactivation Plan.*

w. *Air Force War and Mobilization Plan.*

Intentionally Blank

APPENDIX K
ADMINISTRATIVE INSTRUCTIONS

1. User Comments

Users in the field are highly encouraged to submit comments on this publication to: Joint Staff J-7, Deputy Director, Joint and Coalition Warfighting, Joint and Coalition Warfighting Center, ATTN: Joint Doctrine Support Division, 116 Lake View Parkway, Suffolk, VA 23435-2697. These comments should address content (accuracy, usefulness, consistency, and organization), writing, and appearance.

2. Authorship

The lead agent and JS doctrine sponsor for this publication is the Director for Operational Plans and Joint Force Development (J-7).

3. Supersession

This publication supersedes JP 5-0, 26 December 2006, *Joint Operation Planning.*

4. Change Recommendations

a. Recommendations for urgent changes to this publication should be submitted:

    TO: JOINT STAFF WASHINGTON DC//J-7-JEDD//
               JOINT STAFF WASHINGTON DC//J-5-JOWPD//

Routine changes should be submitted electronically to the Deputy Director, Joint and Coalition Warfighting, Joint and Coalition Warfighting Center, Joint Doctrine Support Division and info the lead agent and the Director for Joint Force Development, J-7/JEDD.

b. When a Joint Staff directorate submits a proposal to the CJCS that would change source document information reflected in this publication, that directorate will include a proposed change to this publication as an enclosure to its proposal. The Services and other organizations are requested to notify the Joint Staff J-7 when changes to source documents reflected in this publication are initiated.

5. Distribution of Publications

Local reproduction is authorized, and access to unclassified publications is unrestricted. However, access to and reproduction authorization for classified JPs must be in accordance with DOD 5200.1-R, *Information Security Program.*

a. Joint Staff J-7 will not print copies of JPs for distribution. Electronic versions are available on JDEIS at https://jdeis.js.mil (NIPRNET), and http://jdeis.js.smil.mil (SIPRNET), and on the JEL at http://www.dtic.mil/doctrine (NIPRNET).

b. Only approved JPs and joint test publications are releasable outside the CCMDs, Services, and Joint Staff. Release of any classified JP to foreign governments or foreign nationals must be requested through the local embassy (Defense Attaché Office) to DIA, Defense Foreign Liaison/IE-3, 200 MacDill Blvd., Joint Base Anacostia-Bolling, Washington, DC 20340-5100.

c. JEL CD-ROM. Upon request of a joint doctrine development community member, the Joint Staff J-7 will produce and deliver one CD-ROM with current JPs. This JEL CD-ROM will be updated not less than semi-annually and when received can be locally reproduced for use within the combatant commands and Services.

7. Lessons Learned

a. CJCSI 3150.25D, dated 10 October 2008, codifies JLLIS as the DOD System of Record for the Joint Lessons Learned Program (JLLP).

b. JLLIS provides a Web-enabled information management system to meet the JLLP's operational needs. The JLLP provides for the transfer of knowledge within the DOD and USG organizations that are involved in joint operations or supported by military operations. This is done by the rapid distribution of observations and recommendations; after action reports; tactics, techniques, and procedures; topic papers; briefings; and interviews (lessons learned information). The JLLIS Web site can be found at https://www.jllis.mil or http://www.jllis.smil.mil.

GLOSSARY
PART I—ABBREVIATIONS AND ACRONYMS

AFDD	Air Force doctrine document
AJP	allied joint publication
ALERTORD	alert order
AOR	area of responsibility
APEX	Adaptive Planning and Execution
BDA	battle damage assessment
BPLAN	base plan
C2	command and control
CAP	crisis action planning
CCDR	combatant commander
CCIR	commander's critical information requirement
CCMD	combatant command
C-day	unnamed day on which a deployment operation begins
CJCS	Chairman of the Joint Chiefs of Staff
CJCSI	Chairman of the Joint Chiefs of Staff instruction
CJCSM	Chairman of the Joint Chiefs of Staff manual
COA	course of action
COCOM	combatant command (command authority)
COG	center of gravity
CONOPS	concept of operations
CONPLAN	concept plan
CONUS	continental United States
CSA	combat support agency
D-day	unnamed day on which operations commence or are scheduled to commence
DEPORD	deployment order
DOD	Department of Defense
DODD	Department of Defense directive
DODI	Department of Defense instruction
DOS	Department of State
DSM	decision support matrix
DST	decision support template
DTA	dynamic threat assessment
EXORD	execute order
FCC	functional combatant commander
FDO	flexible deterrent option
FFIR	friendly force information requirement
FM	field manual (Army)

FRAGORD	fragmentary order
FRO	flexible response option
FTN	force tracking number
FY	fiscal year
GCC	geographic combatant commander
GEF	Guidance for Employment of the Force
GFM	Global Force Management
GFMAP	Global Force Management Allocation Plan
GFMB	Global Force Management Board
GFMIG	Global Force Management Implementation Guidance
H-hour	specific time an operation or exercise begins
HNS	host-nation support
IFO	integrated financial operations
IGO	intergovernmental organization
ILO	in lieu of
IO	information operations
IPR	in-progress review
IPR F	plan approval in-progress review
ISR	intelligence, surveillance, and reconnaissance
J-1	manpower and personnel staff section
J-2	intelligence directorate of a joint staff
J-3	operations directorate of a joint staff
J-5	plans directorate of a joint staff
J-7	Joint Staff Directorate for Joint Force Development
J-8	Joint Staff Director for Force Structure, Resource, and Assessment
JCS	Joint Chiefs of Staff
JEL	Joint Electronic Library
JFC	joint force commander
JFLCC	joint force land component commander
JFP	joint force provider
JIA	joint individual augmentation
JIPOE	joint intelligence preparation of the operational environment
JLLIS	Joint Lessons Learned Information System
JLLP	Joint Lessons Learned Program
JMD	joint manning document
JOA	joint operations area
JOPES	Joint Operation Planning and Execution System
JOPP	joint operation planning process
JP	joint publication

JPEC	joint planning and execution community
JPG	joint planning group
JRSOI	joint reception, staging, onward movement, and integration
JS	the Joint Staff
JSCP	Joint Strategic Capabilities Plan
JSPS	Joint Strategic Planning System
JTF	joint task force
LAD	latest arrival date
L-hour	specific hour on C-day at which a deployment operation commences or is to commence
LOC	line of communications
LOI	letter of instruction
LOO	line of operation
MCDP	Marine Corps doctrinal publication
MEA	munitions effectiveness assessment
MNF	multinational force
MOE	measure of effectiveness
MOP	measure of performance
NAI	named area of interest
NATO	North Atlantic Treaty Organization
NDS	National Defense Strategy
NGO	nongovernmental organization
NIPRNET	Nonsecure Internet Protocol Router Network
NMS	National Military Strategy
NSC	National Security Council
NSS	National Security Strategy
OA	operational area
OPCON	operational control
OPLAN	operation plan
OPORD	operation order
OSD	Office of the Secretary of Defense
OUSD(P)	Office of the Under Secretary of Defense for Policy
PIR	priority intelligence requirement
PLANORD	planning order
PMESII	political, military, economic, social, information, and infrastructure
PPD	Presidential policy directive
PTDO	prepare to deploy order
QDR	quadrennial defense review

RATE	refine, adapt, terminate, execute
RFF	request for forces
ROE	rules of engagement
SC	strategic communication
SecDef	Secretary of Defense
SGS	strategic guidance statement
SOF	special operations forces
SOP	standing operating procedure
TACON	tactical control
TCP	theater campaign plan
TIM	toxic industrial material
TPFDD	time-phased force and deployment data
UCP	Unified Command Plan
USC	United States Code
USD(P)	Under Secretary of Defense for Policy
USG	United States Government
USSTRATCOM	United States Strategic Command
USTRANSCOM	United States Transportation Command
WARNORD	warning order
WMD	weapons of mass destruction

PART II—TERMS AND DEFINITIONS

acceptability. The joint operation plan review criterion for assessing whether the contemplated course of action is proportional, worth the cost, consistent with the law of war, and is militarily and politically supportable. (Approved for incorporation into JP 1-02.)

Adaptive Planning and Execution system. A Department of Defense system of joint policies, processes, procedures, and reporting structures, supported by communications and information technology, that is used by the joint planning and execution community to monitor, plan, and execute mobilization, deployment, employment, sustainment, redeployment, and demobilization activities associated with joint operations. Also called **APEX system.** (Approved for inclusion in JP 1-02.)

adequacy. The joint operation plan review criterion for assessing whether the scope and concept of planned operations can accomplish the assigned mission and comply with the planning guidance provided. (JP 1-02. SOURCE: JP 5-0)

alert order. 1. A crisis action planning directive from the Secretary of Defense, issued by the Chairman of the Joint Chiefs of Staff, that provides essential guidance for planning and directs the initiation of execution planning for the selected course of action authorized by the Secretary of Defense. 2. A planning directive that provides essential planning guidance, directs the initiation of execution planning after the directing authority approves a military course of action, but does not authorize execution. Also called **ALERTORD.** (Approved for incorporation into JP 1-02.)

allocation. Distribution of limited forces and resources for employment among competing requirements. (Approved for incorporation into JP 1-02.)

allocation (nuclear). None. (Approved for removal from JP 1-02.)

alternate command post. None. (Approved for removal from JP 1-02.)

annex. None. (Approved for removal from JP 1-02.)

appendix. None. (Approved for removal from JP 1-02.)

apportionment. In the general sense, distribution of forces and capabilities as the starting point for planning. (Approved for incorporation into JP 1-02.)

assumption. A supposition on the current situation or a presupposition on the future course of events, either or both assumed to be true in the absence of positive proof, necessary to enable the commander in the process of planning to complete an estimate of the situation and make a decision on the course of action. (Approved for incorporation into JP 1-02 with JP 5-0 as the source JP.)

augmentation forces. Forces to be transferred from a supporting combatant commander to the combatant command (command authority) or operational control of a supported combatant commander during the execution of an operation order approved by the President and Secretary of Defense. (JP 1-02. SOURCE: JP 5-0)

available-to-load date. A date specified for each unit in a time-phased force and deployment data indicating when that unit will be ready to load at the point of embarkation. Also called **ALD.** (Approved for incorporation into JP 1-02 with JP 5-0 as the source JP.)

base plan. A type of operation plan that describes the concept of operations, major forces, sustainment concept, and anticipated timelines for completing the mission without annexes or time-phased force and deployment data. Also called **BPLAN.** (Approved for incorporation into JP 1-02.)

branch. 1. A subdivision of any organization. 2. A geographically separate unit of an activity, which performs all or part of the primary functions of the parent activity on a smaller scale. 3. An arm or service of the Army. 4. The contingency options built into the base plan used for changing the mission, orientation, or direction of movement of a force to aid success of the operation based on anticipated events, opportunities, or disruptions caused by enemy actions and reactions. (Approved for incorporation into JP 1-02.)

campaign. A series of related major operations aimed at achieving strategic and operational objectives within a given time and space. (JP 1-02. SOURCE: JP 5-0)

campaign plan. A joint operation plan for a series of related major operations aimed at achieving strategic or operational objectives within a given time and space. (JP 1-02. SOURCE: JP 5-0)

campaign planning. The process whereby combatant commanders and subordinate joint force commanders translate national or theater strategy into operational concepts through the development of an operation plan for a campaign. (Approved for incorporation into JP 1-02.)

C-day. The unnamed day on which a deployment operation commences or is to commence. (Approved for incorporation into JP 1-02.)

center of gravity. The source of power that provides moral or physical strength, freedom of action, or will to act. Also called **COG.** (Approved for incorporation into JP 1-02 with JP 5-0 as the source JP.)

coalition. An arrangement between two or more nations for common action. (Approved for incorporation into JP 1-02.)

coalition action. None. (Approved for removal from JP 1-02.)

combat support agency. A Department of Defense agency so designated by Congress or the Secretary of Defense that supports military combat operations. Also called **CSA.** (JP 1-02. SOURCE: JP 5-0)

commander's concept. None. (Approved for removal from JP 1-02.)

commander's estimate. A developed course of action designed to provide the Secretary of Defense with military options to meet a potential contingency. (Approved for incorporation into JP 1-02.)

commander's required delivery date. The original date relative to C-day, specified by the combatant commander for arrival of forces or cargo at the destination; shown in the time-phased force and deployment data to assess the impact of later arrival. (Approved for replacement of "combatant commander's required date" and its definition in JP 1-02.)

completeness. The joint operation plan review criterion for assessing whether operation plans incorporate major operations and tasks to be accomplished and to what degree they include forces required, deployment concept, employment concept, sustainment concept, time estimates for achieving objectives, description of the end state, mission success criteria, and mission termination criteria. (JP 1-02. SOURCE: JP 5-0)

concept of operations. A verbal or graphic statement that clearly and concisely expresses what the joint force commander intends to accomplish and how it will be done using available resources. Also called **CONOPS.** (Approved for incorporation into JP 1-02.)

concept plan. In the context of joint operation planning level 3 planning detail, an operation plan in an abbreviated format that may require considerable expansion or alteration to convert it into a complete operation plan or operation order. Also called **CONPLAN.** (JP 1-02. SOURCE: JP 5-0)

constraint. In the context of joint operation planning, a requirement placed on the command by a higher command that dictates an action, thus restricting freedom of action. (JP 1-02. SOURCE: JP 5-0)

contingency. A situation requiring military operations in response to natural disasters, terrorists, subversives, or as otherwise directed by appropriate authority to protect US interests. (JP 1-02. SOURCE: JP 5-0)

contingency plan. A plan for major contingencies that can reasonably be anticipated in the principal geographic subareas of the command. (Approved for inclusion in JP 1-02.)

contingency planning. None. (Approved for removal from JP 1-02.)

course of action. 1. Any sequence of activities that an individual or unit may follow. 2. A scheme developed to accomplish a mission. 3. A product of the course-of-action development step of the joint operation planning process. Also called **COA.** (Approved for incorporation into JP 1-02.)

crisis action planning. The Adaptive Planning and Execution system process involving the time-sensitive development of joint operation plans and operation orders for the deployment, employment, and sustainment of assigned and allocated forces and resources in response to an imminent crisis. Also called **CAP.** (Approved for incorporation into JP 1-02.)

critical capability. A means that is considered a crucial enabler for a center of gravity to function as such and is essential to the accomplishment of the specified or assumed objective(s). (JP 1-02. SOURCE: JP 5-0)

critical requirement. An essential condition, resource, and means for a critical capability to be fully operational. (JP 1-02. SOURCE: JP 5-0)

critical vulnerability. An aspect of a critical requirement which is deficient or vulnerable to direct or indirect attack that will create decisive or significant effects. (JP 1-02. SOURCE: JP 5-0)

culminating point. The point at which a force no longer has the capability to continue its form of operations, offense or defense. (Approved for incorporation into JP 1-02.)

current force. The actual force structure and/or manning available to meet present contingencies. (Approved for incorporation into JP 1-02.)

date-time group. The date and time, expressed as six digits followed by the time zone suffix at which the message was prepared for transmission (first pair of digits denotes the date, second pair the hours, third pair the minutes, followed by a three-letter month abbreviation and two-digit year abbreviation.) Also called **DTG.** (Approved for incorporation into JP 1-02.)

D-day consumption/production differential assets. None. (Approved for removal from JP 1-02.)

D-day materiel readiness gross capability. None. (Approved for removal from JP 1-02.)

D-day pipeline assets. None. (Approved for removal from JP 1-02.)

decision. In an estimate of the situation, a clear and concise statement of the line of action intended to be followed by the commander as the one most favorable to the successful accomplishment of the assigned mission. (Approved for incorporation into JP 1-02 with JP 5-0 as the source JP.)

decision point. A point in space and time when the commander or staff anticipates making a key decision concerning a specific course of action. (JP 1-02. SOURCE: JP 5-0)

decisive point. A geographic place, specific key event, critical factor, or function that, when acted upon, allows commanders to gain a marked advantage over an adversary or contribute materially to achieving success. (Approved for incorporation into JP 1-02 with JP 5-0 as the source JP.)

Defense Planning Guidance. None. (Approved for removal from JP 1-02.)

deliberate planning. 1. The Adaptive Planning and Execution system process involving the development of joint operation plans for contingencies identified in joint strategic planning documents. 2. A planning process for the deployment and employment of apportioned forces and resources that occurs in response to a hypothetical situation. (Approved for inclusion in JP 1-02.)

deployment database. None. (Approved for removal from JP 1-02.)

deployment order. A planning directive from the Secretary of Defense, issued by the Chairman of the Joint Chiefs of Staff, that authorizes and directs the transfer of forces between combatant commands by reassignment or attachment. Also called **DEPORD.** (Approved for incorporation into JP 1-02.)

deployment planning. Operational planning directed toward the movement of forces and sustainment resources from their original locations to a specific operational area for conducting the joint operations contemplated in a given plan. (Approved for incorporation into JP 1-02.)

deterrent options. A course of action, developed on the best economic, diplomatic, and military judgment, designed to dissuade an adversary from a current course of action or contemplated operations. (Approved for incorporation into JP 1-02.)

direction of attack. None. (Approved for removal from JP 1-02.)

earliest arrival date. A day, relative to C-day, that is specified as the earliest date when a unit, a resupply shipment, or replacement personnel can be accepted at a port of debarkation during a deployment. Also called **EAD.** (Approved for incorporation into JP 1-02.)

employment. The strategic, operational, or tactical use of forces. (JP 1-02. SOURCE: JP 5-0)

essential task. A specified or implied task that an organization must perform to accomplish the mission that is typically included in the mission statement. (Approved for incorporation into JP 1-02.)

estimate. 1. An analysis of a foreign situation, development, or trend that identifies its major elements, interprets the significance, and appraises the future possibilities and the prospective results of the various actions that might be taken. 2. An appraisal of the capabilities, vulnerabilities, and potential courses of action of a foreign nation or combination of nations in consequence of a specific national plan, policy, decision, or contemplated course of action. 3. An analysis of an actual or contemplated clandestine operation in relation to the situation in which it is or would be conducted in order to identify and appraise such factors as available as well as needed assets and potential obstacles, accomplishments, and consequences. (Approved for incorporation into JP 1-02 with JP 5-0 as the source JP.)

execute order. 1. An order issued by the Chairman of the Joint Chiefs of Staff, at the direction of the Secretary of Defense, to implement a decision by the President to initiate military operations. 2. An order to initiate military operations as directed. Also called **EXORD.** (JP 1-02. SOURCE: JP 5-0)

execution planning. The Adaptive Planning and Execution System translation of an approved course of action into an executable plan of action through the preparation of a complete operation plan or operation order. Also called **EP.** (Approved for incorporation into JP 1-02.)

feasibility. The joint operation plan review criterion for assessing whether the assigned mission can be accomplished using available resources within the time contemplated by the plan. (JP 1-02. SOURCE: JP 5-0)

flexible deterrent option. A planning construct intended to facilitate early decision making by developing a wide range of interrelated responses that begin with deterrent-oriented actions carefully tailored to create a desired effect. Also called **FDO.** (Approved for incorporation into JP 1-02.)

flexible response. The capability of military forces for effective reaction to any enemy threat or attack with actions appropriate and adaptable to the circumstances existing. (Approved for incorporation into JP 1-02 with JP 5-0 as the source JP.)

force module package. None. (Approved for removal from JP 1-02.)

force planning. 1. Planning associated with the creation and maintenance of military capabilities by the Military Departments, Services, and US Special Operations Command. 2. In the Joint Operation Planning and Execution System, the planning conducted by the supported combatant command and its components to determine required force capabilities to accomplish an assigned mission. (Approved for incorporation into JP 1-02.)

force requirement number. None. (Approved for removal from JP 1-02.)

force(s). None. (Approved for removal from JP 1-02.)

force sourcing. The identification of the actual units, their origins, ports of embarkation, and movement characteristics to satisfy the time-phased force requirements of a supported commander. (Approved for incorporation into JP 1-02 with JP 5-0 as the source JP.)

fragmentary order. An abbreviated form of an operation order issued as needed after an operation order to change or modify that order or to execute a branch or sequel to that order. Also called **FRAGORD.** (JP 1-02. SOURCE: JP 5-0)

governing factors. In the context of joint operation planning, those aspects of the situation (or externally imposed factors) that the commander deems critical to the accomplishment of the mission. (JP 1-02. SOURCE: JP 5-0)

handover. None. (Approved for removal from JP 1-02.)

H-hour. The specific hour on D-day at which a particular operation commences. (Approved for incorporation into JP 1-02.)

implementation. Procedures governing the mobilization of the force and the deployment, employment, and sustainment of military operations in response to execution orders issued by the Secretary of Defense. Also called **IMP.** (Approved for incorporation into JP 1-02 with JP 5-0 as the source JP.)

implied task. In the context of joint operation planning, a task derived during mission analysis that an organization must perform or prepare to perform to accomplish a specified task or the mission, but which is not stated in the higher headquarters order. (JP 1-02. SOURCE: JP 5-0)

intensive management. None. (Approved for removal from JP 1-02.)

joint operation planning. Planning activities associated with joint military operations by combatant commanders and their subordinate joint force commanders in response to contingencies and crises. (Approved for incorporation into JP 1-02.)

Joint Operation Planning and Execution System. An Adaptive Planning and Execution system technology. Also called **JOPES.** (Approved for incorporation into JP 1-02.)

joint operation planning process. An orderly, analytical process that consists of a logical set of steps to analyze a mission, select the best course of action, and produce a joint operation plan or order. Also called **JOPP.** (Approved for incorporation into JP 1-02.)

joint planning and execution community. Those headquarters, commands, and agencies involved in the training, preparation, mobilization, deployment, employment, support, sustainment, redeployment, and demobilization of military forces assigned or committed to a joint operation. Also called **JPEC.** (Approved for incorporation into JP 1-02.)

joint planning group. A planning organization consisting of designated representatives of the joint force headquarters principal and special staff sections, joint force components (Service and/or functional), and other supporting organizations or agencies as deemed necessary by the joint force commander. Also called **JPG.** (JP 1-02. SOURCE: JP 5-0)

Joint Strategic Capabilities Plan. A plan that provides guidance to the combatant commanders and the Joint Chiefs of Staff to accomplish tasks and missions based on current military capabilities. Also called **JSCP.** (Approved for incorporation into JP 1-02.)

Joint Strategic Planning System. One of the primary means by which the Chairman of the Joint Chiefs of Staff, in consultation with the other members of the Joint Chiefs of Staff and the combatant commanders, carries out the statutory responsibilities to assist the President and Secretary of Defense in providing strategic direction to the Armed Forces. Also called **JSPS.** (Approved for incorporation into JP 1-02.)

latest arrival date. A day, relative to C-Day, that is specified by the supported combatant commander as the latest date when a unit, a resupply shipment, or replacement personnel can arrive at the port of debarkation and support the concept of operations. Also called **LAD.** (Approved for incorporation into JP 1-02.)

leverage. In the context of joint operation planning, a relative advantage in combat power and/or other circumstances against the adversary across one or more domains or the information environment sufficient to exploit that advantage. (Approved for incorporation into JP 1-02.)

L-hour. The specific hour on C-day at which a deployment operation commences or is to commence. (Approved for incorporation into JP 1-02.)

limiting factor. A factor or condition that, either temporarily or permanently, impedes mission accomplishment. (Approved for incorporation into JP 1-02.)

line of effort. In the context of joint operation planning, using the purpose (cause and effect) to focus efforts toward establishing operational and strategic conditions by linking multiple tasks and missions. Also called **LOE.** (Approved for inclusion in JP 1-02.)

line of operation. A line that defines the interior or exterior orientation of the force in relation to the enemy or that connects actions on nodes and/or decisive points related in time and space to an objective(s). Also called **LOO.** (Approved for replacement of "line of operations" and its definition in JP 1-02.)

major combat element. None. (Approved for removal from JP 1-02.)

major fleet. None. (Approved for removal from JP 1-02.)

major force. A military organization comprised of major combat elements and associated combat support, combat service support, and sustainment increments. (Approved for incorporation into JP 1-02.)

military options. None. (Approved for removal from JP 1-02.)

mission statement. A short sentence or paragraph that describes the organization's essential task(s), purpose, and action containing the elements of who, what, when, where, and why. (Approved for incorporation into JP 1-02.)

mobility analysis. None. (Approved for removal from JP 1-02.)

movement directive. None. (Approved for removal from JP 1-02.)

multinational. Between two or more forces or agencies of two or more nations or coalition partners. (JP 1-02. SOURCE: JP 5-0)

nonstandard unit. None. (Approved for removal from JP 1-02.)

non-unit record. None. (Approved for removal from JP 1-02.)

objective. 1. The clearly defined, decisive, and attainable goal toward which every operation is directed. 2. The specific target of the action taken which is essential to the commander's plan. (Approved for incorporation into JP 1-02.)

operational approach. A description of the broad actions the force must take to transform current conditions into those desired at end state. (Approved for inclusion in JP 1-02.)

operational characteristics. Those military characteristics that pertain primarily to the functions to be performed by equipment, either alone or in conjunction with other equipment; e.g., for electronic equipment, operational characteristics include such items as frequency coverage, channeling, type of modulation, and character of emission. (Approved for incorporation into JP 1-02 with JP 5-0 as the source JP.)

operational design. The conception and construction of the framework that underpins a campaign or major operation plan and its subsequent execution. (Approved for incorporation into JP 1-02 with JP 5-0 as the source JP.)

operational design element. A key consideration used in operational design. (Approved for incorporation into JP 1-02 with JP 5-0 as the source JP.)

operational limitation. An action required or prohibited by higher authority, such as a constraint or a restraint, and other restrictions that limit the commander's freedom of action, such as diplomatic agreements, rules of engagement, political and economic conditions in affected countries, and host nation issues. (JP 1-02. SOURCE: JP 5-0)

operational pause. A temporary halt in operations. (JP 1-02. SOURCE: JP 5-0)

operational reserve. An emergency reserve of men and/or materiel established for the support of a specific operation. (Approved for incorporation into JP 1-02 with JP 5-0 as the source JP.)

operation annexes. None. (Approved for removal from JP 1-02.)

operation order. A directive issued by a commander to subordinate commanders for the purpose of effecting the coordinated execution of an operation. Also called **OPORD.** (JP 1-02. SOURCE: JP 5-0)

operation plan. 1. Any plan for the conduct of military operations prepared in response to actual and potential contingencies. 2. A complete and detailed joint plan containing a full description of the concept of operations, all annexes applicable to the plan, and a time-phased force and deployment data. Also called **OPLAN.** (Approved for incorporation into JP 1-02.)

personnel increment number. A seven-character, alphanumeric field that uniquely describes a non-unit-related personnel entry (line) in a Joint Operation Planning and

Execution System time-phased force and deployment data. Also called **PIN.** (Approved for incorporation into JP 1-02 with JP 5-0 as the source JP.)

phase. In joint operation planning, a definitive stage of an operation or campaign during which a large portion of the forces and capabilities are involved in similar or mutually supporting activities for a common purpose. (JP 1-02. SOURCE: JP 5-0)

plan identification number. 1. A command-unique four-digit number followed by a suffix indicating the Joint Strategic Capabilities Plan year for which the plan is written. 2. A five-digit number representing the command-unique four-digit identifier, followed by a one-character, alphabetic suffix indicating the operation plan option, or a one-digit number numeric value indicating the Joint Strategic Capabilities Plan year for which the plan is written. Also called **PID.** (Approved for incorporation into JP 1-02.)

plan information capability. None. (Approved for removal from JP 1-02.)

planning factor. A multiplier used in planning to estimate the amount and type of effort involved in a contemplated operation. (Approved for incorporation into JP 1-02.)

planning order. A planning directive that provides essential planning guidance and directs the initiation of execution planning before the directing authority approves a military course of action. Also called **PLANORD.** (JP 1-02. SOURCE: JP 5-0)

prepare to deploy order. An order issued by competent authority to move forces or prepare forces for movement (e.g., increase deployability posture of units). Also called **PTDO.** (JP 1-02. SOURCE: JP 5-0)

Programmed Forces. None. (Approved for removal from JP 1-02.)

ready-to-load date. The date when a unit will be ready to move from the origin, i.e., mobilization station. Also called **RLD.** (Approved for incorporation into JP 1-02 with JP 5-0 as the source JP.)

required delivery date. The date that a force must arrive at the destination and complete unloading. Also called **RDD.** (Approved for incorporation into JP 1-02 with JP 5-0 as the source JP.)

requirements capability. None. (Approved for removal from JP 1-02.)

restraint. In the context of joint operation planning, a requirement placed on the command by a higher command that prohibits an action, thus restricting freedom of action. (JP 1-02. SOURCE: JP 5-0)

risk. Probability and severity of loss linked to hazards. (Approved for incorporation into JP 1-02.)

scheduled arrival date. None. (Approved for removal from JP 1-02.)

scheduling and movement. None. (Approved for removal from JP 1-02.)

scheduling and movement capability. None. (Approved for removal from JP 1-02.)

scheme of maneuver. The central expression of the commander's concept for operations that governs the design of supporting plans or annexes of how arrayed forces will accomplish the mission. (Approved for incorporation into JP 1-02.)

security cooperation planning. None. (Approved for removal from JP 1-02.)

sequel. The subsequent major operation or phase based on the possible outcomes (success, stalemate, or defeat) of the current major operation or phase. (Approved for incorporation into JP 1-02.)

shortfall. The lack of forces, equipment, personnel, materiel, or capability, reflected as the difference between the resources identified as a plan requirement and those apportioned to a combatant commander for planning that would adversely affect the command's ability to accomplish its mission. (Approved for incorporation into JP 1-02 with JP 5-0 as the source JP.)

specified task. In the context of joint operation planning, a task that is specifically assigned to an organization by its higher headquarters. (JP 1-02. SOURCE: JP 5-0)

staff estimates. None. (Approved for removal from JP 1-02.)

strategic concept. The course of action accepted as the result of the estimate of the strategic situation which is a statement of what is to be done in broad terms. (Approved for incorporation into JP 1-02.)

strategic direction. The processes and products by which the President, Secretary of Defense, and Chairman of the Joint Chiefs of Staff provide strategic guidance to the Joint Staff, combatant commands, Services, and combat support agencies. (Approved for incorporation into JP 1-02.)

strategic estimate. The broad range of strategic factors that influence the commander's understanding of its operational environment and its determination of missions, objectives, and courses of action. (Approved for incorporation into JP 1-02.)

strategic mobility. None. (Approved for removal from JP 1-02.)

strategic plan. A plan for the overall conduct of a war. (Approved for incorporation into JP 1-02 with JP 5-0 as the source JP.)

subordinate campaign plan. A combatant command prepared plan that satisfies the requirements under a Department of Defense campaign plan, which, depending upon the circumstances, transitions to a supported or supporting plan in execution. (Approved for inclusion in JP 1-02.)

supporting plan. An operation plan prepared by a supporting commander, a subordinate commander, or an agency to satisfy the requests or requirements of the supported commander's plan. (JP 1-02. SOURCE: JP 5-0)

threat identification and assessment. None. (Approved for removal from JP 1-02.)

time-phased force and deployment data. The time-phased force data, non-unit-related cargo and personnel data, and movement data for the operation plan or operation order, or ongoing rotation of forces. Also called **TPFDD.** (Approved for incorporation into JP 1-02.)

time-phased force and deployment data maintenance. None. (Approved for removal from JP 1-02.)

time-phased force and deployment data refinement. None. (Approved for removal from JP 1-02.)

times. The Chairman of the Joint Chiefs of Staff coordinates the proposed dates and times with the commanders of the appropriate unified and specified commands, as well as any recommended changes when specified operations are to occur (C-, D-, M-days end at 2400 hours Universal Time [Zulu time] and are assumed to be 24 hours long for planning). (Approved for incorporation into JP 1-02.)

transportation feasible. A determination made by the supported commander that a draft operation plan can be supported with the apportioned transportation assets. (Approved for replacement of "grossly transportation feasible" and its definition in JP 1-02.)

Universal Time. A measure of time that conforms, within a close approximation, to the mean diurnal rotation of the Earth and serves as the basis of civil timekeeping. Also called **ZULU** time. (Formerly called Greenwich Mean Time.) (Approved for incorporation into JP 1-02.)

validate. Execution procedure used by combatant command components, supporting combatant commanders, and providing organizations to confirm to the supported commander and United States Transportation Command that all the information records in a time-phased force and deployment data not only are error-free for automation purposes, but also accurately reflect the current status, attributes, and availability of units and requirements. (Approved for incorporation into JP 1-02.)

war game. None. (Approved for removal from JP 1-02.)

warning order. 1. A preliminary notice of an order or action that is to follow. 2. A planning directive that initiates the development and evaluation of military courses of action by a supported commander and requests that the supported commander submit a commander's estimate. 3. A planning directive that describes the situation, allocates forces and resources, establishes command relationships, provides other initial planning guidance, and initiates subordinate unit mission planning. Also called **WARNORD.** (Approved for incorporation into JP 1-02 with JP 5-0 as the source JP.)

wartime manpower planning system. None. (Approved for removal from JP 1-02.)

Intentionally Blank

JOINT DOCTRINE PUBLICATIONS HIERARCHY

```
                              ┌──────────────┐
                              │    JP 1      │
                              │   JOINT      │
                              │  DOCTRINE    │
                              └──────┬───────┘
                                     │
     ┌──────────┬──────────┬─────────┼─────────┬──────────┬──────────┐
┌─────────┐┌─────────┐┌─────────┐┌─────────┐┌─────────┐┌─────────────┐
│ JP 1-0  ││ JP 2-0  ││ JP 3-0  ││ JP 4-0  ││ JP 5-0  ││   JP 6-0    │
│PERSONNEL││INTELLI- ││OPERATIONS││LOGISTICS││ PLANS   ││COMMUNICATIONS│
│         ││ GENCE   ││         ││         ││         ││   SYSTEM    │
└─────────┘└─────────┘└─────────┘└─────────┘└─────────┘└─────────────┘
```

All joint publications are organized into a comprehensive hierarchy as shown in the chart above. **Joint Publication (JP) 5-0** is in the **Plans** series of joint doctrine publications. The diagram below illustrates an overview of the development process:

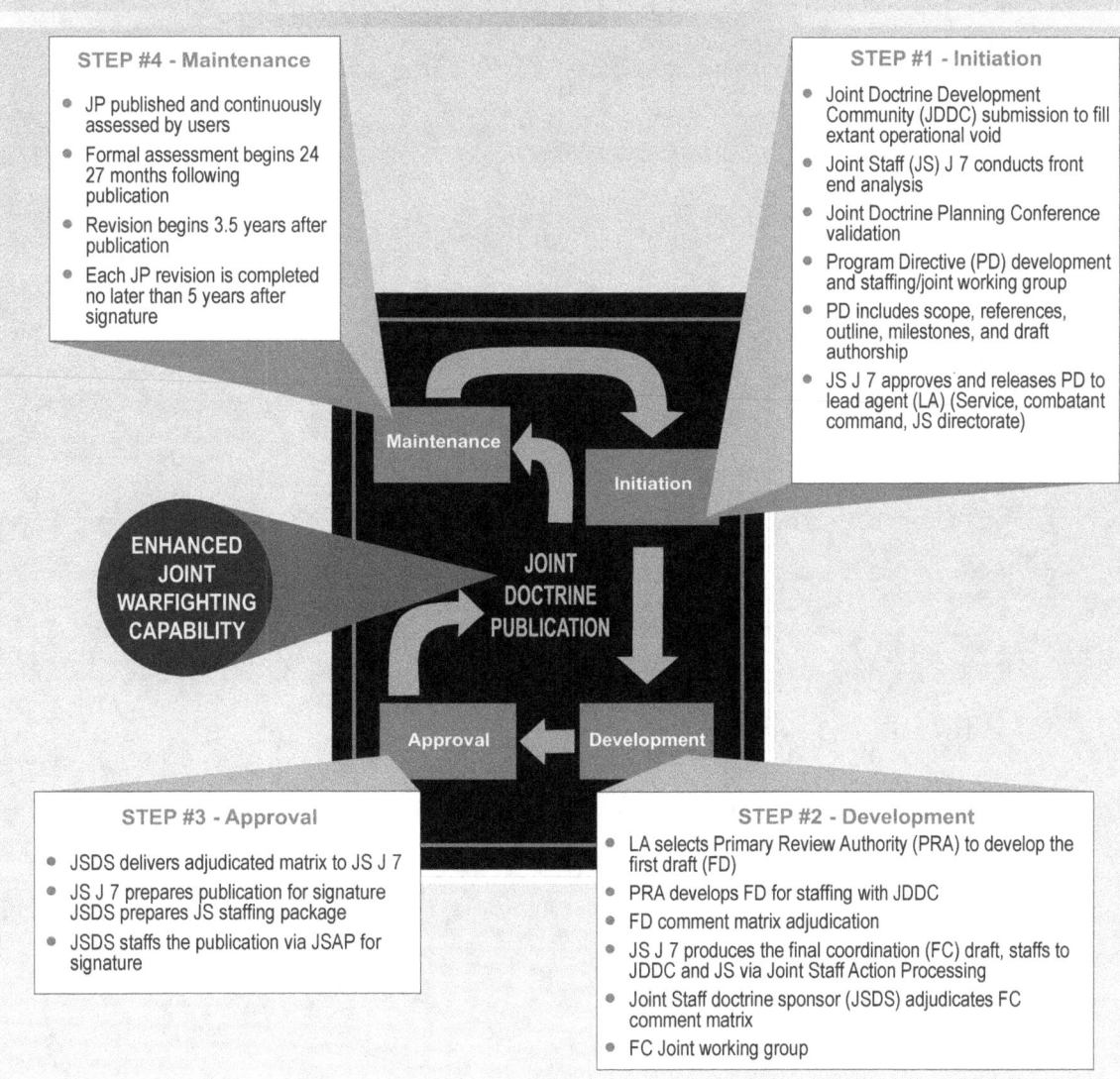

STEP #4 - Maintenance

- JP published and continuously assessed by users
- Formal assessment begins 24 27 months following publication
- Revision begins 3.5 years after publication
- Each JP revision is completed no later than 5 years after signature

STEP #1 - Initiation

- Joint Doctrine Development Community (JDDC) submission to fill extant operational void
- Joint Staff (JS) J 7 conducts front end analysis
- Joint Doctrine Planning Conference validation
- Program Directive (PD) development and staffing/joint working group
- PD includes scope, references, outline, milestones, and draft authorship
- JS J 7 approves and releases PD to lead agent (LA) (Service, combatant command, JS directorate)

ENHANCED JOINT WARFIGHTING CAPABILITY

JOINT DOCTRINE PUBLICATION

Maintenance — Initiation — Development — Approval

STEP #3 - Approval

- JSDS delivers adjudicated matrix to JS J 7
- JS J 7 prepares publication for signature JSDS prepares JS staffing package
- JSDS staffs the publication via JSAP for signature

STEP #2 - Development

- LA selects Primary Review Authority (PRA) to develop the first draft (FD)
- PRA develops FD for staffing with JDDC
- FD comment matrix adjudication
- JS J 7 produces the final coordination (FC) draft, staffs to JDDC and JS via Joint Staff Action Processing
- Joint Staff doctrine sponsor (JSDS) adjudicates FC comment matrix
- FC Joint working group